An Introduction to Indian Philosophy

This wide-ranging introduction to classical Indian philosophy is philosophically rigorous without being too technical for beginners. Through detailed explorations of the full range of Indian philosophical concerns, including some metaphilosophical issues, it provides readers with non-Western perspectives on central areas of philosophy, including epistemology, logic, metaphysics, ethics, philosophy of language, and philosophy of religion. Chapters are structured thematically, with each including suggestions for further reading. This provides readers with an informed overview, whilst enabling them to focus on particular topics if needed. Translated Sanskrit texts are accompanied by authorial explanations and contextualizations, giving the reader an understanding of the argumentative context and philosophical style of Indian texts. A detailed glossary and a guide to Sanskrit pronunciation equip readers with the tools needed for reading and understanding Sanskrit terms and names. The book will be an essential resource for both beginners and advanced students of philosophy and Asian studies.

ROY W. PERRETT is a Research Associate of the School of Historical and Philosophical Studies at the University of Melbourne, Australia. He is the author of *Hindu Ethics: A Philosophical Study* (1998) and *Death and Immortality* (1987).

An Introduction to Indian Philosophy

ROY W. PERRETT

CAMBRIDGE
UNIVERSITY PRESS

CAMBRIDGE
UNIVERSITY PRESS

University Printing House, Cambridge CB2 8BS, United Kingdom

Cambridge University Press is part of the University of Cambridge.

It furthers the University's mission by disseminating knowledge in the pursuit of education, learning and research at the highest international levels of excellence.

www.cambridge.org
Information on this title: www.cambridge.org/9780521618694

First published 2016
4th printing 2018

Printed and bound in Great Britain by Clays Ltd, Elcograf S.p.A.

A catalogue record for this publication is available from the British Library

ISBN 978-0-521-85356-9 Hardback
ISBN 978-0-521-61869-4 Paperback

An old style can be translated, as it were, into a newer language; it can, one might say, be performed afresh at a tempo appropriate to our own times. To do this is really only to reproduce . . .

But what I mean is *not* giving an old style a fresh trim. You don't take the old forms and fix them up to suit the latest taste. No, you are really speaking the old language, perhaps without realizing it, but you are speaking it in a way that is appropriate to the modern world, without on that account necessarily being in accordance with its taste.

Ludwig Wittgenstein, *Culture and Value*

Contents

Figures

Preface

I would like to thank especially the following persons who have – both through their writings and through conversation or correspondence over the years – significantly shaped the way I think about Indian philosophy: in alphabetical order, they are Arindam Chakrabarti, Eli Franco, Jonardon Ganeri, Jay Garfield, Jitendra Mohanty, Stephen Phillips, Karl Potter, Chakravarthi Ram-Prasad, Jay Shaw, Mark Siderits, John Taber, and Tom Tillemans. Naturally, it should not be inferred that any of them would agree with all of what I have written here.

A very special debt of gratitude is also due to Hilary Gaskin, my editor at Cambridge University Press, who commissioned this book and continued to believe in it – patiently combining the right mix of editorial acumen, encouragement and reproof – over the inordinately lengthy time I took to deliver the final manuscript. Without her efforts this book would certainly not have come into being. Many thanks!

Two other persons' efforts were also essential in transforming the submitted manuscript into the final book: those of the anonymous clearance reader for Cambridge University Press, who offered a number of valuable suggestions for improvement, and of Rosemary Crawley, Assistant Editor, who skilfully shepherded me through the production process.

In writing this book I have made use of some of my own previously published articles (in varying degrees of revision). Thus the Introduction and Chapter 2 incorporate material from my 'Truth, Relativism and Western Conceptions of Indian Philosophy', *Asian Philosophy* 8, 1998. Chapter 1 includes material from my article 'Hindu Ethics' in Hugh LaFollette (ed.), *International Encyclopedia of Ethics* (Blackwell, 2013). Chapter 3 includes material originally published in 'The Problem of Induction in Indian Philosophy', *Philosophy East and West* 34, 1984. Chapter 4 reuses some material from my 'Musical Unity and Sentential Unity', *British Journal of Aesthetics* 39, 1999. Chapter 5 includes material from 'The Momentariness of Simples', *Philosophy* 79, 2004, and 'Causation, Indian Theories of' in Edward Craig (ed.), *Routledge Encyclopedia of Philosophy* (Routledge, 1998). Chapter 6 draws on 'Computationality, Mind and Value: The Case of Sāṃkhya-Yoga', *Asian Philosophy* 11, 2001, and 'Personal Identity, Minimalism, and Madhyamaka', *Philosophy East and West* 52, 2002. I am grateful to the editors and publishers involved for permission to reprint these materials here. Finally, the book's epigraph is reprinted (with the permission of Wiley) from Ludwig Wittgenstein, *Culture and Value* (Blackwell, 1980).

A note on the pronunciation of Sanskrit

The vast majority of classical Indian philosophical texts are in Sanskrit, as too are the names of their authors. Following standard scholarly practice, all Sanskrit words in this book are written phonetically according to the International Alphabet of Sanskrit Transliteration (IAST). A few very basic points about the pronunciation of Sanskrit for readers unfamiliar with the language are set out below. (For more detailed information on Sanskrit phonology see Coulson 1976 or Goldman and Sutherland 1987.)

The vowels *a*, *i*, *u*, *e* and *o* are pronounced roughly as are the English vowels in (respectively) 'but', 'pin', 'pull', 'they' and 'go'. The use of a macron indicates a lengthening of the corresponding vowel: so *ā*, *ī*, and *ū* are pronounced as are the corresponding English vowels in 'father', 'police' and 'rude'. The diphthongs *ai* and *au* are pronounced like the *ie* in 'pie' and the *ow* in 'now'. The vowel *ṛ* is pronounced as the *ri* in the name 'Rita'. Sanskrit *ṃ* indicates nasalization of the preceding vowel.

An *h* following a consonant indicates it is aspirated: so *ph* and *th* are pronounced as in 'uphill' and 'boathouse'. A dot under a consonant indicates that the tongue is to be pointed to the roof of the mouth when uttering it. *S* with an accent (*ś*) or a dot (*ṣ*) is pronounced approximately as *sh*.

The general rule in pronouncing Sanskrit words is to stress the penultimate syllable, if it is long, or the nearest long syllable preceding it. If none is long, the first syllable is stressed. (A long syllable is one containing a long vowel or one in which a vowel is followed by two or more consonants.)

Introduction

Preliminaries

As its title suggests, this book is an introduction to Indian philosophy (or more specifically, classical Indian philosophy) – one of the world's great philosophical traditions. But while it aims to be an introduction to classical Indian philosophy suitable for the philosophically curious, it does not aim to be an introduction to philosophy. Instead the expected typical audience will include undergraduates who have taken at least a first course in philosophy, graduate students in philosophy seeking to broaden their philosophical horizons, and interested general readers with some prior background in philosophy.

In philosophy there are two common ways of structuring an introductory work. One approach is to structure the exposition chronologically; the other approach is to structure it thematically. This book strongly favours the thematic approach: each of the seven succeeding chapters is devoted to a particular philosophical topic discussed extensively by the classical Indian philosophers.

Chapter 1 'Value' deals with Indian views about ethics, about which there were both major commonalities and some significant differences. Chapter 2 'Knowledge' deals with some of the epistemological concerns central to classical Indian philosophy. Chapter 3 'Reasoning' focuses on Indian 'logic', broadly conceived. Chapter 4 'Word' deals with Indian philosophy of language. Chapter 5 'World' focuses on metaphysics: specifically, the matter of which fundamental entities make up the world and how causation holds them together. Chapter 6 'Self' deals with Indian theories of the self. Chapter 7 'Ultimates' deals with philosophy of religion, especially the variety of differing conceptions of a maximally great being to be found in the Indian tradition.

This thematic organization permits the book to be used in at least two different ways. A reader wanting a moderately comprehensive overview of

Indian philosophy should definitely read it straight through. But a reader wanting instead only a sense of Indian contributions to a particular philosophical theme – say, the nature of knowledge, or the metaphysics of the self – can just turn to the relevant chapter (and then follow this up with the suggested readings at the end of it).

Similarly, this whole book – appropriately supplemented with translations from the Sanskrit primary sources – could be used as the text for an introductory survey course on Indian philosophy; or particular chapters (plus readings) could be used either for more advanced courses on selected topics in Indian philosophy, or to provide a non-Western perspective in a general introductory course on, say, epistemology or philosophy of language.

Each chapter spends some time teasing out the presuppositions and arguments of the Indian philosophers. Hence, unlike some introductions to Indian philosophy, sustained attention is paid here to various of the technical details of the Indian debates in order to enable us better to pursue the paradigmatically philosophical tasks of evaluating proposed analyses and justifications of beliefs. While both Indian and Western philosophers are certainly concerned to offer some sort of synoptic account of reality, the route to that end is usually strongly connected with the rigorous tasks of analysis and argumentation. This is why so much of this book is devoted to Indian materials drawn from the classical and medieval periods, periods of outstanding philosophical creativity and rigour in India.

Before plunging into the details of the competing theories and arguments to be canvassed, however, it will also be helpful for the reader to have at least some prior sense of the general historical context of these Indian debates and the chronology of the Indian authors mentioned. Accordingly, I shall presently offer a brief historical overview of Indian philosophy. But before I do so it seems appropriate to raise first a metaphilosophical question that this book might otherwise seem naively to presuppose an affirmative answer to: namely, 'Is there Indian *philosophy*?'

Is there Indian *philosophy*?

Indologists are often understandably exasperated by the question 'Is there Indian *philosophy*?' when they encounter it being asked in a snide tone conveying that the questioner is already convinced – typically from a position of textual ignorance – that the correct answer is a negative one. After all, so far as most Indologists are concerned, the obviously correct answer is an affirmative one! But the question can also be raised quite sincerely as a genuine metaphilosophical question.

Metaphilosophy is that branch of philosophy concerned with the nature of philosophy and hence questions like: What is philosophy? What is philosophy for? How should philosophy be done? From a metaphilosophical perspective, then, the question 'Is there Indian *philosophy*?' can be more charitably construed as raising genuine issues of clarification about what is to count as philosophy.

We need to begin by distinguishing two senses of 'philosophy'. One is a familiar non-technical sense of that term: roughly, a complete world-view that could be regarded as providing a fully coherent explanation of everything. Uncontroversially, there is Indian philosophy in this non-technical sense of 'philosophy'. But there is also a second, more technical sense of 'philosophy'. Philosophy in this latter sense occurs when we begin to reflect critically on the traditional explanatory world-view: when, for instance, we begin to ask questions about precisely what is explained, how the proffered explanation works, and whether it is superior to rival explanatory candidates. The development of Western philosophy is associated with the growth of such a tradition of critical reflection. And, as we shall see, the Indian tradition too developed a comparable critical tradition.

The second point to make is that the question 'Is there Indian *philosophy*?' is ambiguous because the term 'philosophy' may be being used descriptively or evaluatively. Compare the question 'What is art?' When someone says of something, 'That is not art', they may be saying (*descriptively*) that it is not a member of the class of artworks, or they may be saying (*evaluatively*) that while it may be a member of the class of artworks, it is not a member of the class of *good* artworks. After all, something can be art without being good art. Similarly, to say something is not philosophy may be a descriptive claim or an evaluative one, for something can be philosophy without being *good* philosophy. But determining the descriptive range of the term is, in an important fashion, logically prior to determining its evaluative range: although something can be philosophy without being *good* philosophy, nothing can be *good* philosophy without being philosophy.

Matters would obviously be simpler if we could all agree on a set of necessary and sufficient conditions for something's being (descriptively) philosophy, in the technical sense of that term. But, alas, no such consensus obtains among philosophers – Western or Indian. Some have felt, however, that at least we can specify some plausible *necessary* conditions, conditions that would exclude Indian thought from being *philosophy*.

The difficulty for such a project, however, is to specify plausible necessary conditions on philosophy such that they are satisfied by Western philosophy, but not Indian philosophy. For example, it is sometimes complained that the Indian thinkers were motivated by religious concerns, and hence were not really philosophers. Call this *the secularity condition* on philosophy. But such a condition is clearly unsatisfactory, for while it is true that many Indian philosophers were motivated by religious concerns, so too were many Western philosophers. A purportedly *descriptive* account of philosophy that excludes the work of (among others) Descartes, Leibniz, Berkeley, Kant and almost all of the Western medievals is plainly inadequate.

A much more plausible condition on being philosophy is *the argumentation condition*: philosophy is concerned with analyzing and evaluating arguments for and against competing positions. This requirement flows directly from the point made earlier that the occurrence of philosophy (in the technical sense of the term) is associated with the growth of a tradition of critical reflection. And it is easy to see how a Western philosopher, turning from the works of Kant or Russell to dip into translations of the Upaniṣads, the *Bhagavadgītā* or the *Dhammapada*, might be inclined to deny that these Indian texts are genuine works of *philosophy* – whatever their other merits as 'wisdom literature'.

But the argumentation condition needs to be wielded delicately. On the one hand, philosophical arguments can be presented more or less explicitly or formally, and even Western philosophers have made use of a variety of literary styles and genres to present their views, including myths, dramatic dialogues and epigrams. An overly austere conception of argumentation risks giving us a purportedly descriptive account of philosophy that banishes works of, inter alia, the pre-Socratics, Plato and Nietzsche from the shelves of philosophy. On the other hand, if we are willing to tough it out and insist on construing the argumentation condition so austerely, then it is still the case that huge amounts of Indian *śāstra* literature from the classical and medieval periods, packed with explicit technical argumentation, will satisfy the condition. And these are exactly the kind of Indian philosophical texts we shall be particularly attending to in the succeeding chapters of this book.

A third proposed condition on philosophy is *the historicist condition*. In 2001 the French philosopher Jacques Derrida visited Shanghai, causing much consternation in China when he was reported as having said:

> There is no problem with talking about Chinese thought, Chinese history, Chinese science, and so forth, but obviously, I have a problem with talking about the Chinese 'philosophy' of this Chinese thought and culture before the introduction of the European model... Philosophy in essence is not just thought. It is linked with a sort of specific history, with one type of language, and with an ancient Greek invention. It is an ancient Greek invention which then underwent 'transformation' by Latin translation and German translation and so on. It is something European. There may be various kinds of thought and knowledge of equal integrity beyond Western European culture, but it is not reasonable to call them 'philosophy'. (Jing 2006: 60–1)

A similar argument would, of course, rule out the existence of Indian *philosophy* too.

Once again, however, the proposed necessary condition seems implausibly restrictive for a *descriptive* account of philosophy. No musicologist wants to insist that there is no Indian *music* because the concept of music is linked with a specific (European) history and (European) type of language. So what is so special about philosophy that it is supposed to be so very different?

Finally, we have *the lexical equivalence condition*, which effectively claims that since there is no single traditional Indian word for 'philosophy', there was no philosophy in India. True, there are two Sanskrit words that might seem promising candidates for terminological analogues of 'philosophy': namely, *darśana* and *ānvīkṣikī* (see further Halbfass 1988). But although *darśana* ('view') is used in the Indian doxographic tradition to name philosophical 'schools', the Sanskrit term has no serious methodological implications. In contrast, while the term *ānvīkṣikī* ('investigation through reasoning') does have methodological implications, it is too narrowly focused to serve as an equivalent to 'philosophy'.

Why assume, however, that philosophy cannot occur in a culture without a clearly corresponding (single) term also occurring in that culture? After all, in the West earlier practices came to be retrospectively interpreted, redescribed and appropriated as 'philosophy'. Why can we not do the same with the Indian practices we now call 'Indian philosophy'?

In sum, then, the secularity condition, the historicist condition, and the lexical equivalence condition all seem implausible candidates for being a necessary condition for philosophy. The argumentation condition is a much more plausible candidate, if construed generously enough, but then the standard works of Indian philosophy would also satisfy that condition. True, a more austere construal of the argumentation condition might disqualify some of these

Indian texts from being counted as philosophy, but there would still remain a very large number of Indian texts that would satisfy even such a strengthened condition. Moreover, the strengthened argumentation condition would also risk excluding a significant amount of what would be generally accepted as Western philosophy.

Of course, defusing some sceptical arguments about the existence of Indian philosophy is not the same as offering a positive argument for the existence of Indian philosophy. One promising positive strategy for locating Indian philosophy as *philosophy* is to proceed recursively: that is, begin with some paradigms of philosophy, then count anything as philosophy that resembles these paradigms (at least as closely as they resemble each other).

For the sake of the argument, let us allow the sceptic about Indian philosophy to choose the standard works and figures of Western philosophy (from the pre-Socratics onwards) as the paradigms of philosophy. This enables us to construct a resemblance class of philosophical paradigms such that members of the relevant resemblance class are all more similar to one another than they all are to any one thing outside the class (i.e. each non-member of the class differs more from some member than that member differs from any member). Faced with a new candidate for inclusion as philosophy, we ask whether it differs more from some member of the class of paradigms than that member differs from any member of the class. If the answer is negative, then it can be added to the class of paradigms.

This recursive strategy also recognizes the historicity of the notion it seeks to capture, for the construction of a resemblance class takes place over time and often involves the use of different paradigms, which is why the notion of philosophy can seem to involve a class that lacks unity. But this alleged lack of unity of the relevant class of paradigm objects may be a misperception caused by the multiplicity of paradigms around which the notion has been constructed over time. Accordingly, some things within the resemblance class cluster together more closely than others, even though all members of the class are sufficiently similar to count as members of the similarity circle we call 'philosophy'.

The term 'philosophy' does not need, then, to refer to an unchanging, ahistorical essence in order to be intelligible, and the obvious dissimilarities between some of the things that can be claimed as instances of philosophy should not be allowed to obscure the existence of a network of relevant similarities that unify the resemblance class. It is the presence of these very similarities that justifies the inclusion of Indian philosophy into the resemblance class; that is, justifies acknowledging Indian philosophy as *philosophy*.

Indian philosophy: a brief historical overview

The study of the history of Indian philosophy is notoriously fraught with problems in establishing chronology and dates. Hence for many of even the major figures of Indian philosophy it is very difficult to give any precise details of their lives (this is why in this book only an assignment of an author to a particular century is attempted). True, there is more of a consensus among scholars about *relative* chronology, but even this is a very much more disputed matter than it is in the case of Western philosophy.

Furthermore, among Indologists the periodization of Indian philosophy is another highly contested matter (see Franco 2013). All historical periodization, however, involves a certain amount of arbitrariness, so perhaps the following may serve as a useful first pass for our purposes:

1 The Ancient Period (900 BCE–200 CE)
2 The Classical Period (200 CE–1300 CE)
3 The Medieval Period (1300 CE–1800 CE)
4 The Modern Period (1800 CE–present)

Some authors treat the third period here as more seamlessly continuous with the classical period, so that the term 'classical Indian philosophy' then refers to work of both the second and third periods above. Unless otherwise indicated, we too shall follow this practice of using 'classical Indian philosophy' to refer indiscriminately to Indian philosophy of what is, according to the periodization above, either the classical or medieval periods.

The ancient period of Indian philosophy is the period of the composition of Vedas and the Upaniṣads. It is also the period of the growth of the anti-Vedic movements: Buddhism, Jainism and Cārvāka. The classical period of Indian philosophy is the period of the rise of the philosophical systems (*darśanas*). The medieval period is the period of the great commentaries on the *sūtras* of these various systems. And the modern period is the period characterized by the contact of inheritors of the earlier tradition with new influences, particularly from the West. While the primary focus in succeeding chapters of this book is on texts from the classical and medieval periods of Indian philosophy, a few words more about all four periods may be helpful to the reader in contextualizing what is to follow.

The ancient period of Indian philosophy

The earliest Indian religious texts are the Vedas. These include hymns to the gods and manuals of sacrificial ritual, but also the beginnings of Indian philosophy proper. Thus we find in the early Vedic texts speculations about the origins of existence and prefigurements of important later concepts like karma and moral order (*ṛta*). More importantly still, among the late Vedic texts are the Upaniṣads, a set of dialogues on philosophical themes.

The main philosophical themes that the Upaniṣads explore are the nature of the Absolute (*Brahman*) as the ground of being and the importance of knowledge of *Brahman* as the key to liberation. Crucial for the attainment of this goal is a correct understanding of the nature of the Self (*ātman*), which according to some texts is identical to *Brahman*. This Upaniṣadic emphasis on the importance of a correct understanding of the nature of the self for the attainment of liberation meant that metaphysical and epistemological issues about knowledge and the self became fundamental for many later Indian philosophers.

The Upaniṣads thus represent a shift in world-view away from the earlier Vedic literature's emphasis on ritual action towards a focus on self-realization and the attainment of liberation from suffering and rebirth. Correspondingly, we find two competing ethical ideals in the Vedic literature: an earlier ideal of the householder embedded in society and committed to the performance of social duties (*dharma*), and a later ideal of the renunciant who has withdrawn from the world to pursue liberation (*mokṣa*).

The Vedic legacy in later Indian philosophy, then, is a continuing tension between two competing strands in Brahmanical (or 'Hindu') thought: activism (*pravṛtti*), exemplified in the early Vedic ritualistic tradition, and quietism (*nivṛtti*), exemplified in the later Upaniṣadic renunciant tradition. One popular attempt to resolve this tension is to be found in the *Bhagavadgītā* (*c.* 500 BCE), part of the great *Mahābhārata* epic.

The Upaniṣads are sometimes represented as the quintessence of Indian philosophy. This is unfortunate for at least two reasons. First, although these texts are philosophically suggestive, they are nowhere near as systematic or rigorously argumentative as classical Indian philosophical works from, say, the fifth century onwards. Indeed, given a more austere conception of what *philosophy* is, the Upaniṣads are probably better represented as Indian *proto-philosophy*. They do, however, significantly contribute to the development of later Indian philosophy, particularly shaping the schools of Vedānta.

The second reason why it is important not to identify the Upaniṣads with Indian philosophy is that even in the ancient period there were rival anti-Vedic philosophies being vigorously championed by (among others) the Buddhists, the Jainas and the Cārvākas. Most of these philosophies are associated with the influence of the *śramaṇa* or ascetic movement. Vedic orthodoxy was built upon commitment to the authority of the Vedas, belief in a world creator, the path of ritualism, and a social structure based upon a hereditary hierarchy of caste. The diverse heterodox schools, collectively known as the *śramaṇas*, rejected all of these in favour of the path of asceticism.

The two most important heterodox schools were Buddhism and Jainism, both arising around the sixth century BCE. Buddhism's historical founder was the prince Gautama Siddhārtha (known after his enlightenment as Gautama Buddha), and the path to freedom from suffering that he preached was called the 'middle way' between the extremes of sensuality and asceticism. While Gautama accepted his own versions of the Upaniṣadic doctrines of rebirth, karma and liberation, a crucial Buddhist theme was the rejection of the Upaniṣadic doctrine of *ātman* or the Self. Gautama also rejected the Brahmanical beliefs in a world creator and in caste as a principle of social order. He attracted many followers, both monastics and laypersons, during his lifetime and established a large Buddhist community in India that flourished there for around seventeen centuries, during which time it successfully spread Buddhist teachings throughout Asia.

Jainism's historical founder was Mahāvīra, and (like Gautama) he was not born of the priestly brahmin class, but of the *kṣatriya* or warrior class. Like Gautama, Mahāvīra too was unimpressed by Brahmanical commitments to sacrificial rituals, a world creator and a social order based on caste. Before he was 30 years old he had renounced the householder life and become a mendicant, leading a life of severe austerities before achieving enlightenment and being recognized by his followers as a *tīrthaṅkara* or 'ford crosser', and establishing a large Jaina community of both monastics and laypersons. Although Jainism was never as popular as Buddhism in India, it has continued to flourish there right up to the present day. It has also counted among its adherents some of the sharpest philosophical minds in classical Indian philosophy.

While both Buddhism and Jainism rejected many tenets central to Brahmanism, they were nevertheless both still committed to the pursuit of liberation (*mokṣa*). The Cārvāka materialists, in contrast, were anti-Vedic atheists who rejected the goal of liberation and all of the ascetic practices said to be required to achieve it. Their original texts did not survive, but through quotations in the writings of the opponents they enjoyed a polemical longevity.

The classical period of Indian philosophy

The classical period of Indian philosophy is the period of the rise of the philosophical schools or *darśanas*. Some of these were Brahmanical schools that accepted the authority of the Vedas and hence were classified as orthodox (*āstika*). Others (like the Buddhists, the Jainas and the Cārvākas) did not accept the authority of the Vedas and were classified as heterodox (*nāstika*). In both cases the characteristic textual genre adopted by a *darśana* is the *sūtra*, a systematic arrangement of memorizable aphorisms organized systematically around reasons and arguments so as to present a world-view. This basic framework subsequently requires the development of a second genre, the *bhāṣya* or more extended commentary on the gnomic original *sūtra*.

According to a later Indian doxographical tradition, the orthodox Hindu philosophical schools are six in number, arranged in three pairs: Sāṃkhya–Yoga, Nyāya–Vaiśeṣika, Mīmāṃsā–Vedānta. (This schema is inadequate historically, but still useful for our present purposes.)

Sāṃkhya is the oldest of these six schools, but its classical redaction is to be found in Īśvarakṛṣṇa's *Sāṃkhyakārikā* (second century). It teaches a dualistic metaphysics that is usually taken to underpin the practical psychology of Yoga, as presented in Patañjali's *Yogasūtra* (third century).

Nyāya is the school of logic and argument and Vaiśeṣika is the atomistic tradition. Their root *sūtras* are, respectively, Gautama's *Nyāyasūtra* (second century) and Kaṇāda's *Vaiśeṣikasūtra* (second century). Although Nyāya and Vaiśeṣika were originally two separate schools with separate *sūtras*, they soon come to be regarded as a single syncretic school (Nyāya-Vaiśeṣika) specializing in logic, epistemology and metaphysics.

Mīmāṃsā is the school of scriptural exegesis, focusing on the earlier Vedic texts, and its root *sūtra* is Jaimini's *Mīmāṃsāsūtra* (first century). Vedānta, in contrast, focuses on the later Upaniṣadic texts and its root *sūtra* is Bādarāyaṇa's *Brahmasūtra* (second century BCE).

Finally, for each root *sūtra* there is a later *bhāṣya* or commentary on it that became particularly influential: for example, Vyāsa's *Yogabhāṣya* (fourth century) for Yoga, Vātsyāyana's *Nyāyabhāṣya* (fifth century) for Nyāya, Praśastapada's *Padārthadharmasamgraha* (fifth century) for Vaiśeṣika, Śabara's *Śābarabhāṣya* (sixth century) for Mīmāṃsā, and Śaṃkara's *Brahmasūtrabhāṣya* (eighth century) for Vedānta.

Turning now to the heterodox schools, we have a later Buddhist doxographical tradition according to which there were four major schools of Indian Buddhist philosophy: Sarvāstivāda, Sautrāntika, Madhyamaka and Yogācāra. (Once again, the schema is inadequate historically, but still useful for our present expository purposes.)

The most important extant source for knowledge about the Sarvāstivāda is Vasubandhu's *Abhidharmakośa* (fourth century), which reviews both Sarvāstivāda doctrines and arguments and Sautrāntika criticisms of them. Metaphysically, both schools affirm varieties of reductionist realism. Epistemologically, Sarvāstivāda favours a kind of direct realism and Sautrāntika a kind of representationalism.

This first pair of Buddhist schools are often referred to (pejoratively) as Hīnayāna ('Lesser Vehicle') schools, in contrast to the Mahāyāna ('Greater Vehicle') schools that emphasize universal compassion. The two main schools of Mahāyāna philosophy are Madhyamaka and Yogācāra. The founder of the Madhyamaka school was Nāgārjuna (second century), author of the *Mūlamadhyamakākarikā*. Madhyamaka (the 'middle' school) seeks to maintain a dialectical middle way between the extremes of eternalism and nihilism. After Nāgārjuna's death, however, Madhyamaka became somewhat marginal to the Indian philosophical scene for centuries because its opponents regarded it as just an implausible variety of nihilism, until the writings of Candrakīrti (seventh century) and Śāntideva (eighth century) began to revive some interest in the school. (As Buddhism spreads to Tibet, the Tibetans valorize the Madhyamaka tradition and promulgate a revisionist history of that school's pre-eminence in India – a tale sometimes still uncritically accepted by modern Western Buddhists.)

The Yogācāra school was founded by the brothers Asaṅga and Vasubandhu (fourth century). Most Indian philosophers took Yogācāra to be advocating a variety of metaphysical idealism (though some modern scholars dispute this reading of their texts). Yogācāra is also associated, through the influence of Dignāga's *Pramāṇasammucaya* (fifth century) and Dharmakīrti's

Pramāṇavārtikka (seventh century), with the rise of a sophisticated school of Buddhist logic and epistemology.

Another development in this period was the appearance of Buddhist philosophers like Śāntarakṣita (eighth century), who tried to synthesize the dialectical approach of Nāgārjuna with the logical and epistemological innovations of Dignāga and Dharmakīrti.

All these Buddhist philosophical challenges to Hindu orthodoxy provoked orthodox replies. Thus the Nyāya realists like Uddyotakara (seventh century), Jayanta (ninth century) and Udayana (tenth century) all engaged in serious and well-informed polemics against Buddhist varieties of reductionism and idealism. The Mīmāṃsā philosopher Kumārila's *Ślokavārttika* (eighth century) defends metaphysical realism and the intrinsic validity of the Vedic scriptures. The Advaitin Śaṃkara (eighth century) sharply critiques Buddhism in his *Brahmasūtrabhāṣya*, but is nevertheless sufficiently influenced by it to be labelled a 'crypto-Buddhist' by his orthodox critics.

Jainism is the other major heterodox school, advocating a distinctive metaphilosophy of non-absolutism (*anekāntavāda*), according to which no metaphysical view is unconditionally true, and an ethic of non-injury (*ahiṃsā*). Among other things, the conjunction of these two features helped incline Jainas to be admirably impartial doxographers of the Indian views.

As warned earlier, these traditional Indian schematizations in terms of opposing schools leave out a lot of the historical detail. To take but one example, the redaction of Pāṇini's Sanskrit grammar (fifth century BCE) and the later commentaries on it generated a model of the formal analysis of language that is accepted by all Indian philosophers. Hence the significance of the Grammarian philosophers – the most important of which was Bhartṛhari (fifth century) – for subsequent Indian philosophy of language.

The medieval period of Indian philosophy

The medieval period is the period of the great commentaries on the *sūtras* of the various systems. The biggest change in the philosophical milieu is the disappearance of Buddhism from India by the end of the fourteenth century. This is very much connected with the waves of Muslim invasions of northern India from the eleventh century on. By then Buddhism was centred in large monastic universities, which were easy targets for looting and destruction by Muslim armies. Accordingly, today the original Sanskrit versions of many

Indian Buddhist texts are lost and only available through early Tibetan and Chinese translations.

Coinciding with the disappearance of Buddhism there arises a new flourishing of Hindu theistic devotionalism (*bhakti*). This influence is evident in the development of theistic forms of Vedānta. One of these is the qualified non-dualism of Viśiṣṭādvaita. The leading figure of that school is Rāmānuja (eleventh century), author of the *Śrībhāṣya*, and his most distinguished successor is the prolific Veṅkaṭanātha (fourteenth century). Another important form of theistic Vedānta is Dvaita dualism, the leading figure of which is Madhva (thirteenth century). Later Dvaita philosophers of special note are Jayatīrtha (fourteenth century) and the dialectician Vyāsatīrtha (sixteenth century).

Both of these theistic schools of Vedānta were much involved with polemics against the non-theistic school of Advaita Vedānta, which also continues to flourish during this period. Post-Śaṃkara Advaita begins with a division into the Vivaraṇa and Bhāmatī subschools, who disagree as to whether *Brahman* or the individual self is the locus of ignorance. The Vivaraṇa position is associated with Padmapāda (eighth century), a direct disciple of Śaṃkara, and is further developed by Prakāśātman (eleventh century) and Vidyāraṇya (fourteenth century). The Bhāmatī position is associated with Vācaspati (tenth century). A more instrumentalist tradition of Advaita takes its inspiration from Sureśvara (ninth century), another of Śaṃkara's direct disciples. A still later development in Advaita are the highly polemical works of Śrīharṣa (twelfth century) and Madhusūdana Sarasvatī (sixteenth century).

During this period Sāṃkhya and Yoga lost much of their status as distinct schools, effectively getting 'Vedanticized' by Vedāntin commentators like Vācaspati (tenth century) and Vijñāna Bhikṣu (sixteenth century). Nyāya-Vaiśeṣika, however, fully retains its independence and develops into a single syncretic school. By far the most important development in Nyāya-Vaiśeṣika is the growth of Navya-Nyāya ('New Logic'). The most influential work of this school is certainly Gaṅgeśa's prodigious *Tattvacintāmaṇi* (fourteenth century). The next most eminent Navya-Naiyāyika is Raghunātha Śiromaṇi (sixteenth century), who further refined the analytical tools of Navya-Nyāya and introduced a number of ontological innovations. The Navya-Naiyāyika philosophers developed a powerful technical language which became the language of all serious discourse, an intentional logic of cognitions increasingly construed by most Indian philosophers as being independent of the realist metaphysics of Nyāya-Vaiśeṣika.

As already mentioned, the medieval period of Indian philosophy is the period of the great commentators. Accordingly, some writers have disparaged the writings of this period as mostly arid scholasticism and polemics, contrasting them unfavourably with the creative work of the preceding classical period. The writings of the medieval period certainly are scholastic in style, usually assuming the reader's familiarity with a specialized technical vocabulary and range of allusions. But that does not at all mean that they were lacking in creativity: instead, we find exhibited everywhere a sustained concern with analytical subtlety and logical rigour, the frequent presence of ingenious technical innovations, and a characteristic drive for philosophical systematization. Hence one interesting and revealing feature of the late medieval period is the appearance of scholastic manuals for various philosophical schools that, for the first time, clearly summarize and systematize the essentials of the systems. Some famous examples are: for Nyāya-Vaiśeṣika, Annaṃbhaṭṭa's *Tarkasaṃgraha* and its *Dīpīka* (seventeenth century), and the *Bhāṣapariccheda* with the *Siddhāntamuktāvalī* autocommentary, traditionally (but now disputably) attributed to Viśvanātha (seventeenth century); the *Mānameyodaya* of Nārāyaṇa (sixteenth century) for Mīmāṃsā; and the *Vedāntaparibhāṣa* of Dharmarāja (seventeenth century) for Advaita.

More important still is the way in which the commentarial genre functions in India as a way of making possible a conception of oneself as engaging the ancient and the alien in conversation. By the end of the late medieval period the ancient texts are no longer thought of as authorities to which one must defer, but are regarded as the source of insight in the company of which one pursues the quest for truth (see further Ganeri 2011).

The modern period of Indian philosophy

The existence of the traditional style of Indian philosophical education in Sanskrit persisted into the modern period – indeed right up to the present day (in a somewhat attenuated form). But the modern period also brought about huge changes in Indian society due to the influence of the encounter with Western culture. In particular, the nineteenth and early twentieth centuries were the age of the British Raj. Whereas the Muslim domination from the tenth century onwards had a very limited impact on the Hindu way of life (though not the Buddhist one), the British transformed matters by in 1835 introducing English education into India with the explicit intention of revolutionizing traditional Indian modes of thought. As Thomas Macaulay's 1835 'Minute on Education' famously put it:

> We must at present do our best to form a class who may be interpreters between us and the millions whom we govern; a class of persons, Indian in blood and colour, but English in taste, in opinions, in morals and in intellect. To that class we may leave it to refine the vernacular dialects of the country, to enrich those dialects with terms of science borrowed from the Western nomenclature, and to render them by degrees fit vehicles for conveying knowledge to the great mass of the population. (de Bary 1958: 601)

In fact, the introduction of English education – particularly the introduction of English-language universities from 1857 – revolutionized Indian modes of thought in a rather more complex manner than the British had intended. Thus the growth of Indian nationalism was inadvertently encouraged by the education of an Indian elite in the liberal ideals of Western thought, ultimately subverting the very colonial authority that education was supposed to support. Moreover, the spirit of nationalism manifested itself in the rediscovery and reinterpretation of India's indigenous intellectual traditions, presented anew in relation to Western thought.

Philosophy is but one example of this trend. We have seen that India has a rich and venerable native tradition in philosophy, including an enormous philosophical literature written in the Sanskrit language. But after 1857 it was *Western* philosophy that formed the basis of the curriculum in the Indian universities, with traditional Indian philosophy being, at least at first, ignored or despised. (Hence even today in India a philosophy department, heavily devoted to Western philosophy, is part of most major universities.) However, the education of Indians in Western philosophy also made possible the growth of a class of Indian philosophers equipped to represent in English the riches of the Sanskritic tradition, particularly in its various relations to Western philosophy. Thus their colonial education in Western philosophy was a necessary condition for Surendranath Dasgupta and Sarvepalli Radhakrishnan being able to write in the 1920s their pioneering English-language histories of Indian philosophy, and these works were followed by other more specialized studies by modern Indian philosophers such as K. C. Bhattacharya, Satischandra Chatterjee, D. M. Datta, Mysore Hiriyanna, T. R. V. Murti and others – an interpretive tradition continued in recent times by Indian philosophers such as Jitendranath Mohanty and Bimal Krishna Matilal. Macaulay's hoped-for class of interpreters began not just to convey Western knowledge to Indians, but also Indian knowledge to Westerners.

Western conceptions of Indian philosophy

The original neglect of traditional Indian philosophy in the philosophy curriculum of Indian English-language universities was obviously a consequence of Macaulay's own exaggeratedly low opinion of Indian literature, an opinion confidently held notwithstanding his own ignorance of Sanskrit. But on this issue Macaulay was undoubtedly influenced by the opinions of the great Hindu reformer Rāmmohun Roy, who in 1823 had written (in his superb English) a letter of appeal against British plans to found and support a new college for Sanskrit studies in Calcutta. And since Roy had steeped himself in Sanskrit learning in Banaras, he felt himself to be all too aware of what a Sanskrit education could offer: 'This seminary . . . can only be expected to load the minds of youth with grammatical niceties and metaphysical distinctions of little or no practical use to the possessors or to society' (de Bary 1958: 593). Roy then goes on to offer a number of examples of what he means, examples which students of classical Indian philosophy will easily recognize as allusions to some of the most central texts and problems in that tradition. Unlike Macaulay, Roy is undoubtedly familiar with what a Sanskrit philosophical education would involve and he vehemently opposes it as something 'best calculated to keep this country in darkness' (de Bary 1958: 595).

Roy's attitude to traditional Indian philosophy, then, is a particularly clear and historically influential instance of what we shall call (borrowing some terminology from Amartya Sen) the *magisterial* conception of Indian philosophy (Sen 1997). Magisterial approaches to India emphasize the inferiority of the country's native traditions and strongly relate to the exercise of the imperial power of guardianship. As such, they are much associated with ideologies of the Raj. Macaulay's comments are clearly within this magisterial tradition; so too are the influential attitudes towards India of both James and John Stuart Mill. But, as we have just seen, magisterial assumptions about the poverty of Indian intellectual traditions are by no means confined to Westerners; indeed such Western conceptions can sometimes be reinforced by similar Indian conceptions of those traditions. Thus Roy is just as magisterially dismissive of the Sanskritic intellectual tradition as, say, James Mill – only much better informed than Mill about the content of that tradition. Moreover Roy's magisterialism is motivated by the same sort of utilitarian considerations as Mill's: like Mill, Roy believes that 'the improvement of the native population' will be best served by 'a more liberal and enlightened system of instruction' in the 'useful sciences' of the West (de Bary 1958: 595).

Sen contrasts magisterial approaches to India with *exoticist* and *curatorial* approaches. Exoticist approaches concentrate on the wondrous aspects of India, emphasizing the positive value of India's supposed differences from the West. Curatorial approaches are more catholic, including a host of various attempts to note, classify and exhibit diverse aspects of Indian culture. Unlike the exoticist approaches, curatorial approaches are not committed to valorizing India's difference from the West; unlike magisterial approaches, they are not weighed down with a ruler's sense of superiority and guardianhood. However, curatorial approaches do tend to view India as a rather special and fascinating object. Both exoticist and curatorial approaches are instanced in various Western conceptions of Indian philosophy.

Exoticism dominated the Romantic vision of Indian philosophy propounded by Herder, the Schlegels, Schelling, Schopenhauer and others. In their different ways these writers constructed an image of India as an 'Other' that exemplified those valuable qualities that Europe lacked: in particular, various forms of spirituality, transcendentalism and anti-materialism. But romantic exoticism of this type fits ill with a closer acquaintance with Indian thought, and nowadays such romanticism is more common in 'New Age' circles than in academic ones. Nonetheless, a number of important modern works on Indian philosophy are markedly exoticist, including not just those of Indian authors like Sarvapalli Radhakrishnan, but also those of Western writers like Heinrich Zimmer and Mircea Eliade.

It is curatorial approaches, however, that dominate contemporary Indological treatments of Indian philosophy. Indological approaches to Indian philosophy are focused on philological-cum-historical-cum-grammatical analyses of the Sanskrit texts. Such purely curiosity-driven research has a venerable pedigree from Alberuni and William Jones through to contemporary Western scholars such as Erich Frauwallner, Paul Hacker and Daniel Ingalls (and, of course, their numerous Japanese counterparts). In terms of numbers of publications, this would surely be the dominant Western academic approach to Indian philosophy.

Two clarificatory points about these categories are worth making. First, it is important to understand that it is not being claimed here that these three categories exhaust all the Western approaches to India (indeed we shall shortly suggest a fourth, without even then claiming completeness). The schema here is not supposed to be definitive, only useful for our present purposes. Second, this typology is not to be confused with Edward Said's influential notion of 'Orientalism', which takes the idea of the 'Orient' to be a construct of the Western imagination (Said 1978). Perhaps Romantic exoticism, with its imaginative construction of India as Europe's 'Other', is a kind of Orientalism in Said's sense. However, Sen's typology emphasizes the *conflicting variety* of Western conceptions of India, whereas Said's notion assumes the uniformity of Western conceptions of the Orient.

Our own central claim is that none of these three approaches gives us an adequate conception of Indian philosophy. The magisterial approach is overly dismissive of the very real intellectual achievements of Indian philosophy. The exoticist approach does not denigrate Indian philosophy in the way the magisterial approach does, but it valorizes the non-rationalist parts of the Indian philosophical tradition. By presenting Indian philosophy as being about spirituality and mysticism, rather than about logic and epistemology, exoticism importantly misrepresents the analytical achievements of Indian philosophy. (Ironically these two apparently opposed approaches between them manage to underwrite the almost total neglect of Indian philosophy by contemporary Western philosophers, for they imply that Indian philosophy is either simply false and hence not worth bothering with, or else it is non-rational mysticism and hence not really *philosophy*.)

In some respects the curatorial approach to Indian philosophy fares better than the other two. Its emphasis on careful philological and historical research means that it is less likely to ignore the analytical tradition of Indian philosophy (there are just too many extant Sanskrit texts that would have to be ignored). Nor is it burdened with the magisterial need to denigrate in order to justify the assumption of power. But there is still one crucial respect in which the curatorial approach fails to do justice to Indian philosophy *as philosophy*: it refuses to try to rationally assess the theories and arguments of the texts it studies, to ask whether the theses affirmed there are true and the arguments offered in support of them are good ones. In other words, the curatorial approach (especially as practised by Indologists) fails to take seriously Indian philosophy's concern with *truth*.

In this respect the curatorial approach is markedly opposed to the other two approaches. The magisterial approach takes Indian philosophy's concern with truth seriously; indeed it disparages Indian philosophy precisely because its central claims are thought to be *false*. The exoticist approach, on the other hand, valorizes Indian philosophy because what are taken to be its central claims are thought to be *true*. The curatorial approach, however, simply ignores the truth or falsity of those central claims as irrelevant to its concerns – sometimes, indeed, because of a scepticism about the very notion of cross-cultural evaluation of truth claims. Against this trend we want to affirm the importance of truth for our understanding of Indian philosophy and its significance for Western philosophy.

What is the relevance of all this to our concerns with Western conceptions of Indian philosophy? Briefly, that it suggests the possibility of a fourth Western conception of Indian philosophy: what we shall call the *interlocutory* approach. Like their Indian counterparts, Western philosophers have typically aspired to the truth, whatever their differing views about the nature and criterion of truth. What the classical Indian debates about truth (reviewed in Chapter 2) suggest is that such differences are quite compatible with a shared acceptance of a broad notion of coherence and workability as at least providing our best epistemic access to truth. But for this irenic claim to be plausible, we also need to suppose that we are talking about coherence/workability in the face of rigorous attempts to refute the theories we provisionally hold to be true. However truth is conceived, our confidence in the truth of our theories reasonably increases in the face of their survival of rigorous philosophical scrutiny by interlocutors also committed to a search for the truth, but reflecting disparate backgrounds and theoretical presuppositions. Thus a commitment to the philosophical search for truth implies the need to bring new interlocutors into the conversation. (Indeed historically the Indian tradition has done just this, ever incorporating new opponents (*pūrvapakṣin*) into the philosophical dialogue that leads to the true view (*siddhānta*). Arguably, periods of stagnation and scholasticism in that tradition have coincided with a shortage of such new interlocutors.)

This is the interlocutory approach to Indian philosophy favoured here. Unlike the curatorial approach, it takes seriously Indian philosophy's own aspirations to truth. Unlike the magisterial and exoticist approaches, it neither disparages nor valorizes Indian philosophy's truth claims. It is indeed something like a global version of the way in which, in classical India, orthodox Hindu philosophers approached the theories and arguments of their heterodox Buddhist and Jaina counterparts, and vice versa. It gives proper weight to cultural diversity – indeed requires it – but eschews any kind of relativism that would prohibit cross-cultural criticism. The results of the systematic pursuit of such a global philosophical dialogue are perhaps likely to be the closest to objective truth that we can hope to get. Insofar as it is plausible to suppose that such a result is one desired by Western (and Indian) philosophers, then such philosophers need to embrace this interlocutory conception of Indian philosophy.

Suggestions for further reading

Recommended alternative introductory surveys of Indian philosophy include Hiriyanna 1932, Potter 1963, Smart 1964 and Mohanty 2000. Useful collections of translated primary sources include Radhakrishnan and Moore 1957, Koller and Koller 1991, Sarma 2011, Frauwallner 2007, Edelglass and Garfield 2009 and Deutsch and van Buitenen 1971. On the broader Indian cultural background, see Basham 1971. On the ancient period of Indian philosophy, see further Edgerton 1965, van Buitenen 1973 and Jaini 1973. For readings on the classical and medieval periods of Indian philosophy, see the suggestions at the end of each of the successive thematic chapters of this book. On the modern period, see Raghuramaraju 2006, 2013 and Bhusan and Garfield 2011. There is no adequate single history of Indian philosophy: Dasgupta 1922–55 is a venerable classic attempt, but it is both dated and partial – albeit full of useful information. The multivolume *Encyclopedia of Indian Philosophies* series under the general editorship of Karl Potter, however, is currently an invaluable source of historical information and philosophical synopses: for details of the volumes published to date and still forthcoming, together with an authoritative online bibliography of Indian philosophy, see http://faculty.washington.edu/kpotter. On the history of Western interpretations of Indian philosophy, see Halbfass 1988. On the importance of engaging philosophically with Indian philosophical texts, see too Taber 2013.

1 Value

Introduction

While classical Indian philosophy is incredibly rich in rigorous discussions of topics in epistemology, logic and metaphysics, comparable discussions in the areas of ethics, politics and aesthetics were not as extensive as might have been expected. Certainly, ethics was not a distinct field within Indian philosophy in the manner of *pramāṇavāda* (the part of Indian philosophy that corresponds roughly to epistemology and logic). Instead, Indian ethical discussions are to be found scattered acoss many works and genres. However, although classical Indian ethics is thus underdeveloped relative to other branches of Indian philosophy, the Indian philosophers did have a good deal to say about the theory of value insofar as they vigorously discussed topics like the ends of life and the relation of virtuous action to those ends. Moreover, there are major commonalities between both the orthodox Hindu and heterodox Buddhist and Jaina philosophers – though there are also some significant differences.

In this chapter we begin by outlining the structure of classical Hindu ethics and its theories of the good and the right. We then consider some arguments for the primacy of the value of liberation, a claim common to both orthodox and heterodox Indian value theorists, before focusing on some of the distinctive features of Buddhist and Jaina ethics. It seems appropriate to begin our introduction to Indian philosophy here because these crucial normative presuppositions underpin so many of the more fully articulated and technical debates in classical Indian epistemology and metaphysics.

The structure of value: the *puruṣārthas*

The Hindu ethical tradition is complex and by no means monolithic, but arguably the most developed parts of classical Hindu ethics are its theory of the good and its theory of the right. The former is articulated in terms of the *puruṣārthas* or ends of human life.

A traditional Hindu classification recognizes four classes of values: the *puruṣārthas* or ends of human life. The most common traditional ordering of these is: *dharma, artha, kāma* and *mokṣa*. The first three are sometimes grouped together as the *trivarga* ('group of three'); the addition of *mokṣa* constructs the *caturvarga* ('group of four'). *Artha* is wealth and political power; *kāma* is sensual pleasure, particularly as associated with sexual and aesthetic experience; *dharma* is the system of obligations and prohibitions enshrined in the legal and religious texts. As the *trivarga* these three values are arranged hierarchically with *artha* as the lowest and *dharma* as the highest. One argument for this arrangement appeals to the distinction between intrinsic and instrumental values. *Artha* is clearly an instrumental value, a means rather than an end, and hence inferior. However, this argument cannot serve to distinguish *kāma* and *dharma*, for pleasure is surely an intrinsic value and the Indians do not seek to deny this. While *artha* is valued ordinarily as a mere means to *kāma*, *kāma* is valued for itself. In order to elevate *dharma* over *kāma* other arguments are invoked. First, that *dharma* is a higher value because it is restricted to humans; other animals pursue wealth and pleasure, but only humans can consciously pursue morality. Second, that although all desire pleasure, pleasure is not always desirable. In distinguishing higher and lower pleasures, *dharma* is offered as the regulative principle: the type of pleasure that is truly valuable is that in accordance with the demands of *dharma*. In this sense *dharma* as a regulative principle is a higher value than *kāma*.

The highest value is *mokṣa*, a state of complete liberation from the bondage of the cycle of rebirth (*saṃsāra*). Since all *saṃsāric* existence is held to be marked by universal suffering (*duḥkha*), *mokṣa* is the ultimate end of Hindu ethics. It can be characterized in both positive and negative terms. Thus some (like the Vedāntins) hold it to be a state of absolute bliss; others (like Sāṃkhya-Yoga and Nyāya-Vaiśeṣika) hold it merely to be the absence of all pain and suffering. But this difference may not be as significant as it might first appear, for the philosophical psychology of the latter schools tends to regard pleasure as but the temporary and relative absence of pain. In any case, *mokṣa* as absolute bliss (or absence of suffering) is distinct from *kāma* in that it is both hedonically unmixed and permanent once achieved.

According to some schools the state of *mokṣa* is here and now attainable. That is, one can be liberated while still alive, a *jīvanmukta* (Fort and Mumme

1996). Others hold that the ideal can only be fully attained after physical death (*videhamukti*). But again the difference may not amount to as much as all that. For all parties agree that persons can in this life attain a state such that immediately upon the destruction of the physical body they will attain *mokṣa*, without any further actions being required of them.

Mokṣa and its relation to knowledge and action are extensively discussed in the *darśana* treatises that are the paradigm Indian philosophical texts. However, there are separate classes of Sanskrit treatises devoted to expositions of *dharma* (religious and moral laws), of *artha* (political and economic power), and of *kāma* (sexual and aesthetic pleasure).

While all the orthodox Hindu philosophers were committed to recognizing the value of *dharma*, the highest value is not *dharma* but *mokṣa*. Moreover, the relation of *dharma* to *mokṣa* is controversial. The oldest tradition (present in the Dharmaśāstra and the Epics) claims an essential continuity between *dharma* and *mokṣa*: selfless performance of one's *dharma* leads ineluctably to *mokṣa*. A different tradition (particularly associated with Śaṃkara and other Vedāntins) insists on a sharp opposition between *dharma* and *mokṣa*. But even then, the cultivation of *dharma* is considered a prerequisite for the moral development of the *adhikārin*, the qualified aspirant to *mokṣa*. Hence the supreme ideal of *mokṣa* is not so easily separable from the lesser ideal of *dharma*.

The Hindu political philosophers too acknowledged that *mokṣa* is the ultimate end of human activity, but insisted that *artha* and *dharma* are legitimate worldly goals which, if properly pursued, lead to *mokṣa*. The most famous political treatise is the *Arthaśāstra* (fourth century BCE), which argues for the advantages of monarchy over other forms of government. The king's duty is to maintain the order and stability necessary for the people to promote their economic well-being and practise *dharma*. Such order is upheld by proper use of *daṇḍa* ('the rod'), that is, by the just use of force to punish breaches of the rules of *dharma*.

The rules of *dharma* are presented in the Dharmaśāstras, the best known of which is the *Manusmṛti* (Olivelle 2005). *Dharma* involves two distinct sets of duties. Firstly, there are universal duties (*sādhāraṇa-dharma*) incumbent on all, regardless of age or occupation. These include non-injury (*ahiṃsā*), truthfulness, patience, respect for others' property and so on. Secondly, and more important for determining one's particular personal responsibilities or *svadharma*, are the demands of social duty. Indeed, in the case of a conflict between the two sets of obligations, it is the particular rather than the universal duty that prevails.

The content of one's personal *dharma* is determined by caste and stage in life (*varṇāśrama-dharma*). The four social classes (*varṇa*) are: the *brāhmaṇa* or priestly caste; the *kṣatriya*, the ruler and warrior caste; the *vaiṣya* or merchant caste; and the *śūdra* or labourers. Various duties accrue to members of these *varṇas*, appropriate to the function each class has in the operation of society as a whole.

But it is not just caste that determines a person's *dharma*. Also crucial is their stage in life (*āśrama*). The ideal Hindu life pattern (at least for male members of the three higher *varṇas*) is in four stages. First there is the period of student life (*brahmacarya*). Then there is the stage of the householder (*gārhasthya*). Having fulfilled these obligations, it is appropriate in later life to enter the stage of the anchorite (*vānaprastha*). Finally, one may enter the renunciant stage (*saṃnyāsa*), abandoning all worldly concerns, focused entirely on the attainment of liberation (*mokṣa*). Ideally, then, a full life allows for each of the *puruśārthas* to be realized in one's lifetime: the student studies *dharma*; the householder pursues *artha* and *kāma* (in accordance with *dharma*); the anchorite pursues *mokṣa*, but still upholds *dharma* through the performance of the daily sacrifices; and the *saṃnyāsin* is devoted entirely to *mokṣa*.

There are two sorts of texts that deal directly with the value of *kāma* or pleasure. Sexual pleasure is the subject matter of the well-known *Kāmasūtra* and other texts in the same genre. Aesthetic pleasure is one of the subject matters of a developed body of writing on aesthetic theory. The central concept of Indian aesthetics is *rasa* ('flavour'), the special feeling or enjoyment that pervades an artwork or is aroused in its contemplator. The theory of *rasa* was discussed by a number of writers, including Abhinavagupta (eleventh century). Aesthetic enjoyment is commonly seen as detached from the aims and concerns of ordinary life; it even, some suggest, provides a foretaste of the bliss of *mokṣa*.

Dharma and *mokṣa*: moral and non-moral values

As already mentioned, while all the orthodox Hindu philosophers were committed to recognizing the value of *dharma*, the highest value is not *dharma* but *mokṣa*. If we are inclined to think of morality as a concept focused upon forbidden and obligatory actions, then it seems that it is *dharma* that comes closest to such a notion of morality: compare, for instance, the explicit Prābhākara Mīmaṃsaka identification of *dharma* with the performance of obligatory actions (*nitya-karma*) and the avoidance of forbidden ones (*pratiṣiddha-karma*). Moreover, the Prābhākaras take *dharma* to be an end and not a means: virtue consists in practising *dharma* for its own sake, not for the sake of any benefits (like *mokṣa*) that might accrue to the agent. The Prābhākara position, however, is very much a minority opinion in the Hindu tradition.

The superior value of *mokṣa*, in contrast, appears to be a non-moral value considered higher than morality. But the relation of *dharma* to *mokṣa* (and hence, too, the relation of morality to non-moral value) was a controversial topic among Hindu philosophers, and it is worth exploring the Indian debates about this in a bit more detail.

The oldest tradition (present in the Dharmaśāstra and the Epics) claims an essential continuity between *dharma* and *mokṣa*: selfless performance of one's *dharma* leads ineluctably to *mokṣa*. The Hindu political philosophers also concurred, acknowledging the religious goal of *mokṣa* as the ultimate end of human activity, but also insisting that *artha* and *dharma* are legitimate intermediate worldly goals which, if properly pursued, lead to *mokṣa*. Thus the *Arthaśāstra* acknowledges *artha* or material wealth as an important instrumental value insofar as it enables the performance of *dharma* and the enjoyment of pleasure (*kāma*). However, it is *dharma* that is the superior value, for it is the way to heaven and salvation:

> [The observance of] one's *dharma* leads to heaven and eternal bliss. When *dharma* is transgressed, the resulting chaos leads to the extermination of this world. Whoever upholds his own *dharma*, adheres to the customs of the Aryas and follows the rules of the *varnas* and the stages of life, will find joy here and in the hereafter. For the world, when maintained in accordance with the Vedas, will ever prosper and not perish. Therefore, the king shall never allow the people to swerve from their *dharma*. (*Arthaśāstra* 1.3.14–7; Rangarajan 1987: 107–8)

Accordingly the king's duty is to maintain the order and stability necessary for the people to promote their economic well-being and practise *dharma*. Such order is upheld by proper use of *daṇḍa* ('the rod'), in other words, by the just use of force to punish breaches of the rules of *dharma*: 'The people of a society, whatever their *varna* or stage of life, will follow their own *dharma* and pursue with devotion their occupations, if they are protected by the king and the just use of *danda* [coercion and punishment]' (*Arthaśāstra* 1.4.16; Rangarajan 1987: 99).

The content of a person's particular *svadharma* is determined, of course, by his or her caste and stage of life, as laid down in the Dharmaśāstra. The idea that the practice of *dharma* leads naturally to the attainment of *mokṣa* is there connected with the *āśrama* schema: the exclusive pursuit of *mokṣa* is placed at the end of life after a lifetime of selfless practice of one's *dharma* has enabled the cultivation of the requisite self-discipline and detachment. Indeed the *Manusmṛti* (6.34–7) goes so far as to insist:

> A man who has gone from one stage of life to another, made the offerings into the fire, conquered his sensory powers, exhausted himself by giving alms and propitiatory offerings, and then lived as a wandering ascetic – when he has died, he thrives. When a man has paid his three debts, he may set his mind-and-heart on Freedom [*mokṣa*]; but if he seeks Freedom when he has not paid the debts, he sinks down. When a man has studied the Veda in accordance with the rules, and begotten sons in accordance with his duty, and sacrificed with sacrifices according to his ability, he may set his mind-and-heart on Freedom. But if a twice-born man seeks Freedom when he has not studied the Vedas, and has not begotten progeny, and has not sacrificed with sacrifices, he sinks down. (Doniger and Smith 1991: 120–1)

In this sense *dharma* is continuous with *mokṣa*.

In direct conflict with this emphasis on the continuity of *dharma* and *mokṣa* is the view of the great Advaitin philosopher Śaṃkara (eighth century), which instead opposes *dharma* and *mokṣa*. This opposition is a logical consequence of the metaphysics of Advaita Vedānta, according to which *mokṣa* is the realization of the identity of the Self (*ātman*) with the Absolute (*Brahman*). But *mokṣa* thus conceived is a state of non-duality, whereas all action presupposes a duality between self and other. Thus *mokṣa* precludes action, and hence *dharma* with its concern for obligatory and forbidden actions. As Śaṃkara puts it in the *Upadeśasāhasrī*:

> In fact action is incompatible with knowledge [of *Brahman*], since [it] is associated with misconception [of *Ātman*]. And knowledge [of *Brahman*] is declared here [in the Vedānta] to be the view that *Ātman* is changeless. [From the notion] 'I am agent; this is mine' arises action. Knowledge [of *Brahman*] depends upon the real, [whereas] the Vedic injunction depends upon an agent. Knowledge destroys the factors of action as [it destroys] the notion that

> there is water in the salt desert. After accepting this true view, [how] would one decide to perform action? Because of the incompatibility [of knowledge with action] a man who knows thus, being possessed of this knowledge, cannot perform action. For this reason action should be renounced by a seeker after final release. (I.1.12–3; Mayeda 1992: 104)

True, Śaṃkara recognizes the demands of *dharma* on those still enmeshed in the worldly life. Indeed the cultivation of *dharma* is considered a prerequisite for the moral development of the *adhikārin*, the qualified aspirant to *mokṣa*, and hence the supreme ideal of *mokṣa* is not so easily separable from the lesser ideal of *dharma*. But for the *saṃnyāsin*, who recognizes no distinctions, the injunctions of *dharma* have no force. The knowledge of *Brahman*, Śaṃkara insists, puts an end to any activity; including, of course, the ritual actions traditionally incumbent on the twice-born caste male:

> For Self-knowledge is inculcated through the obliteration of the very cause of rites, viz the consciousness of all its means such as the gods. And one whose consciousness of action, its factors and so forth has been obliterated cannot presumably have the tendency to perform rites, for this presupposes a knowledge of specific actions, their means and so on. One who thinks that he is Brahman unlimited by space, time, etc. and not-gross and so on has certainly no room for the performance of rites. (*Bṛhadaraṇyakopaniṣadbhāṣya* I.iii.1; Mādhavānanda 1988: 36)

Śaṃkara's position is a complete rejection of the original Vedānta view that *mokṣa* is attained by a combination of both knowledge and action (*jñānakarmasamuccaya*). Other Vedāntin philosophers are closer to the older view, while still modifying it. Thus Rāmānuja (eleventh century) both allows a place for *dharma* on the path to *mokṣa*, and also denies that liberation is attainable by fulfilment of the obligations of *dharma*. But the motivation here is different from Śaṃkara's. Rāmānuja is a theist who wishes to insist upon a proper creaturely dependence upon the Lord. Liberation is dependent upon God's grace and hence cannot be a direct effect of our own actions. However, if actions are performed not for their results but solely as divine worship, then they are an aid to devotion (*bhakti*) and thereby to release, 'for works enjoined by Scripture have the power of pleasing the Supreme Person, and hence, through his grace, to cause the destruction of all mental impressions obstructive of calmness and concentration of mind' (*Śrībhāṣya* 3.4.27; Thibaut 1971: 701). Rāmānuja's position, then, is a sort of modification of Śaṃkara's. Like

Śaṃkara, he denies that action can be a direct cause of release, but unlike Śaṃkara he insists that one should never abandon the obligatory actions (*nitya-karma*) demanded by *dharma*. The knowledge of *Brahman* that conduces to liberation is understood by Rāmānuja to be that 'knowing' which is synonymous with meditation and meditative worship (*dhyāna*, *upāsanā*):

> Such meditation is originated in the mind through the grace of the Supreme Person, who is pleased and conciliated by the different kinds of acts of sacrifice and worship duly performed by the Devotee day after day... so knowledge, although itself the means of Release, demands the co-operation of the different works. (*Śrībhāṣya* 3.4.26; Thibaut 1971: 699)

Dharma and *mokṣa* are thus still in a sense opposed, though not as radically as in Advaita, for the acts enjoined by *dharma* have no significance in themselves; only the intention of the agent counts, not the result of the action. This is why Rāmānuja insists that his own position is quite different from the Mīmāṃsā idea that the end of life is the performance of (ritual) duty: 'Knowledge of that [devotional] kind has not the most remote connexion even with works [in the Mīmāṃsā sense]' (*Śrībhāṣya* 3.4.12; Thibaut 1971: 692).

Rāmānuja's account is indubitably indebted to the *Bhagavadgītā* (*c.* 500 BCE). But the *Gītā*'s position is nevertheless distinct. The *Gītā* insists upon the absolute importance of *dharma* in sustaining the cosmic and social order. *Dharma* and *mokṣa* are not opposed; rather the *Gītā's* teaching of *karma-yoga* is that it is not action that binds, but attachment to the fruits of action. Thus *mokṣa* does not involve renunciation of action and hence *dharma*, but abandonment of attachment to the fruits of action, while still continuing to perform actions: 'Acts of sacrifice, donation, and askesis of penance are *not* to be renounced: They are one's task – sacrifice, donation, and askesis sanctify the wise. It is my final judgement, Partha, that these acts are to be performed, but with the performer renouncing all self-interest in them and all their rewards' (18.5–6; van Buitenen 1981). *Mokṣa* is not defined in terms of the abandonment of action and hence *dharma*, but instead in terms of the performance of one's *svadharma* with the correct attitude (*niṣkāma karma*):

> Each man achieves perfection by devoting himself to his own task: listen how the man who shoulders his task finds this perfection. He finds it by honoring, through the performance of his own task, him who motivates the creatures to act, on whom all this is strung. One's own Law [*svadharma*] imperfectly observed is better than another's Law carried out with perfection. As long as one does not abandon the work set by nature, he does not incur blame. One

should not abandon his natural task even if it is flawed, Kaunteya, for all undertakings are beset by flaws as fire is by smoke. (18.45–8)

We can distinguish, then, at least four different Hindu views about the relations between *dharma* and *mokṣa*: that of the Dharmaśāstra and the *Arthaśāstra*, of Śaṃkara, of Rāmānuja, and of the *Bhagavadgītā*. Hence notwithstanding the orthodox Hindu insistence that *mokṣa* is the supreme value, there is a significant diversity of Hindu thinking about the relation between moral and non-moral values.

Hindu value pluralism

We have seen that classical Hindu value theory is both pluralistic about value and elevates the non-moral value of *mokṣa* above morality. Perhaps the simplest general characterization of ethical pluralism is that it is the thesis that there is an irreducible plurality of values. Pluralism thus understood is opposed to value monism: the thesis that ultimately there is only one kind of value.

As we have seen, the Hindu philosophers are value pluralists: they affirm the existence of an irreducible plurality of values (this is implicit in the traditional *puruṣārtha* schema). And they are also unanimously *ordered pluralists*, affirming that the plurality of values admits of a single rational ordering.

There is, however, significant disagreement between them about whether the irreducible plurality of values can conflict with one another. The Dharmaśāstrins and the *Gītā* both espouse varieties of *ordered weak pluralism*: there is an irreducible plurality of values that admits of a single rational ordering, but these values do not actually conflict. Śaṃkara, Rāmānuja and Prābhākara Mīmāṃsā all espouse varieties of *ordered strong pluralism*: they affirm that there is an irreducible plurality of values subject to a single rational ordering, and these values can conflict (in which case the ordering resolves the conflict).

Obligation, desire and liberation

Turning now to the Hindu theory of the right, recall the Mīmāṃsā tradition mentioned earlier according to which there are three kinds of deeds that need to be recognized: (1) obligatory deeds (*nitya-karma*); (2) optional deeds (*kāmya-karma*); and (3) forbidden deeds (*pratiṣiddha-karma*). *Dharma* is then identified with the performance of the obligatory actions and the avoidance of the forbidden. This might suggest that right action simply involves performing the obligatory and eschewing the forbidden. But things are a bit more complicated than that because *all* actions are held to accrue karma (good or bad) and yet the state of liberation is supposed to involve freedom from all karma. Thus the demands of right action are in apparent tension with the attainment of the highest good.

Historically, this tension has its sources in two competing strands in Hindu thought: activism (*pravṛtti*), exemplified in the early Vedic ritualistic tradition, and quietism (*nivṛtti*), exemplified in the later Upaniṣadic renunciant tradition. The activist ideal recommends living in society, scrupulously fulfilling all our implied social obligations (including strict adherence to Vedic ritual duties); the quietist ideal recommends instead withdrawing entirely from ordinary society, giving up all karma associated with the performance of social duties and devoting ourselves entirely to contemplation. The primary goal of the discipline recommended by the activistic tradition is the attainment of heaven after death by the earning of merit in this life through the fulfilment of all obligations prescribed by *dharma*; the primary goal of the contemplative discipline recommended by the quietist tradition is the attainment of *mokṣa*, conceived of as a state of liberation from all karma.

Philosophically, this historical tension manifests itself in various ways: one is in the presence of the divergent Hindu views about the relation between the values of *dharma* and *mokṣa* that we reviewed earlier; another is in certain interesting technical details of disputes about the theory of moral motivation.

Theories of moral motivation

Hindu ethicists discussing the nature of right action developed complex theories of moral motivation. According to one standard Indian account, a voluntary action requires the presence of a number of factors, representable as a causal chain: agent, knowledge, desire to act, and effort (*Siddhāntamuktāvalī* 149–51; Mādhavānanda 1977: 243–55). There were significant differences of opinion, however, about the details of this causal chain.

According to the philosophers of the Nyāya school, the relevant kind of desire here requires that the agent believes that (i) the action in question is achievable by the agent, (ii) performing the action is conducive to the agent's good, and (iii) the action is also incapable of causing harm to the agent. In the absence of any of these three factors, the desire to perform the action will not arise in the agent. Moreover, a Vedic injunctive sentence has the power of conveying these three meanings.

The Bhāṭṭa Mīmāṃsā philosophers accept a broadly similar account of voluntary action, but deny that injunctive sentences directly mean that an action can be accomplished by one's volition. Instead, when we understand a Vedic injunctive sentence we also come to believe that the action enjoined is conducive to the desired goal of achieving the highest good and it is this belief that causes us to act.

The Prābhākara Mīmāṃsā philosophers have a simpler theory still. Conduciveness to good is not a sufficient condition for action; all that is necessary for action is the belief that the action should be done. And 'being something to be done' (*karyātva*) is a quite different property from 'being conducive to the good of the agent'.

The major difference between the first two theories and the third is that the former party claims that a belief about an action's conduciveness to good necessarily plays a mediating role, whereas the latter denies that it plays such a role.

Each of these three theories has features relevant to the aforementioned tension between right action and promoting the highest good. The Nyāya account of moral motivation, for instance, is clearly *externalist*: recognizing that an action is morally obligatory is in itself insufficient for moral motivation. What is required instead is a belief that the action conduces to the good of the agent involved. But since all self-interested action creates negative karma, even voluntarily performing right actions is apparently in tension with achieving the highest good of *mokṣa*, conceived of as a state free of karma.

The Bhāṭṭa account is also a variety of externalism insofar as it is the belief that the action enjoined is conducive to the desired goal of achieving the highest good that causes us to act. If that goal is not desired by the agent, then the act will not be performed. But once again that desire of the agent creates karma apparently in tension with the agent's attainment of the highest good.

The Prābhākara account, on the other hand, is *internalist*: the belief that an action is morally obligatory is itself enough to motivate action. The idea of duty is all that is required to mediate between the hearing of a moral injunction and the performance of the action enjoined. This account is thus able to allow for the agent to perform right actions without thereby creating karma incompatible with the attainment of the highest good.

Desire and action in the *Bhagavadgītā*

The Prābhākara Mīmāṃṣā theory of moral motivation may be seen as an elaborate systematization of an earlier idea, expressed much more informally, in the *Bhagavadgītā* (*c.* 500 BCE). The *Gītā* is an enormously popular philosophical poem that attempts a synthesis of many of the themes in Hindu ethics we have touched on so far, albeit without the argumentative rigour of some of the other sources already alluded to. In particular, it suggests an influential and ingenious resolution of the previously noted tension between the demands of right action and the attainment of the highest good.

The *Gītā* is part of the epic tale of the *Mahābhārata*, which tells of the great war between the virtuous Pāṇḍavas and the wicked Kauravas. The *Gītā* is set on the field of battle at Kurukṣetra, where the war is about to begin and the two armies are arrayed facing each other. One of the Pāṇḍava brothers, the master bowman Arjuna, instructs his charioteer, Kṛṣṇa, to position his chariot between the armies so that he may survey the foe. But assembled in the opposing army are Arjuna's relatives, teachers and childhood friends. Faced with the thought of their forthcoming slaughter, Arjuna lays down his bow and refuses to fight.

The motive for Arjuna's refusal to fight goes much deeper than just his reluctance to harm his old friends and kin. Rather he fears that by slaying them he will initiate a slide into moral anarchy and finally cosmic disorder. Arjuna, then, is caught in a moral dilemma. His duty as a warrior is to fight, but if he does so he undermines the moral foundations of that very duty. Either way he does something wrong, so he opts for what he takes to be the lesser evil, to die unarmed and defenseless on the battlefield. For the rest of the *Gītā* Kṛṣṇa tries to persuade Arjuna to recant and take part in the battle.

Firstly Kṛṣṇa explains that Arjuna should go ahead and fight because abstaining from action in order to evade its karmic consequences is just not a viable option: forbearance from action is just another kind of karma-creating action. Rather what we should do is to perform those actions required by our caste duty. This is our *svadharma* ('own duty') and the *Gītā* is very insistent on the importance of following one's own *dharma*, those duties prescribed by the social norms appropriate to one's caste and stage of life.

However, we are also supposed to perform the actions required by our *svadharma* with a special attitude of detachment. Specifically, we should perform those actions without regard to their 'fruits' (*phala*). The commentarial tradition epitomizes this in a punning Sanskrit slogan: the *Gītā* does not teach non-action (*naiṣkarmya*), but detached action (*niṣkāma karma*, literally 'desireless action').

The *Gītā*'s teaching here is an ingenious attempt at a synthesis of the competing activist and quietist strands in Indian thought already mentioned. The *Gītā* says that one must act and perform the duties appropriate to one's *svadharma*; but that one should also act without attachment, for action (*karma*) without desire (*niṣkāma*) does not lead to bondage. Renunciation is thus rendered compatible with activism. The ideal is the sage, all of whose undertakings are devoid of an intention to achieve an object of desire, a being in the world but not of it.

Later in the *Gītā* Kṛṣṇa indicates that the easiest way to implement this strategy of acting while abandoning concern with the fruits of action is to dedicate the fruits of one's actions to God: this is the way of devotion, *bhakti-yoga*. But it is also apparent that this devotional strategy presupposes the essential point about *karma-yoga*: that it is the renunciation of the fruits of action that permits action without bondage, neutralizing the karmic effects of such action. Thus *karma-yoga* is entirely compatible with the other paths to liberation (devotion and knowledge) also acknowledged in the *Gītā*.

The *Gītā* recommends to us, then, a way of living as if one was disassociated from one's actions. We cannot forbear from action, but we can cease to identify ourselves with our actions by no longer performing them for some end. In this way we can disavow *moral* responsibility for actions that we are *causally* responsible for by virtue of their causal association with our bodies.

The *Gītā*'s advice is to concentrate exclusively on the performance of the duties attendant on our communal roles and, in doing so, to surrender all attachment to the fruits of our action. Since the *Gītā* prescribes 'desireless' action and classical Hindu theories of action make desire a necessary condition of action, presumably 'desireless' here means free of some particular *kind* of desire (though see Framarin 2009 for a different view). If so, however, then arguably it is attachment to desires that has to be eliminated, rather than desires per se, and disinterested action can be understood as action free from *attached* desires. An attached desire for something might then be explicated as typically involving both a first-order desire for that thing and a second-order desire for that first-order desire (see further Perrett 1998).

For the *Bhagavadgītā*, then, moral action is action performed with a special impersonal psychological attitude of detachment, but where the content of that action is determined by the agent's particular caste, thus ensuring a stable sociopolitical structure in order to maximize the possibilities for pursuing the supramoral ideal of liberation (*mokṣa*) – even if in the case of the warrior Arjuna, this means performing his caste duty and killing hordes of his friends and relatives.

Virtue and the supramoral

What has been said so far about the nature of Hindu ethics is likely to have already suggested that it is unpromising to represent it as a variety of virtue ethics, if by 'virtue ethics' we mean a normative theory that takes the virtues to be more fundamental than other normative factors. However, that does not mean that Hindu ethicists were unconcerned with *virtue theory*, that is, the area of normative enquiry concerned with the virtues in general.

One traditional Hindu classification, for instance, divides the virtues into (1) the virtues of the body (e.g., *dāna* or charity), (2) the virtues of speech (e.g., *satya* or truthfulness), and (3) the virtues of the mind (e.g., *dayā* or benevolence). A particularly highly praised virtue is non-violence (*ahiṃsā*), the presence of which is taken to imply other virtues to the extent that other virtues like truthfulness, non-stealing, continence, and greedlessness are all said to be based on the spirit of non-injury.

But while the cultivation of these ideal virtues is always praiseworthy, it need not be obligatory for ordinary persons. Although *mokṣa* is the highest value, it is not considered morally blameworthy to fail to exemplify it in one's own life. In this way the ideal of the saint is acknowledged (and even valorized), but a tolerance of the limitations of ordinary human nature means that failure to live up to the ideal of sainthood will not be seen as a moral failure. In other words, a place is made in Hindu ethics for both the ordinary ideal of morality and the supramoral ideal of the saint.

To be a candidate for *mokṣa*, an *adhikārin*, requires being able to discriminate between the eternal and non-eternal, being able to give up desires for the fruits of one's actions, being able to control the mind and senses, and having an ardent desire for liberation. Liberation, then, is only available to those who by disposition and training are equipped for the demands of the quest, typically the ascetic *saṃnyāsin*.

However, the Hindu tradition also acknowledges the material dependence of the ascetic aspirant to *mokṣa* on the generosity of the householder. Thus even if there is no moral obligation for everyone to exemplify in their own person the supramoral ideal of liberation, there is an obligation to ensure a society that best promotes this ideal. We need a sociopolitical structure that effectively harmonizes the demands of morality and the supramoral, as does the traditional *varṇāśrama-dharma* scheme, which assigns duties to agents according to their caste and stage of life.

Defending the primacy of liberation

A major commonality between orthodox Hindu ethics and the ethics of the heterodox Buddhist and Jaina was their shared commitment to the primacy of liberation as the supreme good. A variety of Sanskrit terms were introduced for the notion of liberation, including *mokṣa*, *mukti*, *nirvāṇa*, *kaivalya*, and *apavarga*. Some of these terms are specific to particular philosophical schools and hence incorporate special theoretical connotations. Thus the Yoga term *apavarga* ('completion, end') connotes that liberation is escape from rebirth, while the Sāṃkhya term *kaivalya* ('isolation') connotes the nature of the state of being of a liberated soul. The term *nirvāṇa* is used by both the Buddhists and the Jainas, but whereas the Buddhists use it as a synonym for *mokṣa*, the Jainas use it to refer to the final death of an enlightened being, followed immediately by *mokṣa*. The Vedāntin philosophers, on the other hand, tend to favour the general terms *mokṣa* or *mukti*, both ultimately derived from the root *muc*, meaning 'free, release'. But one thing all of these philosophers agree on is the primacy of the value of liberation, however this is conceived.

That liberation is the highest good is taken by most Indian philosophers to be an implication of the fact that all ordinary worldly life is characterized by our bondage to suffering (*duḥkha*), even though this quality may not be obvious to the unreflective. Thus the *Sāmkhyakārikā* begins, 'Because of the torment of the threefold suffering arises the desire to know the means of terminating it'; but the *Yogasūtra* (II.15) adds, 'To the discerning all is but suffering.' Similarly, the ubiquity of suffering is the First Noble Truth of Buddhism, but the Buddha is also reported to have added: 'It is difficult to shoot from a distance arrow after arrow through a narrow key hole, and miss not once. It is more difficult to shoot and penetrate with the tip of a hair split a hundred times a piece of hair similarly split. It is more difficult still to penetrate to the fact that "all this is ill"' (*Saṃyutta Nikāya* 56.45; Conze 1951: 45).

The claim about the ubiquity of suffering is thus (at least partially) an evaluative thesis that is supposed to be objectively true: ordinary human life is deeply unsatisfactory, whether or not worldlings perceive it as so. Most Indian philosophers also agree that what keeps us bound to suffering is karma, that is, our actions and their consequences, particularly the habits and further desires they create. They usually agree too that the route to freedom is through renunciation. There is much less agreement, however, on the details of the metaphysics of karma and on the issue of precisely how renunciation works its liberating magic.

Scepticism with respect to these sorts of claims about the ubiquity of suffering and the value and feasibility of liberation was certainly not unknown in India. The Cārvāka materialists, for instance, maintained that sensual enjoyment is the only rational end of human action and that a state of *mokṣa* is effectively no better than death. Moreover, they argued that even if liberation were conceded to be a superior good, it would still need to be shown that such a good is readily attainable. Otherwise it is irrational to renounce certain worldly pleasures in pursuit of the wildly uncertain hope of *mokṣa*.

In the face of such objections the liberation-oriented philosophers try to show that liberation is both desirable and attainable. In order to show that *mokṣa* is desirable, they develop an interestingly nuanced account of the evil of suffering and its place in the structure of value. Thus in the Buddhist tradition *duḥkha* is classified as of three kinds (*Abhidharmakośa* 6.3; *Visuddhimagga* 16.3). The first is *duḥkha* as physical pain (*duḥkha-duḥkha*); the second is *duḥkha* due to change (*vipariṇāma-duḥkha*); and the third is *duḥkha* through the fact of being conditioned (*saṃskāra-duḥkha*). The first type of suffering is straightforwardly a disvalue. The second type of *duḥkha* is a bit more subtle: the transitoriness of phenomena is *duḥkha* because we cannot hold on to the objects of our cravings and this gives rise to a continual frustration which again is an obvious disvalue. In this sense even happy states of experience may be called suffering or *duḥkha*. The third type of suffering is subtler still. It is not just physical pain, nor mental frustration caused by the impermanence of phenomena, but rather the *duḥkha* that is associated with the conditioned nature of phenomena. The idea here seems to be that we want the good life to be resilient, that is, not hostage to fortune. But the goodness of worldly life is irretrievably fragile since all things are conditioned. Our enjoyment of a present good is inevitably contingent upon innumerable conditions outside of our control; we are the impotent recipients of moral luck. This sense of fragility undermines the goodness of whatever we are fortunate enough to enjoy temporarily, leading in reflective agents to a felt unease.

This latter emphasis on the fragility of goodness is also present in the Hindu tradition. Thus the *Manusmṛti* explicitly says: 'Everything under another person's control is unhappiness [*duḥkha*], and everything under one's own control is happiness; it should be known that this sums up the distinguishing marks of unhappiness and happiness' (4.160; Doniger and Smith 1991: 89). Compare also the way in which the *Yogabhāṣya*, commenting on Patañjali's claim that 'to the discerner all is but *duḥkha*' (II.15), classifies suffering as being of three types: the suffering associated with change (*pariṇāma*), with anxiety (*tāpa*), and with habituation (*saṃskāra*). The first type of suffering is associated with the fact that fulfilment of our desires increases our attachment to them and hence too the subsequent frustration attendant upon their future non-fulfilment. Knowledge of this takes away from our present enjoyment of states of pleasure. The frustration by change of our need for security is associated with the second type of suffering: the anxiety or anguish that is common to all human experience. The third type of suffering is that of habituation, the way in which our desires and the habits they create make for a locus with not only a potential for pleasure, but also an inevitable potential for pain. Insofar as we are conditioned beings, our enjoyment of the good life is fragile.

As in Buddhism, it is not that there are no agreeable or pleasurable experiences. Rather the idea is that because of the continual transformation of nature, our experience is permeated with a deep dissatisfaction and anxiety. The radical contingency and fragility of those pleasures we do experience causes the discriminating to experience even these as sorrowful. In the Buddhist simile, the pursuit of worldly pleasures is like licking honey from a razor blade (*Bodhicaryāvatāra* 7.65).

Buddhist ethics

The ethics of Buddhism and Jainism are a bit different from Hindu ethics since the Buddhists and the Jainas do not accept the *puruṣārtha* schema, or the *varṇāśrama* system. However, the heterodox systems of Buddhism and Jainism also affirm the pre-eminence of *mokṣa* (or *nirvāṇa*). In Indian Buddhist ethics typically we find a two-tiered system, with the monks committed to the pursuit of the supramoral goal of *nirvāṇa* and the laity committed to the ordinary ideal of morality as expressed in the five precepts. The laity revere and serve the monks and through these activities strive for a favourable rebirth so as to be better placed in the future to pursue *nirvāṇa* for themselves. In other words, as laypersons they seek to promote the supramoral value of *nirvāṇa* through their support of the monks, but they do not seek to exemplify that value themselves. This is instead the goal of the monks, the specialists of the supramoral. True, the Mahāyāna ethical ideal of the compassionate *bodhisattva* allows more of a place for laypersons, but even then the monastic community effectively gets prioritized since the conditions of monastic life better allow for the serious cultivation of the *bodhisattva* path.

The most widely known list of ethical requirements in Buddhism is the set of general duties expressed in the Five Precepts (*pañcaśīla*): the duties to refrain from killing, stealing, sexual immorality, wrong speech and the use of intoxicants. On becoming a Buddhist one formally accepts these precepts in the ceremony of 'going for refuge'. Laypersons may then elect to take on additional precepts, but monastics have in addition to the Five Precepts a much more elaborate set of special duties, described in the *Vinaya* literature. These special duties are set out in the *prātimokṣa* codes, the set of rules regulating the behaviour of monks and nuns. The total number of such rules varies in the texts of different Buddhist schools, ranging from 218 to 263 for monks and from 279 to 380 for nuns.

In addition to all these moral rules there is also a significant emphasis on the virtues, for accordance with the rules must be properly motivated in order to be optimally moral. For laypersons one of the most important virtues is generosity (*dāna*), particularly as manifested in material support for the monastic community. Two other highly valued virtues are non-injury (*ahiṃsā*) and compassion (*karuṇā*). Buddhist virtue theory is further developed in the Mahāyāna schools where the ideal of the *bodhisattva*, a being who seeks enlightenment for the benefit of others, is associated with the practice of the 'Six Perfections' (*pāramitā*): generosity (*dāna*), morality (*śīla*), patience (*kṣānti*), perseverance (*vīrya*), meditation (*samādhi*), and wisdom (*prajñā*). Mahāyāna ethics also allows that the precepts can sometimes be justifiably overridden by a skilful *bodhisattva* in furtherance of the ideal of compassion.

The proper classification of the nature of Indian Buddhist ethics is a matter of controversy among contemporary Buddhist scholars. Some favour an understanding of Buddhist ethics as a variety of *virtue ethics* (Keown 2001, 2005). As already noted, there is certainly an emphasis on the cultivation of various virtues in Buddhist ethical texts. But it is also important once again to distinguish *virtue theory* from *virtue ethics*. Any developed normative ethical theory will have to include some place for the virtues and hence offer some sort of virtue theory (i.e., some sort of account of what the virtues are and why they matter, their logical structure and their interrelations with other relevant phenomena). On the other hand, a normative ethical theory is often only considered to be a variety of virtue ethics if it insists that the virtue notions are somehow logically prior to other moral notions. So although Buddhist ethics unquestionably exhibits a concern with virtue theory, this does not entail that it is a variety of virtue ethics. Instead other scholars (Goodman 2009; Siderits 2003, 2007) believe that Buddhist ethics is better classified as a form of *consequentialism*, that is, an ethical theory that takes the rightness of an action to be a function of its consequences. The importance of the cultivation of the virtues is then to be justified in terms of their positive contribution to the overall consequentialist project of acting so as to promote the best consequences.

Intention (*cetanā*) in Buddhist ethics

One source of a reluctance to view Buddhist ethics as a variety of consequentialism is the obvious importance Buddhism places on intention (*cetanā*), even to the point where the moral value of an action might seem to be just a function of the agent's intentions. After all, Buddhism's distinctive contribution to the ethicization of the doctrine of karma was to make the crucial act a mental one, a 'volition' or 'intention' (*cetanā*). It is the presence of this intentional factor, rather than the external act alone, that is held to be the karmically significant force. Thus the oft-quoted words of the Buddha as recorded in the *Aṅguttara Nikāya* (3.295): 'O monks, it is volition [or intention, *cetanā*] that I call karma. Having willed, one acts through body, speech and thought.'

Furthermore, in the Theravādin legalistic tradition embodied in the *Vinayapiṭaka* it is clear that the moral assessment of actions requires assessment of the condition of the agent. Unfortunately, the Pali *Vinayapiṭaka* does not explicitly discuss the principles involved here. This is because Buddhist law is traditionally casuistic: rather than enunciate general principles from which particular judgments can be derived, it prefers extensive listing of individual cases and the Buddha's judgments thereon. However, certain principles are implicit in such individual case judgments. For instance, the agent's intention to commit a forbidden act seems at least a *necessary* condition for moral responsibility. This is well brought out in relation to the precept concerning sexual restraint by the following interesting case from the *Suttavibhaṅga*:

> Now at that time a certain monk was lying down, having gone into the Great Wood at Vesālī for the day-sojourn. A certain woman, sat down on him, and having taken her pleasure, stood laughing near by. The monk, waking up, spoke thus to this woman: 'Have you done this?' 'Yes, I have,' she said. On account of this he was remorseful... 'Monk, did you consent?' 'I did not, lord,' he said. 'Monk, there is no offence as you did not know.' (Horner 1938: 59)

However, although intentionality is thus crucial for the assignment of responsibility, Theravādin thought does allow consequences to play some role in grading the moral severity of various intentional actions. Hence we find the *Suttavibhaṅga* juxtaposing three similar cases where a monk gets meat stuck in his throat and is struck on the neck by a fellow monk (Horner 1938: 139–40). In the first case the striker kills the monk inadvertently. In the second case the striker intends to kill the monk and does so by striking him on the neck. In the third case the striker intends to kill the monk but fails to do so, though he strikes him. The first case is ruled to be no offence; the second case is ruled to be an offence involving 'defeat' (*pārājika*), that is, expulsion from the order of monks; the third case is ruled to be a grave offence, but not one involving defeat.

An unsuccessful attempt at an intentional killing, then, is to be viewed less severely than a successful killing. The latter fulfils the traditional conditions for the gravest sort of violation against the precept to avoid taking life: (1) it is a living being that is destroyed; (2) it is known by the killer that it is a living being; (3) there is a desire or intention (*cetanā*) to kill that living being; (4) an endeavour was made to kill that living being; and (5) that living being was killed through the efforts made by the would-be killer. Thus whether or not death actually results from an intended act of killing does affect the moral gravity of the offence. In this sense Theravādin Buddhist ethics is not *purely* intentionalistic since it does not hold that the moral value of an action is simply a function of the agent's intentions.

Buddhist consequentialism

Not only is the presence of a concern with virtue and intentions insufficient to show that Buddhist ethics is not consequentialist, there are also positive reasons to think that it may indeed be a form of consequentialism. Consequentialism as a theory of the right holds that actions are right insofar as they promote the good. For Buddhists this good is the elimination of suffering (*duḥkha*). Motives too are important in Buddhist ethics, but consequentialists can admit the importance of motives, provided the goodness of a motive depends on how good its overall consequences are – and similarly for the virtues. For Buddhists this means that the goodness of a motive or virtue depends upon whether it promotes the elimination of suffering.

As a matter of ethical theory, then, we need to distinguish between the normative *factors* relevant to determining the moral status of an act and the normative *foundations* that generate and explain the favoured list of normatively relevant factors (Kagan 1998). Admitting the moral relevance of factors in addition to outcomes does not preclude all of these factors being given a purely consequentialist explanation at the foundational level. Hence the Buddhist can quite consistently be a consequentialist at the foundational level without being a consequentialist at the factoral level.

This idea that Buddhist ethics is *foundationally* consequentialist is obviously very explicitly marked in the Mahāyāna conception of 'skilful means' (*upāya-kauśalya*), according to which a compassionate *bodhisattva* may justifiably override other ethical considerations if doing so would prevent or reduce suffering. But we can find even early canonical Theravādin texts (e.g., *Majjhima Nikāya* 61.88) which affirm that whatever action – bodily, verbal or mental – leads to suffering for oneself, for others or for both, that action is wrong; while whatever action – bodily, verbal or mental – does not lead to suffering for oneself, for others or for both, that action is right.

Some of the most striking affirmations of Buddhist consequentialism, however, are to be found in the writings of the Madhyamaka philosopher Śāntideva (eighth century). Consider, for instance, this passage from his *Śikṣāsamuccaya*, which explicitly sets forth a universal characteristic of wrongdoing for a *bodhisattva*:

> Through actions of body, speech, and mind, the Bodhisattva sincerely makes a continuous effort to stop all present and future suffering and depression, and to produce present and future happiness and gladness, for all beings. But if he does not seek the collection of the conditions for this, and does not strive for what will prevent the obstacles to this, or he does not cause small suffering and depression to arise as a way of preventing great suffering and depression,

> or does not abandon a small benefit in order to achieve a great benefit, if he neglects to do these things even for a moment, he is at fault. (I.15: Goodman 2009: 89–90)

In his *Bodhicaryāvatāra* Śāntideva goes further, apparently seeking to derive something like this sort of impartialist act-consequentialism from the distinctive Buddhist metaphysics of 'no-self'.

'No-self' and selflessness

There are some famous verses in Śāntideva's *Bodhicaryāvatāra* (8.90–103) that offer an interesting set of arguments for impartialist altruism, some of which appeal directly to Buddhist reductionism about the self (i.e., the metaphysical thesis that personal identity just consists in the holding of certain facts that can be described without making reference to personal identity).

The altruistic thesis that Śāntideva wants to defend is that 'All equally experience suffering and happiness, and I must protect them as I do myself' (8.91). In support of this he begins with a fundamental impartialist claim:

> I should eliminate the suffering of others because it is suffering, just like my own suffering... When happiness is equally dear to others and myself, then what is so special about me that I strive after happiness for myself alone? When fear and suffering are equally abhorrent to others and myself, then what is so special about me that I protect myself but not others? (8.94–6; Wallace and Wallace 1997)

Śāntideva then goes on to respond to an anticipated objection to the effect that there is an all-important metaphysical distinction between my future self and other future selves. Not so, he says, because the connection between me and the sufferings of my future body is metaphysically no closer than that between me and other future bodies. In support of this he appeals to Buddhist reductionism:

> The continuum of consciousness, like a series, and the aggregate of constituents, like an army and such, are unreal. Since one who experiences suffering does not exist, to whom will that suffering belong? All sufferings are without an owner, because they are not different. They should be warded off simply because they are suffering. Why is any restriction made in this case? Why should suffering be prevented? Because everyone agrees. If it must

be warded off, then all of it must be warded off; and if not, then this goes for oneself as it does for everyone else. (8.101–3)

Note that there are two distinct arguments here for altruism. The first claims that we should regard the well-being of others impartially with our own because suffering is equally bad regardless of where it happens to occur. The second claims that a reductionist view of the self undermines egoism by showing the ultimate unreality of persons. Let us take the latter argument first.

What Śāntideva is arguing is that since Buddhists hold that persons are ultimately unreal, ultimately they have to admit that there is suffering but none who suffer. When we realize the truth of reductionism, we see that our thinking of ourselves as self-existent separate beings is without ontological grounding. Ultimately our intrinsic separateness from other beings is a conceptual fiction. But suffering itself remains real enough, though 'ownerless'. Hence since everyone admits it reasonable to attempt to alleviate their 'own' present and future suffering, everyone should admit that it is only reasonable to alleviate the present and future suffering of 'others' too.

The argument is contentious (see Williams 1998a). To go through it requires not only the truth of reductionism about the self, but also that such reductionism really does entail that one should be equally concerned for the well-being of all. But it is hard to see why this should be so. Of course, Buddhism tells us that at the level of ultimate truth there are no real persons and hence no distinctions to be made between them. But then neither, ultimately, is there suffering to be relieved, or any moral duty to relieve it. At the conventional level of truth, on the other hand, where moral agency occurs, there certainly are still persons whose suffering we ought to relieve. However, in that context there is also an important conventional distinction to be made between my suffering and the suffering of others. In other words, it is unclear that we have here a convincing justification of our obligations of moral selflessness as following from the Buddhist metaphysics of the self.

Note, however, that this metaphysical argument appeals also in part to Śāntideva's other argument to the effect that since suffering is equally bad wherever it appears, we should work to overcome others' suffering just as we work to overcome our own suffering. After all, Śāntideva asks, what is so special about me that I should seek to further only my well-being? Implicit here is perhaps a distinct argument from Śāntideva's metaphysical argument; indeed it seems to be an argument quite independent of any particular metaphysics of the self. How might it best be developed?

It is commonly conceded that moral judgments need to be *universalizable*, namely moral judgments must be capable of being universal and involve no ineliminable reference to a particular person. Moreover there is a kind of rational inconsistency in making different moral judgments about cases that are admitted to be identical in all their non-moral universal properties, whether these cases are actual or hypothetical. Moral judgments are also arguably *prescriptive*: they involve willing their applications to actual or hypothetical cases. Hence if I assert that I ought to act in a particular way towards a certain person, I am thereby committed to asserting too that the same ought to be done to me if I were in precisely his situation. Although different individuals would occupy the two roles, their universal properties would be identical. But then my judgment that it is permissible to fail to alleviate another's suffering when it is within my power to do so implies that the same ought to be done to me if I were in precisely his situation, though I know that if I were in that situation I would not agree to this. Furthermore in the case of suffering there is no plausible difficulty in determining what the other's preferences might be: as Śāntideva says, suffering is equally abhorrent to others and myself. But then what is so special about me that I seek to protect myself from suffering but not others? How can my interests have a special moral weight just because they are *my* interests? There seems, then, to be a kind of rational inconsistency in refusing to give at least prima facie equal weight to the interests of others, actual or hypothetical.

Jaina ethics

The Jainas are also opposed to ethical egoism, but they do not defend their ethical position by appeal to a reductionist theory of the self (on the contrary, they are fervent non-reductionists about the self). Like the Buddhists, however, they do emphasize the moral importance of a sense of fellowship and reciprocity for the agent's own wellbeing:

> He who knows what is bad for himself knows what is bad for others, and he who knows what is bad for others knows what is bad for himself. This reciprocity should always be borne in mind. Those whose minds are at peace

> and who are free from passions do not desire to live [at the expense of others]. (*Ācārāṅga Sūtra* 1.1.7; de Bary 1958: 60)

Moreover, a similar pattern to the Buddhist two-tiered social system of monastics and laity exists in Jainism, where the ascetic community of mendicants whose practice is focused on the attainment of *mokṣa* is materially supported by a lay community committed to a much more restricted set of moral ideals expressed in the five 'lesser vows' (*aṇuvrata*).

There is no doubt that Jaina ethics is very demanding in its ideal demands on the individual agent. The individual's ethical task is to undertake a rigorous process of self-purification and self-cultivation so as to eliminate the karma that entangles us in suffering and thereby achieve liberation. This goal is indeed the source of the Sanskrit word *Jaina*: from *jina* or 'conqueror', one who has successfully subdued their passions and achieved liberation from suffering.

For Jaina monks and nuns this process of purification involves following the five 'Great Vows' (*mahāvrata*): non-violence (*ahiṃsā*), truthfulness (*satya*), non-stealing (*asteya*), celibacy (*brahmacarya*) and non-attachment (*aparigraha*). The first vow is a commitment to total abstinence in thought, word and deed from injury to all life forms. The second is a commitment both to abstain from lying, and to take care not to use violent or harmful speech. The third is a general commitment not to take what has not been given. The fourth is a commitment to lead a life of complete sexual continence. The fifth is a commitment to renounce attachment to the objects of the world, that is, to renounce possession of property. In each case, the point of the vow is to foster a state of internal purification necessary for the attainment of liberation.

Although these five Great Vows capture the Jaina ethical ideal, they are recognized by Jainas to be feasible only for ascetics. For laypersons a less severe code of conduct is expected. The lay vows are twelvefold, the core being the five 'Lesser Vows' (*aṇuvrata*), which parallel the five ascetic Great Vows both in their content and in the lifelong commitment they require. The major difference between the two sets of vows is that for the laity the last two of the Great Vows are replaced with vows of chastity and contentment or strict limitation of the accumulation of wealth.

The most fundamental of both sets of five vows is *ahiṃsā*, the unique and cardinal virtue in Jaina ethics. Here is the Great Vow version:

> I renounce all killing of living beings, whether subtle or gross, whether movable or immovable. Nor shall I myself kill living beings, nor cause others to do so, nor consent to it. As long as I live I confess, and blame, and exempt myself of these sins, in mind, speech and body. (*Ācārāṅga Sūtra* II.15; Jacobi 1884: 202)

For the ascetic, this vow is taken to imply five further clauses:

> A Nirgrantha [ascetic, 'one without attachments'] is careful in his walk, not careless.
>
> A Nirgrantha searches into his mind. If his mind is sinful, acting on impulses, produces quarrels, pains, he should not employ such a mind.
>
> A Nirgrantha searches into his speech. If his speech is sinful, produces quarrels, pains, he should not utter such speech.
>
> A Nirgrantha is careful in laying down his utensils of begging.
>
> A Nirgrantha eats and drinks after inspecting his food and drink. If a Nirgrantha would eat and drink without inspecting his food and drink, he might hurt and displace or injure or kill all sorts of living beings.

Clearly, this ideal degree of commitment to non-injury is not feasible for laypersons, and so Jainism later introduced the element of intention, such that the observance of *ahiṃsā* need not totally inhibit normal behaviour. Jinabhadra (seventh century) explains:

> It is the intention that ultimately matters. From the real point of view, a man does not become a killer only because he has killed or because the world is crowded with souls, or remain innocent only because he has not killed physically . . . Even if a person does not actually kill, he becomes a killer if he has the intention to kill; while a doctor has to cause pain but is still noninjuring and innocent because his intention is pure . . . For it is the intention which is the deciding factor, not the external act. (Dundas 2002: 164)

The demands of *ahiṃsā*, however, still remain very rigorous for all Jainas. For instance, according to Jaina metaphysics the class of sentient beings (*jīva*) includes not only humans and animals, but also innumerable *nigoda* (the myriad single-sense creatures that inhabit almost every part of the universe). Thus Jainas are not only strict vegetarians, they also avoid all occupations that involve harm to living creatures. (For laypersons, this usually means favouring the choice of a livelihood as a merchant.) In addition, this ideal of non-violence is famously extended to include intellectual life too, and is sometimes even claimed to have influenced the development of Jaina pluralistic logical theory (*syādvāda*).

Given the centrality of *ahiṃsā* to Jaina ethics, it is important to understand that the harm (*hiṃsā*) to be avoided is not just the harm to others, but also the harm done to oneself by such violent actions. Indeed for the Jainas, the primary reference of *hiṃsā* is to such self-injury, that is, to behaviour that by creating further karmic entanglements inhibits the self's ability to attain *mokṣa*. Morality, then, is seen as a means for progressing towards liberation.

This raises an interesting issue about the Jaina practice of ritual self-starvation (*sallekhanā*). Faced with old age or a terminal illness, a Jaina may permissibly opt to die by gradual fasting. This kind of death is available to both ascetics and laity (though it is more common among mendicants). *Sallekhanā* is a practice that properly 'thins out' both the physical body and the internal passions. Such voluntary deaths have occurred throughout the history of Jainism (even in modern times) and, if done in the proper manner, are celebrated by Jainas as ensuring a rapid passage to liberation.

Jainism is very insistent, however, that this special kind of voluntary death is quite different from the usual sort of death through suicide. Jainas eschew the latter because passions of attachment, aversion or infatuation are involved. In contrast, *sallekhanā* involves the aspirant merely withdrawing conscientiously from the taking of food in a gradual fashion that does not disrupt their inner peace or mindfulness. By virtue of its excellence, this passionless death performed under strict conditions is regarded as the most effective ascetic practice to rid the soul of binding passions and to bring to an end an ethical life. In this sense, *sallekhanā* is a voluntary death that is not a self-harming incompatible with *ahiṃsā*.

Conclusion

Even if ethics was not a distinct field within Indian philosophy, we have seen that the Indian philosophers certainly presented us with a challenging set of substantive proposals concerning how to live, how to act, and what sort of person to be. We have also seen that there was a broad consensus among Hindu, Buddhist and Jaina philosophers both that liberation is the highest good and that the observance of a variety of moral restraints is at least a preliminary condition for the attainment of that good. But most Indian philosophers were also agreed that *knowledge* is a condition for the attainment of the highest good, and on the issue of knowledge they had a great deal to say – as we shall see in the next chapter.

Suggestions for further reading

On the nature of Hindu ethics, see further Hiriyanna 1975, Maitra 1956, Perrett 1998 and Crawford 1982. For more on the Dharmaśāstra literature, see Lingat 1973, Olivelle 2005 and Davis 2010. On ethics in the Epics, see Das 2009 and Matilal 1989, 2002b. On Indian political theory, see Brown 1953, Spellman 1964 and Kangle 1960–5. For Indian aesthetic theory, see Gerow 1997, Chari 1990 and Trivedi 2013. For divergent accounts of the nature of Buddhist ethics, see Keown 2005, 2001, Goodman 2009 and Harvey 2000. On Jainism, see Jaini 1998, Dundas 2002. An interesting study of desire and moral motivation in Indian philosophy is Framarin 2009. For Indian debates about the relation of knowledge to the highest good, see Ram-Prasad 2001.

2 Knowledge

Introduction

Epistemological concerns were explicitly central to classical Indian philosophy. This followed naturally from the fact that the avowed goal of most Indian philosophers was liberation (*mokṣa*), conceived of as the highest good. Such liberation was deemed worth pursuing because worldly life was widely accepted to be inevitably characterized by suffering (*duḥkha*). The usual philosophical strategy for finding a route to liberation from suffering involved isolating a crucial causal condition for our entanglement in such suffering and seeking to overturn it. The most popular candidate for such a condition was ignorance (*avidyā*): we are caught in the cycle of suffering due to our ignorance. Accordingly, eliminating our ignorance through the acquisition of knowledge is the way to liberation.

The beginning of the *Nyāyasūtra*, for example, provides a characteristic statement of the leading idea here:

> Supreme felicity is attained by the knowledge about the true nature of the sixteen categories . . . Pain, birth, activity, faults [defects] and misapprehension [wrong notion] – on the successive annihilation of these in the reverse order, there follows release. (Radhakrishnan and Moore 1957: 358)

This soteriological premise, with its implied epistemological optimism about the instrumental relations between knowledge and the attainment of the highest good, then naturally generates a number of more technical epistemological questions. Questions like: What is knowledge? What are its sources? What are its objects? How do we fall into error? These sorts of questions deeply engaged Indian philosophers and the competing theories they developed to answer them gave rise to *pramāṇavāda*, that is, that part of Indian philosophy concerned with the nature and sources of knowledge.

It is worth remarking, however, that although Indian epistemology has an explicit soteriological motivation, much of the detailed technical literature frequently proceeds in a fashion largely independent of this commitment. This is unsurprising since the instrumental view of knowledge can easily be generalized, and indeed explicitly was so generalized. Thus the Buddhist logician Dharmakīrti (ninth century), although personally firmly committed to the soteriological premise, clearly indicates that it is but a special case of a more general feature about knowledge which should motivate the study of epistemology: 'The attainment of all human ends is preceded by right knowledge and therefore it is here expounded' (*Nyāyabindu* 1.1).

The structure of knowledge according to *pramāṇa* theory

Classical Indian theory of knowledge is centred around *pramāṇa* theory. In Indian epistemology the *pramāṇas* are the *means* of knowledge, providing knowledge through modes like perception, inference and testimony. The *prameyas* are the knowables, cognizable entities that constitute the world. A *pramā* is a knowledge episode and the relation between such a cognitive episode and its object (*prameya*) is structured by the *pramāṇas*. A *pramāṇa* provides both an authoritative source for making a knowledge claim and a means for (or way of) knowledge. In other words, a *pramāṇa* has a dual character: both evidential and causal. It provides evidence or justification for regarding a cognitive episode as a knowledge episode, but it is also supposed to be the most effective causal route to such an episode. Thus the theory of *pramāṇas* becomes both a theory of epistemic justification and a metaphysical theory of the causal requirements necessary for the validity of such justification. The *pramāṇas* are not simply justification procedures, but also those methods that match the causal chains with the justification chains so as to validate knowledge claims. (It is perhaps worth noting here, however, that the Buddhist *pramāṇavādins* of the school of Dharmakīrti dissent from this general conception of *pramāṇas* as what leads to right cognition: for them the *pramāṇas are* right cognition.)

Indian philosophers vigorously debated the number and nature of the *pramāṇas*. The Cārvāka admitted only perception as a valid means of knowledge, and accordingly rejected a belief in karma as unjustified. Vaiśeṣika and the Buddhists admitted both perception and inference as *pramāṇas*. Sāṃkhya allowed testimony as third means. Vaiśeṣika added analogy (*upamāna*). Prābhākara Mīmāṃsā added presumption (*arthāpatti*) to these four. Bhāṭṭa

Mīmāṃsā and Advaita Vedānta added yet a sixth source, non-cognition (*anupalabdhi*). Most agreed, however that perception and inference are the most important sources of knowledge. Hence elaborate rival theories of sense perception and (especially) of perceptual error were developed, as well as sophisticated theories of inference.

All schools of Indian philosophy agreed that truth is a differentiating characteristic of knowledge episodes (*pramā*). However, the various schools differed as to their theories of truth (*pramātva* or *prāmāṇya*). Rival theories were offered not only about the meaning and criterion of truth, but also about the apprehension of truth. The central issue that the theory of the apprehension of truth (*prāmāṇyavāda*) addresses is whether the truth of a cognition is apprehended intrinsically (*svataḥ*) or extrinsically (*parataḥ*): in other words, whether a cognition and its truth are apprehended together, or whether it is only through a second cognition that one apprehends the truth of the first cognition.

A traditional typology gives us Mīmāṃsā, Advaita and Sāṃkhya as all supporters of some variant of the theory of intrinsic truth apprehension (*svataḥprāmāṇyavāda*) and Nyāya and the Buddhists as both supporters of the theory of extrinsic truth apprehension (*parataḥprāmāṇyavāda*). Intrinsic theorists all agree that there is no *criterion* of truth, even if there are criteria of error. That is, since a cognition as such is true or apprehended as true, no criterion can *prove* its truth (even though a criterion of error may prove error to be error). Extrinsic theorists oppose these claims and insist that no cognition is true on its own account. Nyāya holds that the truth of a cognition depends upon its correspondence to reality; the Buddhist logician Dharmakīrti instead defines truth pragmatically in terms of 'successful activity' (*arthakriyā*). All parties in the debate, however, accept that coherence and workability are at least marks of truth.

In discussing the idea that truth or falsity is extrinsically apprehended, some Indian philosophers introduced the concept of a second-order cognition, that is, a cognition that is itself the cognition of a cognition. Thus the question 'How is the truth (or falsity) of a cognition determined?' is intertwined with the question 'How is a cognition itself cognized?' With respect to the latter question Indian theorists hold either that a cognition is intrinsically cognized or 'self-illuminating' (*svaprakāśa*) in that its very occurrence makes its own existence known, or that it is extrinsically cognized only by a subsequent cognition (*parataḥprakāśa*). Variants of the self-illumination theory are upheld by Prābhākara Mīmāṃsā, Advaita and some Buddhists;

variants of the extrinsic cognition theory are upheld by Nyāya and Bhāṭṭa Mīmāṃsā.

Indian and Western epistemologies

This brief and partial sketch of the nature and scope of *pramāṇa* theory indicates both its similarity to and difference from Western epistemology. On the one hand, the Indian *pramāṇavādins* concerned themselves with many topics that have also occupied Western epistemologists: the nature and sources of knowledge, theories of sense perception and of perceptual error, the meaning and criterion of truth. On the other hand, there is also much in *pramāṇavāda* that is foreign to Western epistemology. In the Indian context, for instance, knowledge is treated as a species of awareness or cognition (*jñāna*), not of belief, and hence knowledge (*pramā*) is episodic rather than dispositional. Doubt too is a cognitive episode or awareness, one which arises under certain specifiable conditions that do not allow for the possibility of meaningful foundational scepticism. Correspondingly, most Indian philosophers are relatively sanguine about the limits of knowledge, some even going so far as to identify the real with the knowable. The Indian epistemologists also often recognize independent sources of knowledge unfamiliar to Western epistemologists, including testimony (*śabda*), analogy (*upamāna*) and presumption (*arthāpatti*). Moreover, since Indian logical theory is primarily concerned with the nature of inference (*anumāna*) as an independent source of knowledge, it too falls within the scope of *pramāṇa* theory.

These important similarities and differences are philosophically pregnant. There is enough in common between Western epistemology and Indian *pramāṇa* theory to suggest that the philosophers in both traditions are often engaged with similar problems and hence should be able to communicate with each other. However, there are also sufficient differences between the traditions to suggest that they may have some novel perspectives to offer each other. The rest of this chapter explores some of these commonalities and differences in more detail.

Knowledge and *pramā*

While the Sanskrit term *pramā* best translates as 'knowledge', a *pramā* has various features that differentiate it somewhat from what Western epistemologists usually think of as knowledge. These differences can perhaps be more sharply focused by contrasting *pramā* with the venerable (albeit not uncontroversial) Western account of knowledge as justified true belief.

First, as already explained, a *pramā* is really a knowledge episode, a 'knowing'. Although episodic notions of knowledge and belief are not wholly unfamiliar to Western epistemologists, they have tended to favour instead dispositional theories of knowledge according to which knowledge or belief are capacities, rather than episodes or occurrences. In Indian epistemology not only are perceptions and inferences episodic in character, but a knowing episode is an awareness that is the culmination of a perceptual or inferential process. In this sense, the episodic cognitions (*jñāna*) involved in knowledge are not quite the same as beliefs in Western epistemology.

Second, not every cognitive episode amounts to a knowledge episode; only such cognitive episodes as yield truth are knowledge episodes. Not all cognitions (*jñāna*) are veridical and those cognitions that are false are not knowledge but 'non-knowledge' (*apramā*). Whereas Western epistemology typically takes truth to be a property only of propositions, statements or beliefs, Indian theorists take truth to be a property of some (but not all) episodic cognitions. However, just as mere true belief is usually taken to be insufficient for knowledge in Western epistemology, so too true cognition is insufficient for *pramā*: the Advaitin philosopher Śrīharṣa (twelfth century) offers the counterexample of the gambler's confident lucky guess, which does not amount to knowledge (Jha 1986: 138).

For the Indian epistemologists knowledge is a special kind of momentary mental episode: a true cognition revealing the nature of reality as it is, via a reliable causal route (a *pramāṇa*). This last condition is the feature of *pramā* most closely related to the justification condition in Western epistemology. In Western epistemology, however, there are two rival conceptions of justification: internalism and externalism. According to internalism, knowledge requires that the justification of the true belief be transparent to the believer, who thus knows that she knows. Externalism holds that knowledge only requires that the true belief be produced by an appropriate causal route, whether or not the believer is aware of this. Broadly speaking, we can say that Indian epistemology is externalist about justification, even though there is also sometimes something of an internalist flavour to the debates.

A familiar worry for externalist accounts of epistemic justification are imaginary cases where a true belief is produced via a wayward causal chain in such a way as to ensure we have a justified true belief that is not really knowledge. Interestingly, Śrīharṣa offers some ingenious sceptical cases that might seem apposite here. These cases are designed to challenge the idea that specifying the appropriate causal chains for genuine knowledge is unproblematic: for example, someone mistaking fog for smoke and inferring correctly the presence of a fire which just happens to be present (Jha 1986: 140). To a Western epistemologist such cases might look like putative counterexamples to the justified true belief account of knowledge. In the Indian context, however, it is arguable that *pramāṇa* theorists typically would want to deny that these cases are really cases of *justified* true belief (see Stoltz 2007).

Consider, for instance, this striking example (deriving from the eighth-century Buddhist philosopher Dharmottara). There is a fire on which some meat is beginning to cook. Although the fire has not yet produced any smoke, the presence of the meat has attracted a cloud of flies that swarm above the fire. A person observing the scene from a distance cannot see the fire but does see the swarm of flies, which he mistakes for smoke. Hence he comes to believe correctly that there is a fire. For Dharmottara (and other *pramāṇavādins*) this case would not be regarded as a knowledge episode, but arguably neither would it count for them as a case of justified true belief. What we have here instead is the occurrence of a cognition caused by a pseudo-*pramāṇa*, a mistaken belief that is not epistemically justified. Hence if we take *pramāṇa* to be the Indian analogue of the concept of justification, then in Indian epistemology justification and truth are not logically independent: you cannot, for instance, really be justified in believing something false because a genuine *pramāṇa* cannot give rise to a false cognition.

Of course, though the *pramāṇas* are what enable us to identify ideal cognitive processes and they cannot generate false cognitions, our attempts to employ such knowledge generating processes are not infallible. We can indeed mistake a pseudo-*pramāṇa* for the real thing. Thus Indian epistemology also makes room for a kind of fallibilism.

A final implication of the general Indian conception of knowledge that is worth remarking on is highlighted by the fact that the overwhelming majority of Indian epistemologists denied memory to be a source of knowledge. Basically, memory (*smṛti*) is ruled out as a *pramāṇa* for most because of three reasons (though not everyone accepted all three of these arguments). First, memory does not give us new knowledge, but only revives old knowledge. Genuine knowledge has to be both true (*pramā*) and novel (*anadhigata*).

Second, a genuine knowledge episode is true in virtue of corresponding to its object, but the objects of memory no longer exist. The object as remembered is not the object as originally presented, but a representation of what was once presented. Third, a *pramāṇa* must be capable of making its objects known independently, but memory reveals its objects only through the traces of past experience. These three conditions of novelty, correspondence and independence, it is argued, jointly and severally preclude memory being a means of knowledge. All three conditions appeal to those features of memory which entail that a memory experience is not a presentative (*anubhava*) cognition. Genuine knowledge, it is assumed, is presentative, not representative.

Truth and *prāmāṇya*

A feature of both Western and Indian philosophy is the existence of a considerable body of literature explicitly discussing the problem of truth. In Western philosophy the problem of truth has typically been conceived of as involving two questions: 'What is the nature of truth?' and 'What is the test for truth?' An answer to the first question is a theory of the meaning of truth; an answer to the second question is a theory of the criterion of truth.

In Western philosophy it is traditional to distinguish three major rival theories about the nature of truth. The oldest and traditionally most popular theory is that truth is what corresponds to the facts. As Aristotle put it, 'to say what is is, or that what is not is not, is true' (*Metaphysics* 1011b). This is the *correspondence theory* of truth. Notwithstanding its immediate intuitive appeal, there are a number of difficulties that attend any attempt to give the theory a more rigorous explication. Firstly, while the theory claims that the truth of a statement consists in a special 'correspondence' relationship to reality, an adequate account of this relationship still remains to be given. Secondly, it is often complained that the correspondence theory does not tell us how we are to compare our claims with objective reality in order to determine whether they correspond with the facts. Finally, this difficulty of epistemic access to the objective reality that truths are supposed to correspond to can generate a scepticism about the very existence of such a reality.

The *coherence theory* of truth tells us that a statement is true if it coheres or fits with the system of other statements we affirm. A true statement cannot be shown to correspond to an objective reality; indeed for all we know there may be no such reality. Since all we have access to is the reality provided by one or another conceptual scheme, a statement is true to the degree that it coheres with some such favoured scheme (and only true relative to that scheme).

The *pragmatic theory* of truth tells us that a statement is true if it 'works', in other words, if we can act successfully on the basis of it. Once again there is no need to posit any correspondence to an objective reality; all we need to suppose is that true statements are characterized by their utility in promoting particular human purposes.

Of course, all of these theories admit of much more nuanced formulations than the skeletal ones just given. However, let us for the moment focus on how these Western theories relate to Indian theorizing about truth.

All schools of Indian philosophy agree that truth is a differentiating characteristic of knowledge episodes. However, the various schools differ as to their theories of truth (*pramātva* or *prāmāṇya*). Whereas Western philosophers have offered rival theories about both the meaning of truth and the criterion of truth, the classical Indian philosophers principally concerned themselves with issues about the meaning of truth and the apprehension of truth.

The latter debate is peculiarly Indian and hence worth saying a little more about. As already mentioned, the central issue the theory of the apprehension of truth (*prāmāṇyavāda*) addresses is whether the truth of a cognition is apprehended intrinsically (*svataḥ*) or extrinsically (*arataḥ*), that is, whether a cognition and its truth are apprehended together, or whether it is only through a second cognition that one apprehends the truth of the first cognition. This question is also asked for falsity. (The Indian philosophers' concern with this question flows naturally from the *pramāṇa* theory's being a causal theory of knowledge; they wondered whether the originating conditions of a true cognition were in themselves sufficient for producing its truth.)

Following Kumārila Bhaṭṭa (*Ślokavārttika*, II.33–61), it is customary to distinguish four positions on the matter:

(1) Truth is apprehended intrinsically but falsity is apprehended extrinsically.

(2) Both truth and falsity are apprehended intrinsically.

(3) Both truth and falsity are apprehended extrinsically.

(4) Falsity is apprehended intrinsically but truth is apprehended extrinsically.

Position (1) is the view of Mīmāṃsā and Advaita Vedānta, while position (3) is the Nyāya view. These are the two positions that were most fully developed in the literature. According to later doxographic tradition, position (2) is supposed to be the Sāṃkhya view, but this attribution is historically dubious. Position (4) is supposed to be the view of the Buddhists, but this attribution seems even more historically dubious. Certainly, neither of positions (2) and (4) is fully developed in the extant literature, and we know that at least the eighth-century Buddhist philosophers Śāntarakṣita and Kamalaśīla explicitly rejected all four alternatives in favour of the theory that truth and falsity are sometimes intrinsic and sometimes extrinsic (Hattori 1997).

With respect to the apprehension of truth, however, the point to note here is that this (disputable) traditional typology gives us Mīmāṃsā, Advaita and Sāṃkhya as all supporters of some variant of the theory of intrinsic truth apprehension (*svataḥprāmāṇyavāda*) and Nyāya and the Buddhists as both supporters of the theory of extrinsic truth apprehension (*parataḥprāmāṇyavāda*). Moreover, although the different intrinsic theorists disagree significantly as to the details of the theory, they can all agree that there is no *criterion* of truth, even if there are criteria of error. That is, since a cognition as such is true or apprehended as true, no criterion can *prove* its truth (even though a criterion of error may prove error to be error).

Nyāya strongly opposes this approach, insisting that no cognition is true on its own account. Rather the truth of a cognition depends upon its conformity with the way things are (*yathārtha*); or as the *Nyāyabhāṣya* puts it, 'true cognition is knowledge of that as that' (II.1.36). In other words, Nyāya affirms the basic intuition that was also articulated by Aristotle, the intuition that motivates all correspondence theories of the nature of truth. Of course, the Nyāya commitment to a correspondence theory requires them to respond to their opponents' challenge to specify more precisely just what the correspondence relationship consists in. This is no easy task. Thus the great Navya-Naiyāyika logician Gaṅgeśa starts from the relatively accessible proposal that a true cognition is 'an experience whose qualifier is such that it belongs to the object', then further refines this in the face of various objections to reach the following favoured definition of truth expressed in the technical language of Navya-Nyāya: 'the property of having *that* as its qualifier which is limited by the property of having a qualificandum which possesses the *that*' (Mohanty 1989: 39–43).

The theory of extrinsic truth apprehension, however, is logically independent of the correspondence theory of the nature of truth. After all, the Buddhists were also supposed by Kumārila to be *parataḥprāmāṇyavādins*, but in their case presumably because of their belief that truth (like all phenomena) is conditioned by causes. Moreover the Buddhist logicians do disassociate themselves from a correspondence theory of truth. For them reality is just the series of momentary bare particulars, the causally efficient point-instants (*svalakṣaṇa*), and hence no cognition can *correspond* to such a momentary and ineffable reality. Instead Dharmakīrti defines truth in terms of 'successful activity' (*arthakriyā*): true cognitions are those that lead to practical success (*Pramāṇavārttika* II.1). Thus it is unsurprising to find that he was taken by other Indian epistemologists to be espousing a kind of pragmatic theory of truth (though for more nuanced modern accounts of his position, see Katsura 1984, Tillemans 1999, Dunne 2004).

Nyāya assumes this traditional pragmatist interpretation of the Buddhists and argues that they are confused here. Successful activity may be a plausible *criterion* of truth, but it cannot be an adequate account of the *nature* of truth. Some of the opponents of the Nyāya join forces with them on at least this issue, arguing that a false cognition can also lead to the fulfilment of a purpose. A striking Advaitin counterexample is the case where we mistake the lustre of a distant jewel for the jewel itself and, approaching the lustre, actually obtain the desired jewel, that is, a false cognition satisfies our purpose.

Nyāya, however, also accuses the intrinsic truth apprehension theorists of making a similar mistake to the Buddhists. Whatever their internal differences, the *svataḥprāmāṇyavādins* all agree that since the truth of a cognition is intrinsically apprehended, there is no need for a criterion of truth. But, the Naiyāyikas charge, the different theories of the nature of truth then offered are really only plausible as *criteria* of truth. Sāṃkhya, for instance, opts for the view that a true cognition is one in harmony (*saṃvāda*) with other experiences. All this would show, however, is that the cognition has not so far been falsified, not that it is true. Bhāṭṭa Mīmāṃsā and Advaita identify truth with uncontradictedness (*abādhitatva*), where this is understood to mean the property of never being contradicted. However, as Advaita recognizes, an implication of this is that only the knowledge of *Brahman* as ultimate reality is true and no empirical knowledge is ever ultimately true.

Nyāya favours instead combining a correspondence theory of truth with a combined coherence/pragmatist criterion of truth. The nature of truth is correspondence to the facts, but the criterion or test of truth is, in a broad sense, coherence and workability (just as the rival schools imperfectly glimpsed). We cannot directly know whether our cognitions correspond to reality, but we can infer that they do so if they consistently cohere with our other experiences and we can act successfully in terms of them. The Naiyāyikas are fallibilists: they do not think that such inferences guarantee certainty, but they believe nevertheless that such inferences are generally reliable.

One interesting convergence does, however, emerge out of all these disagreements. This is the general Indian acceptance of something like the Nyāya notion of broad coherence and workability as at least a mark of truth. Indeed presumably all parties could agree that the class of cognitions that, broadly speaking, lead to successful action and the class of cognitions that would be pre-theoretically counted as 'true' coincide extensionally. What is disputed is whether they coincide intensionally.

Perception (*pratyakṣa*)

All Indian epistemologists agreed that perception (*pratyakṣa*) was the most fundamental of the *pramāṇas*. A popular folk etymology for the Sanskrit term *pratyakṣa* says it consists of *prati* ('before') and *akṣa* ('eye'): thus 'present to or before the eyes (or other sense organs)'. This etymology is reflected in one important Indian definition of perception in terms of how it is caused: 'Perception is the knowledge resulting from sense-object contact' (*Nyāyasūtra* 1.1.4). Gautama (the author of this verse) immediately goes on to add three further conditions to this definition: that the knowledge involved be non-verbal, non-deviant, and of a definite nature.

Various Indian commentators devote considerable energy to controversies about just what these extra conditions involve. Moreover, the original definition was later rejected by the great Navya-Naiyāyika Gaṅgeśa as both too wide and too narrow: it is too wide because it includes memory and some kinds of inference; it is too narrow because it excludes an omniscient God's perceptions (since his perceptions are eternal and unproduced). In the end Gaṅgeśa ends up defining *pratyakṣa* indirectly as 'cognition that does not have a cognition as its chief instrumental cause' (Phillips and Tatacharya 2004: 335).

For the moment, however, let us focus on the first condition of Gautama's original definition and its suggestion that perception can be (at least partially) defined in terms of sense–object contact.

One small but significant point to note about it is that the contact supposedly involved in perception is between sense and object, not sense organ and object. Thus in visual perception, for example, the Nyāya theory of vision posits an invisible ray of light that rests on the visual organ and goes out to meet the object. The senses (or sense faculties) are thus distinct from the physical sense organs, though for Nyāya the senses too are material.

A more philosophically suggestive point is that this definition seems aimed to capture the commonsense intuition that underpins *direct realism*, that is, the epistemological view that we directly perceive external objects, not just their sensible qualities. Unsurprisingly, then, some version of the definition of *pratyakṣa* in terms of sense contact is espoused not just by the Old Nyāya realists, but also by the equally staunch realists of the Bhāṭṭa Mīmāṃsā school.

Just as in the West, however, not all Indian epistemologists were direct realists. In Western philosophy rival theories include representational realism and phenomenalism. *Representational realism* is the view that perception is an indirect way of acquiring knowledge about the external world based on a causal inference from the sense data that are all we directly see. *Phenomenalism* is the view that 'external' objects are simply logical constructions out of the sense data that are all we directly see.

Analogues of all these views were present in India. As already mentioned, Nyāya and Bhāṭṭa Mīmaṃsā are advocates of direct realism; so too is Vaibhāṣika Buddhism. The Sautrāntika Buddhists are representational realists. Yogācāra Buddhism and Advaita Vedānta advocate variants of phenomenalism. Moreover, these commitments correspondingly influenced competing alternative definitions of perception.

Consider, for instance, the Buddhist *pramāṇavādin* tradition. Dignāga (fifth century) defined perception as a cognition which is 'free from conceptual construction (*kalpanāpoḍha*)', that is, free from association with names and universals (*Pramāṇasamuccaya* 1.3). Responding to the objection that this definition of perception as non-conceptual cognition would allow hallucinations to count as genuine perceptions, Dharmakīrti added (controversially) the extra condition 'and non-erroneous (*abhrānta*)' (*Nyāyabindu* 1.3).

This Buddhist definition is shaped to fit with a particular metaphysical view (itself an interpretation of the Buddha's teaching that all conditioned phenomena are impermanent) that conceives of the world as composed of unique and momentary particulars. If things are momentary and perception cognizes directly what is really there, then only the very first moment of a perceptual act cognizes objective reality because after that moment the object has ceased to exist. Immediate perceptual knowledge can then only be of the bare particular (*svalakṣaṇa*) and the name and universal through which we interpret the particular are supplied by us later. (This argument is viewable as a novel variant of the traditional time-lag argument for representational realism in Western philosophy.)

Opponents of this Buddhist view reject it as failing to underwrite the idea that perception gives us *knowledge*, since the uninterpreted sensation of a pure particular is far too thin to be properly noetic. Direct realists worry too that the theory is unstable and in danger of drifting into idealism, though Dharmakīrti seems unfazed by this since he appears to be favourable to the Yogācāra rejection of extra-mental entities as his preferred ultimate ontology. In company with the direct realists, however, Dharmakīrti does accept that perception requires some kind of *causal* explanation and it is precisely this causal thesis that is denied by Advaita Vedānta.

The Advaitins offer a different definition of perception, not in terms of a causal connection between sense activity and perception, but in terms of immediacy (*aparokṣa*). What is known immediately, however, is just pure consciousness. Or as a famous Advaitin manual on epistemology puts it: 'Valid perceptual knowledge is but consciousness' (*Vedāntaparibhāṣā* I.2). There is no necessary connection between perception and sense stimulation.

Once again, a background metaphysics is helping to shape the definition here. According to the Advaitin interpretation of Upaniṣadic scripture, all that is real is the Absolute (*Brahman*), which is identical with the Self (*ātman*). The Self is in turn characterized as being, consciousness and bliss (*sadcidanānda*). Thus the knower, the objects of knowledge and knowledge are all manifestations of the same pure consciousness (*caitanya*): 'Consciousness is of three kinds: content-consciousness, cognitive-consciousness and cognizer-consciousness. Of these, consciousness defined by pot, etc., is content-consciousness. Consciousness defined by a [modification] of the internal organ is the cognitive-consciousness. That defined by the internal organ is the cognizer-consciousness' (I.17). What, however, of the apparent difference in a perceptual experience between the object seen and the consciousness that sees it? The Advaitin reply is: 'What is called non-difference from the cognizer is not oneness, but rather the non-possession of reality different from the reality of the cognizer' (I.43).

Very briefly then, the Advaitin theory is that perception is immediate and timeless consciousness, which is the Self. An 'external' object like a pot is just a superimposition on consciousness. When we have an experience of perceiving an external object what happens is that the internal organ (*antaḥkaraṇa*) goes out through the senses, assimilates the form of the object and appropriates it to itself: 'Here, just as the water of a tank, going out through a hole and entering fields through channels, comes to have, even like those [fields], a quadrangular or other figure, similarly, the internal organ too, which is of the nature of light, going out through the sense of sight, etc. and reaching the locality of contents like pot, is transformed into the form of contents like pot' (I.18). Since the content-consciousness is but the cognizer-consciousness, the reality of the pot is but the existence of the consciousness associated with it.

The full Advaitin account of the details of this perceptual process is a bit complicated, but in the case of ordinary veridical perception basically it involves two phases. First, in the perception of an external object the mind (*antaḥkaraṇa*) actively goes out, like a beam of light, to the object through the senses (*indriyas*). The mind is then modified so as to assume the 'form' of that object. This modification is called *vṛtti* and when the *vṛtti* coincides with the object, perceptual knowledge arises. Since the *vṛtti* is a mode of the *antaḥkaraṇa*, this coincidence is really the coincidence of the subject and the object such that their being is non-different. Perception is thus the result of a direct communion between knower and known. The Advaitin definition of perception in terms of immediacy offers, then, an account both compatible with their metaphysical non-dualism and sensitive to the phenomenology of (at least some) perceptual experiences as seeming to be unmediated.

Arguably, each of these rival definitions of perception latches on to an intuitively important feature of perception. But the fully developed definitions are clearly not metaphysically innocent. Perhaps the oddest to a Western reader will be the Advaitin definition in terms of immediacy and its attendant metaphysics, but note too that it is the only definition that explicitly tries to capture a purported essence for perception. The Buddhist definition in terms of non-conceptual cognition, however, also serves to introduce another interesting debate in Indian epistemology.

Determinate and indeterminate perception

Indian philosophers vigorously disputed whether perceptual cognitions have conceptual content. Roughly speaking, the issue is whether we can distinguish in perception the bare presentation from the elements read into the presentation by the mind. The most extreme views were, on the one hand, the position that all perception has conceptual content and, on the other hand, the Buddhist position that all perception must be non-conceptual. Occupying the middle ground were those that held there to be two successive kinds of cognition in perception: indeterminate (*nirvikalpaka*) and determinate (*savikalpaka*), with the former being non-conceptual and non-linguistic and the latter involving conceptualization and language.

For a first pass, then, we can set out the battle lines like this:

(1) All perception is determinate (Bhartṛhari, Jainas, Navya-Nyāya).

(2) All perception is indeterminate (Dignāga, Dharmakīrti).

(3) Perceptions are of two kinds: determinate and indeterminate (Nyāya, Mīmāṃsā, Advaita).

This characterization, however, also conceals some significant disagreements about exactly *why* the advocates of these three positions held what they did. In particular, we need to distinguish the issue of whether all *perceptions* (*pratyakṣa*) are determinate from the issue of whether all *cognitions* (*jñāna*) are determinate.

Consider, for example, the differences between the advocates of position (1), the view that all perception is determinate. The grammarian Bhartṛhari held this position because he held that all *cognition*, and hence all perception, is linguistic: 'there is no cognition in the world in which the word does not figure' (*Vākyapadīya* I.123). This is because 'in our cognitions we identify objects with their words and our cognitions are intertwined with words, they are essentially of the nature of the word' (I, comm.). In contrast, the Jainas shunned such a linguistic monism, holding that the world consists of a plurality of things standing in real relations to each other. Indeed, they argue, this is why perception is always determinate. After all, if a perception is a cognition that apprehends the real nature of an object, then there can be no bare indeterminate perception of an object devoid of its relations to anything else. Finally, the Navya-Naiyāyika Gaṅgeśa allows that there are both indeterminate and determinate *cognitions*, but only determinate *perceptions*. Gaṅgeśa happily accepts that there are sensory awarenesses below the level of what we can articulate: indeed, if there were not it is difficult to see how anyone could begin to learn a language. However, *perceptions* are a special type of veridical cognition and veridicality presupposes verbalizability and only determinate awarenesses are verbalizable awarenesses expressible in a propositional form.

Indeterminate awareness is non-propositional and hence neither veridical nor non-veridical. Thus there cannot be indeterminate perceptions, though there are indeterminate cognitions and these indeterminate cognitions are needed in order to explain erroneous cognition.

The Buddhists, in contrast, hold that there are both determinate and indeterminate cognitions, but that perception is only indeterminate. Error occurs precisely when we start to add conceptual constructions onto the deliverances of the original uncontaminated bare awareness. Once again, metaphysical commitments are shaping the epistemological views here. Determinate cognition is a mediate experience wherein categories like name, class and universal are applied to the original indeterminate cognition of an object unassociated with any such categories. But in the ontology of the school of Dharmakīrti all that exists are bare particulars, not universals. Hence all determinate cognitions involve conceptual fictions (*kalpanā*) and cannot be veridical, and so cannot be perceptions.

Finally, while philosophers of the Old Nyāya, Mīmāṃsā and Advaita schools all agree that both cognitions and perceptions can be indeterminate or determinate, they also have their own intramural differences. They all agree that perceptions cannot be just indeterminate and view the Buddhists as unacceptably reducing the richness of genuine perception to the bareness of mere sensation. Nor are they reluctant to admit entities like universals into their ontologies. On the other hand, they reject too the claim that all perceptions are determinate, for in order to have a determinate perception of a pot we have to perceive something presented to us as qualified by potness. But this in turn implies that we must have already had a non-relational indeterminate perception of a pot and potness.

For Nyāya this indeterminate perception is not directly apperceptible; it is only inferred from the rule that to perceive a complex we must have already perceived all its constituents separately. For Mīmāṃsā, however, indeterminate perception is not just a theoretical postulate: it is a real part of the perceptual process and is a cause of action, as evidenced by the fact that animals and infants have only indeterminate perceptions yet act upon them. Lastly, for Advaita an indeterminate perception is a cognition that does not apprehend any relation between a thing and its qualifying attribute, in other words, a cognition of pure indeterminate being. This cognition can be a perception because ultimately there exists but one undifferentiated unity of consciousness.

The theory of error (*khyātivāda*)

Indian epistemologists typically conceived of the problem of perception as being how to explain how knowledge arises in a subject as a result of sense perception. But they also were much concerned with a closely associated problem: how to explain how a subject fails to have knowledge. This latter problem generated the body of theory the Indians called *khyātivāda*, or the theory of error.

Indian concerns with the theory of error connect in an interesting fashion with the soteriological premise mentioned at the beginning of this chapter, in other words, the premise that it is ignorance that causes us to be enmeshed in the cycle of suffering and that, correspondingly, it is knowledge that can eliminate suffering. Exactly how might this work?

Consider a famous Indian example of (perceptual) error. In the dusk a man sees something that he takes to be a dangerous snake and experiences an unpleasant emotion of fear. Looking closer, he realizes that what he took to be a snake is but a rope and his fear dissipates. His new knowledge liberates him from his earlier suffering simply by eliminating permanently his false belief, but the transformation is not due to any change in the nature of the world.

If this example is to serve as a plausible model of how knowledge as the removal of error can free us from suffering, then we need a fuller theoretical articulation of what is going on in such a case. There is nothing in the phenomenal content of the non-veridical cognition of the snake that distinguishes it from a veridical cognition of a snake: they seem exactly alike. Moreover, the non-veridical cognition of the snake is not a cognition of *nothing*; underpinning it is a real rope, to which we ascribe properties that do not belong to it. And what happens when we realize that the cognition of the snake is non-veridical? Well, there is both a cognitive change (what was cognized as a snake is now cognized as a rope) and there is a connative change (the fear of the snake disappears). How are these related? And how is it that having realized that there is no snake we do not lapse back into error, even if we can still recall vividly our mistaken experience? A plausible theory of perceptual error, then, should surely be able to capture all this: the way in which such error arises out of something real but misconstrued and the way in which our false cognition becomes transformed though still remembered.

An influential Indian typology of theories of error, following the *Iṣṭasiddhi* of the eleventh-century Advaitin philosopher Vimuktātman (Sundaram 1980), classifies them as being of three basic types:

(1) Theories where the object of error is real (*sat-khyātivāda*): Nyāya, Mīmāṃsā, Yogācāra Buddhism.
(2) Theories where the object of error is unreal (*asat-khyātivāda*): Madhyamaka Buddhism.
(3) Theories where the object of error is neither real nor unreal (*anirvacanīya-khyātivāda*): Advaita Vedānta.

This useful traditional classification might be a little bit misleading though, for there are some very significant differences between the theorists in the first category. Vimuktātman himself is alive to this point, however, and helpfully divides advocates of the first type of theory into three further subcategories:

(1.1) The theory of self-cognition (*ātmakhyāti*): Yogācāra.
(2.1) The theory of cognition of non-cognition (*akhyāti*): Prābhākara Mīmāṃsā.
(3.1) The theory of cognition as another (*anyathākhyāti*): Bhāṭṭa Mīmāṃsā, Nyāya-Vaiśeṣika.

(Historically speaking, it is dubious that the two Buddhist schools held the positions attributed to them in this typology, though other schools certainly often interpreted them in this way. Dialectically speaking, however, the positions themselves do serve to fill out the logical space of possible theories about the matter.)

Considering the illusory object, the *Iṣṭasiddhi* offers a famous mnemonic verse that sums up the basic arguments for *sat-khyātivāda* and *asat-khyātivāda* and for the superiority of *anirvacanīya-khyātivāda*:

> Because of the impossibility of appearance for the unreal, it is real; because of the impossibility of sublation for the real, it is unreal. For the same reason it is indeterminable. These form the reasons for the three alternatives. (I.4)

The argument against the option of *asatkhyāti-vāda* is simple enough: in cases of error like that of the rope and the snake it is not true that the object of error (the snake) is unreal, for if it were then it could not appear to exist. Non-existent entities (like the sons of barren women) do not even *appear* to exist.

The argument against the option of *satkhyāti-vāda* is a bit more complicated. The basic worry here is that though the object of error cannot be unreal, it cannot be real either because the real cannot be falsified whereas the perception of the snake is indeed falsified. But pressing home this objection requires of the Advaitin a fuller discussion of all three variants of *satkhyāti-vāda*.

The Yogācāra Buddhists are taken to have held a theory of self-cognition (*ātmakhyāti*) according to which the illusory snake is just a real mental state projected outside. Indeed, since the Yogācārin idealists do not accept that there is anything extra-mental, *all* objects are cognitions wrongly taken for external things. The obvious objection to this, however, is that by thus adopting a 'pan-fictionalism' that places all intentional objects on the same level, the Yogācārin is in danger of collapsing the crucial distinction between actual and fictitious entities.

The Prābhākara Mīmāṃsākas held the theory of cognition of non-cognition (*akhyāti*), according to which the supposed erroneous cognition is really two distinct cognitions that the perceiver fails to discriminate. One of these distinct cognitions is a perception (of a rope) and the other a memory (of a snake). The process here is that first there is a perception of an object with various attributes, then association through similarity gives rise to a memory of a different object with some of those perceived attributes. Finally, error occurs when the perceiver then fails to discriminate between the perception and the memory. Furthermore, when the illusion is corrected there is no sublation of the snake but simply a recognition of the confusion. A difficulty for this ingenious theory, of course, is how to explain why this purported failure to discriminate between a perception and a memory occurs only on some occasions. Nor is it clear that non-discrimination is a necessary condition for error, for surely we can be in ignorance though fully discriminative.

The Bhāṭṭa Mīmāṃsakas held a different variant of the Prābhakāra view that erroneous cognition involves a confusion between two distinct cognitions. According to their theory (sometimes called *viparīta-khyāti*), the process that gives rise to error is this. First we perceive the rope, and the perception here is of the rope as qualified by the non-existence of the snake. Thus both the rope and the snake are real in the sense that they are part of the contents of the original perceptual cognition, but only the rope is actually an object of perception. Error occurs, then, when we fail to grasp what is given and wrongly synthesize the presentative and representative factors in a single unitary cognition. The object of error, then, is real enough, but its connection with the time and place in which it is seen is unreal. This theory, however, faces the problem of offering a plausible explanation of how the absent object (the snake) gives rises to its cognition here and now.

The Bhāṭṭa theory of error is very close to the *anyathākhyati* theory advocated by Nyāya-Vaiśeṣika. For the Naiyāyika realists the illusory snake is a real snake all right, but one that is elsewhere and not here in front of us. Directly addressing the difficulty just mentioned for the Bhāṭṭa theory, the Naiyāyikas claim that the absent snake is presented to us here and now through a kind of extraordinary perception called *jñānalakṣaṇa-sannikarṣa* involving contact between a sense and the absent snake. The erroneous cognition is thus presentational with a genuine basis in facts, but the facts are misplaced and misrelated so that what we have is a false apprehension of the real. The obvious difficulty for this account, however, is how to provide any independent evidence for the existence of any such extraordinary perception.

The Advaitin rejects all of the above theories and espouses instead the view that the erroneous cognition is of what is indescribable as real or unreal (*anirvacīnaya-khyāti*). A false cognition cannot be a cognition of *nothing*, since unlike a hare's horn it does occur. But neither can it be a cognition of something real, since it is sublated and unfalsifiability (*abādhitatva*) is the criterion of reality for Advaita. Accordingly, the object of error must have a unique ontological status: neither non-existent nor real. The obvious retort here, however, is that this new Advaitin category is not so much a solution to the problem of error as just a new name for it. Moreover, phenomenologically speaking, an illusory object always presents itself as *real*, not as indescribable: if the illusory snake presented itself as indescribable then the relevant cognition would not be illusory because it would not be falsified by a sublating cognition.

Testimony (*śabda*) and other *pramāṇas*

While all Indian epistemologists agreed that perception (*pratyakṣa*) was the most fundamental of the *pramāṇas*, almost all of them recognized too other independent sources of knowledge. The next most commonly accepted was inference (*anumāna*) and this will be dealt with in some detail in Chapter 3. Some Indian epistemologists recognized additional independent sources of knowledge unfamiliar to most Western epistemologists, including testimony (*śabda*), analogy (*upamāna*) and presumption (*arthāpatti*). The Indian debates about whether analogy and presumption are genuine *pramāṇas* are concerned with whether they really are just varieties of inference, so they too will be discussed in the chapter on inference. The topic of *śabda* or testimony, however, deserves some preliminary discussion here.

Under the topic of *śabda* Indian epistemologists discussed a variety of issues. One of these was the nature of scriptural authority and for most orthodox Hindu philosophers *śabda-pramāṇa* was taken to be the means for justifying the scriptural authority of the Vedas. We shall review some of the philosophical issues at stake there in Chapter 7, the chapter on Indian philosophy of religion. Another set of issues that fell under the rubric of *śabda* was concerned with topics in the philosophy of language and the theory of meaning, some of which will be dealt with in Chapter 4. A third issue about *śabda*, however, is of more direct *epistemological* significance: namely, the question of whether verbal testimony is a distinct and independent means of knowledge and the Nyāya case for an affirmative answer to that question.

The standard Nyāya definition of verbal testimony is that it is 'communication from a trustworthy person (*āpta*)' (*Nyāyasūtra* I.1.7). The *Nyāyabhāṣya* commentary on this definition offers the following gloss: 'A trustworthy person is the speaker who has the direct knowledge of an object and is motivated by the desire of communicating the object as directly known by him'. This particular Indian account explicitly allows that testimony can give us knowledge of both perceptible and imperceptible objects (thus the authority of scriptural testimony is similarly justified by the nature of its author). It also explicitly allows that a trustworthy person can be an ordinary human, as well as a seer or a god.

Naiyāyikas plausibly assume that many will concede that it is relatively uncontroversial that the testimony of competent speakers gives us knowledge about many things (including perhaps even our knowledge of the very meanings of the words that we use to conduct epistemological debates). Naiyāyikas also allow, however, that the objects of some testimonial knowledge may be knowable too through other *pramāṇas* like perception or inference. Hence the real challenge for their general account of testimonial knowledge is to show that *śabda* cannot be reduced to some other *pramāṇa*.

To this end they argue first that perception seems to be an implausible candidate for this reductive role because the phenomenology of a case of learning something through perception seems directly presentative and hence quite different from that of a case of learning something through testimony, which feels more indirect. Secondly, they insist that to say it is indirect is not tantamount to saying it must be inferential, as the Vaiśeṣikas incorrectly maintain. This is because in Indian logic (of which we shall learn more in the next chapter) inferential knowledge requires knowledge of an invariable concomitance (*vyāpti*) between the perception of a sign and the presence of that which is to be inferred from the presence of that sign. Such a relation is fixed and natural, whereas, at least for the Naiyāyikas, the relation between a sentence and its meaning is only conventional. Nor is it helpful here to insist that in a case of testimonial knowledge inference at least gives us knowledge of the speaker's intended meaning. After all, Gaṅgeśa argues, knowledge of the speaker's intention is not knowledge that what the speaker says is *true*, but in a case of testimonial knowledge the hearer does come to know that what the speaker says is true. The only means of knowing this must be a *pramāṇa* distinct from inference: call it *śabda*.

Scepticism in Indian and Western epistemologies

Crucial to the development of Western epistemology is the challenge presented by *philosophical scepticism*, that is, the view that knowledge is impossible, or at least that we can never know for sure that we have attained it. Such scepticism raises doubts about the possibility of knowing anything at all. In Western philosophy the possibility of such scepticism decisively shaped the development of epistemology. Thus the ancient Greek Sceptics first cast doubt upon all forms of knowledge of the real nature of things, apparently motivated by the thought that only by allowing ourselves to rely on appearances can we hope to obtain freedom from anxiety and attain genuine tranquillity of mind. In the seventeenth century René Descartes revived the ancient sceptical arguments, emphasizing the threat to knowledge posed by the mere possibility of universal doubt. Descartes then set out a new agenda for modern philosophy: to rebut the possibility of philosophical scepticism by providing secure and certain foundations for knowledge in the face of doubt. The subsequent development of the rival rationalist and empiricist programmes in Western epistemology continued to pursue this project of epistemic foundationalism, conceived of as an attempt to defeat the sceptical challenge.

The Indian treatment of doubt as itself a species of cognitive awareness pre-empted the development of the kind of foundational scepticism central to the evolution of Western epistemology. Consider, for example, a standard Nyāya definition of doubt (*saṃśāya*): 'Doubt is the contradictory apprehension about the same object which depends on the remembrance of the unique characteristic of each' (*Nyāyasūtra* 1.1.23). A paradigmatic doubt cognition, then, is one like, 'Is it a man or the stump of a tree?', where we waver between two alternate characterizations of a given object. Such a cognition is neither true nor false.

According to Nyāya, everything can be doubted, provided that the specific causal conditions of the cognition called 'doubt' (*saṃśaya*) are present. But the possibility of universal doubt Nyāya thus admits is a 'motivated possibility', rather than a bare logical possibility. This is not the same as a Cartesian-style universal scepticism, built on the premise that anything that is contingent is uncertain and hence doubtful. Since the Indian philosophers do not acknowledge this distinction between necessary and contingent objects or facts, for them nothing possesses any property that in itself makes it liable to be doubted. Meaningful doubt requires that suitable epistemic conditions are satisfied, and radical Cartesian-style scepticism is ruled out as in pragmatic contradiction with everyday practical life.

There were, however, Indian philosophers who are often today taken to be sceptics: thinkers like the Buddhist Nāgārjuna, the Cārvāka Jayarāśi and the Advaitin Śrīharṣa. The writings of these three philosophers are difficult and their interpretation is correspondingly controversial, but it is certainly arguable that none of them was a sceptic in the sense that they denied that we can know anything. However, it is also true that whereas most Indian epistemologists agreed that we can only know anything by having a means of knowledge (*pramāṇa*), our three Indian 'sceptics' all reject this conception of the role of the *pramāṇas*. Accordingly, to most *pramāṇavādins* these three philosophers would seem to be sceptics rejecting the very possibility of knowledge.

But perhaps a better characterization of what they were doing is instead rejecting a particular mistaken *conception* of knowledge, rather than the possibility of knowledge itself. Compare the way in which various twentieth-century Western epistemologists argued that all the sceptic really can show is that some property supposedly essential to knowledge (certainty, for instance) is unattainable, but that the moral to be drawn from this is that any conception of knowledge requiring the presence of such a property must be a mistaken conception of knowledge.

Saul Kripke usefully generalizes the point at issue here thus:

> A *sceptical* solution of a sceptical philosophical problem begins . . . by conceding that the sceptic's negative assertions are unanswerable. Nevertheless our ordinary practice or belief is justified because – contrary appearance notwithstanding – it need not require the justification the sceptic has shown to be untenable. And much of the value of the sceptical argument consists precisely in the fact that he has shown that an ordinary practice, if it is to be defended at all, cannot be defended in a certain way. A sceptical solution may also involve . . . a sceptical analysis or account of ordinary beliefs to rebut their *prima facie* reference to a metaphysical absurdity. (Kripke 1982: 66–7)

With this idea in mind, let us now look a little more closely at the writings of our three Indian 'sceptics'.

Nāgārjuna's critique of the *pramāṇas*

The second-century philosopher Nāgārjuna is the founding figure of Madhyamaka Buddhism. His most important text is the *Mūlamadhyamakakārikā*, which presents the central Madhyamaka teaching of emptiness (*śūnyatā*), that is, the teaching that all things are devoid of essence or intrinsic nature (*svabhāva*). A different text by Nāgārjuna is the *Vigrahavyāvartanī* (Bhattacharya 1978), which sets out a number of Nyāya-style objections to the teaching of emptiness, together with Nāgārjuna's replies.

One of these objections is epistemological (*Vigrahavyāvartanī* 5–6). Basically it amounts to the charge that if the doctrine of emptiness is true, then it cannot be known to be true because its truth would entail that the *pramāṇas* too would be empty and hence unable to supply the epistemic foundations necessary for knowledge.

Nāgārjuna's response (*Vigrahavyāvartanī* 31–2) is to challenge head-on this conception of the *pramāṇas*:

> If such and such objects are established for you through the *pramāṇas*, tell me how those *pramāṇas* are established for you. If the *pramāṇas* are established through other *pramāṇas* there is an infinite series (*anavasthā*) . . . Now, if you think: those *pramāṇas* are established without *pramāṇas*; the objects to be cognized, however, are established through the *pramāṇas*, then your position that [all] objects are established through *pramāṇas* is abandoned . . . And you

should state the special reason why some objects are established through *pramāṇas*, while other are not. But you have not stated this.

In other words, the *pramāṇas* cannot be established by themselves, nor by other *pramāṇas*. Nor can they be unestablished. Furthermore, neither can they be established by the objects (*prameyas*) they reveal because that would lead to a vicious circle: the *pramāṇas* establish the *prameyas* and the *prameyas* establish the *pramāṇas* (*Vigrahavyāvartanī* 47–50). In sum, then, the opponent's confidence that the teaching of emptiness is unknowable rests on 'foundations' that are chimerical.

Clearly Nāgārjuna intends this as a powerful critique of the *pramāṇas*. Does it imply, though, that Nāgārjuna is sceptical about the possibility of knowledge? Surely the structure of Nāgārjuna's argument suggests instead that what he is really sceptical of is the existence of *pramāṇas* that can ground our epistemic practices. Morever, the fact that he bothers to answer the opponent's objection at length suggests that he takes the charge of inconsistency seriously: Nāgārjuna does indeed believe that we can *know* that all things are empty and he implicitly agrees that this would be a problem if all knowledge is grounded in the *pramāṇas*, but he finds the *pramāṇas* are not necessary for knowledge. Moreover, it is fortunate that our ordinary epistemic practices require no grounding in intrinsically existent foundations, for the independent arguments of the *Mūlamadhyamakakārikā* imply that all such intrinsically existent entities are metaphysical absurdities.

Jayarāśi and truthfulnesss

Another powerful sceptical critique of the *pramāṇas* is to be found in *Tattvopaplavasiṃha* of Jayarāśi Bhaṭṭa, a philosopher affiliated with the materialist Lokāyata (or Cārvāka) school who probably lived in the ninth century. This text is the only work that has survived from the Lokāyata school. It is also the only Indian work in which scepticism about the *pramāṇas* is propounded without an affiliation to a religious tradition.

Whereas Nāgārjuna's critique of the *pramāṇas* concentrates on the circularity and interdependence of the means of knowledge, Jayarāśi concentrates instead on what he calls their 'true characteristics' (*sal-lakṣaṇa*). His entire text evolves around the different characteristics, or definitions, of the means of knowledge according to major philosophical schools of his time (in particular, Nyāya, Dharmakīrtian Buddhism and Bhāṭṭa Mīmāṃsā). The most important characteristic of all means of knowledge, Jayarāśi argues, is their truthfulness or reliability. He then argues in considerable detail that all the different criteria of truth favoured by the Indian *pramāṇavādins* fail to make it possible to know that any cognition is true. The *pramāṇas*, then, cannot guarantee knowledge in the way that they are purported to do so.

What did Jayarāśi take to be the upshot of his extensive critique of the *pramāṇas*? That is difficult to determine precisely. He begins his work by quoting the maxim, 'In respect to everyday practice the fool and the wise man are similar' (Franco 1994: 69). But Jayarāśi apparently does not mean to imply by this that the wise man (like the fool) knows nothing. His counterexamples to philosophical theories often make use of cases of pre-critical everyday examples of knowledge that he seemingly endorses as correct. Nor does he even reject all philosophical knowledge claims: Lokāyata materialism is explicitly claimed to be true, for instance. In common with the Mādhyamikas, however, Jayarāśi takes everyday epistemic practices to neither have nor require any deeper epistemic foundation. Moreover, the realization of this is itself taken to be a source of freedom from suffering. Hence his book ends: 'Thus, when the principles are completely annihilated, all everyday practice (or: all thinking, speaking and acting) can be delightful in as much as it no [longer has to be] deliberated' (Franco 1994: 44).

Śrīharṣa and the necessity of the *pramāṇas*

The twelfth-century Advaitin philosopher Śrīharṣa's masterpiece is the *Khaṇḍanakhaṇḍakhādya* (Jha 1986). This voluminous work consists of an introduction, in which he sets out his own philosophical views, followed by a series of debates in which he elaborately refutes the definitions of the categories proposed by his opponents. Right at the beginning of the work Śrīharṣa explicitly addresses a methodological challenge to his philosophical procedures: namely, the *pramāṇavādin* dogma that prior to entering into debate both parties to a philosophical discussion must admit that the *pramāṇas* exist. The silencing implication of this dogma is clear: any refusal to acknowledge the existence of the *pramāṇas* is supposed to place the sceptic completely outside of rational philosophical discourse.

Śrīharṣa responds by analyzing this dogma into four possible claims:

> [T]he existence of the means of valid knowledge, etc. which is to be admitted by the disputants follows from what logical reason? (1) From the fact that discussion, invariably accompanied by the admission of the means of valid knowledge, etc. cannot be undertaken by two debaters who do not admit their existence? (2) From the fact that these things are the causes of the discussion which is to be undertaken by the disputants? or (3) From the fact that these things are commonly accepted? or (4) From the fact that failure to admit their existence would lead to an improper result in the establishment of truth or determination of victory? (Granoff 1978: 71–2)

All four alternatives are rejected. Thus (1) is untenable because philosophers like the Cārvākas and the Mādhyamikas refuse to admit the *pramāṇas* and yet enter into philosophical discussion. Indeed, the very attempts of the *pramāṇavādins* to refute these philosophers imply that they are to be taken seriously. Similar considerations refute alternatives (2) and (3).

The opponent now modifies his thesis. It is not discussion in general that requires the admission of the *pramāṇas*, but discussion that is capable of proving or refuting anything. Śrīharṣa's reply is twofold. First, he denies that there is an invariable concomitance (*vyāpti*) between the admission of the existence of the *pramāṇas* and proof or refutation. The mere admission of *pramāṇas* does not entail that discussion leads to proof or refutation. Secondly, the real determinant of unsuccessful argument is specious reasoning. To indicate specious reasoning, all that is required is a provisional acceptance of the *pramāṇas*. By the use of negative argument the debater can show that if the opponent accepts a particular *pramāṇa*, then certain logical consequences result that are incompatible (on the opponent's own terms) with the original admission.

Śrīharṣa continues:

> We do not say that debate is to be undertaken having admitted that the means of valid knowledge do not exist, but that debate may be undertaken by individuals who are indifferent to the question whether the means of knowledge do exist or whether the means of knowledge do not exist, and yet carry on just as you do having admitted their existence. (Granoff 1978: 75)

Indeed, the very debate in progress between Śrīharṣa and his opponent is an illustration of this! All we require for debate is the acceptance by both parties to the debate of certain conventional rules. Moreover, by insisting on this requirement, alternative (4) in the original analysis is eliminated. Victory in debate is assigned by a neutral judge on the basis of whether or not the debater has violated these conventional rules.

Śrīharṣa's own view seems to be that all definitions are illogical and the bulk of the *Khaṇḍanakhaṇḍakhādya* is devoted to trying to show that the Nyāya definitions in particular all entail contradictions and hence (on Nyāya principles) must be unsound. As an Advaitin, Śrīharṣa believes in the self-luminous *Brahman* of pure consciousness, but the world is indefinable (*anirvacanīya*) as existent or non-existent – as the dialectical attempts at definition show. Like all Advaitins, he holds that the ultimate (and knowable) truth is that the undifferentiated *Brahman* is the only reality. This implies that the *pramāṇas* must be invalid, for they purport to give knowledge of objects that Advaita says are unreal. So the *pramāṇas* too are ultimately 'false', though they may nevertheless assist in facilitating liberation, which is real.

Śrīharṣa helpfully clarifies his own position in the following way:

> In reality, we avoid categorizing the phenomenal world as existent or non-existent; placing our all on the self-established consciousness, the real Brahma alone, we rest in peace, our purpose accomplished. But those who undertake debate by means of a set of proofs and refutations which they themselves design, and hope thereby to establish the truth, to them we say 'These arguments of yours are not correct, for they are contradicted by the very principles which you admit.' And for this reason, all objections to the faults which we adduce are without occasion, for we do no more than point out your principles are contradicted by your own admissions. (Granoff 1978: 141)

Conclusion

Our Indian 'sceptics', then, were not really sceptics who doubted the very possibility of knowledge, but they certainly were sceptical about the epistemic role that most Indian epistemologists wanted to assign to the *pramāṇas*. It is true that they may not have succeeded in convincing the *pramāṇavādins* of this, but by challenging with powerful arguments their opponents' epistemological assumptions the 'sceptics' forced other Indian philosophers to explore more deeply the nature of philosophical reasoning – particularly since one of the most widely acccepted *pramāṇas* was inference (*anumāna*), the topic of our next chapter.

Suggestions for further reading

Valuable accounts of the *pramāṇa* tradition include Matilal 1986, Chatterjee 1950, Datta 1960, Bhatt 1989, Arnold 2005 and Phillips 2012. On *pramāṇyavāda*, see Mohanty 1989, 1992. On Gaṅgeśa's contributions to the epistemology of perception, see Phillips and Tatacharya 2004. For Bhāṭṭa Mīmāṃsā views of perception, see Taber 2005. For the Advaitin theory of perception, see Gupta 1991. On the Dharmakīrtian tradition in Indo-Tibetan Buddhist epistemology, see Dreyfus 1997. On the theory of error, see Hiriyanna 1975, Potter 1963 and Rao 1998. On testimony, see Matilal and Chakrabarti 1994. On Nāgārjuna's critique of *pramāṇa* theory, see Bhattacharya 1978 and Westerhoff 2010. On Jayarāśi, see Franco 1994, Franco (forthcoming) and Mills 2015. On Śrīharṣa, see Granoff 1978 and Phillips 1995.

3 Reasoning

Introduction

Classical Indian *pramāṇa* theory includes not only what Western philosophers would count as epistemology, but also much that they would count as logic and philosophy of language. This is because almost all Indian philosophers recognized inference (*anumāna*) as an independent source of knowledge, and many recognized testimony (*śabda*) as a special kind of word-generated knowledge. This chapter focuses on Indian 'logic' (broadly conceived), and the next chapter addresses Indian debates about selected issues in the philosophy of language.

The history of Indian logic can be roughly divided into three periods (Vidyabhusana 1978): the ancient period (650 BCE–100 CE), dominated by the *Nyāyasūtra* and its commentaries; the medieval period (up to 1200 CE), dominated by the Buddhist logicians Dignāga and Dharmakīrti; and the modern period (from 900 CE), dominated by Gaṅgeśa and the school of Navya-Nyāya, or 'New Logic'.

Since the origins of Indian logic were in the ancient traditions of public debate, there were accordingly two distinct, though intertwined, parts to its development. One part (on which there is a very large literature) is to do with the search for a satisfactory model of inference and the consequent emergence of a formalized canonical inference schema. The other part is more to do with dialectics, and includes a concern with the nature of fallacies (*hetvābhāsa*). Both parts are evident in Gautama's *Nyāyasūtra* (second century), the foundational text for the development of ancient Indian logic.

Early Nyāya logic

In what became the most influential part of the *Nyāyasūtra*, Gautama identifies and systematizes a form of inferential argument used in debate. He defines an inference as having five members: the hypothesis (*pratijñā*); the ground or reason (*hetu*); the corroboration (*dṛṣṭanta*); the application (*upanaya*); and the conclusion (*nigamana*).

This account of inference may be seen as a regimentation of a conversation that might occur if two people were standing together looking at a mountain side from which they could see smoke rising. One of the persons involved remarks that there is a fire on the mountain. When asked for his reasoning he replies that he holds that there is a fire on the mountain side because there is smoke. He then appeals to familiar conjunctions of fire and smoke: as in a kitchen. Furthermore, he reminds his friend that one never sees smoke where there is no fire: as, for example, in a lake. Then we can correctly infer a conclusion (fire on the mountain) from observational evidence (smoke on the mountain) together with a general rule (wherever there is smoke there is fire).

This imaginary exchange can be formalized as what became a stock example of a five-membered inference:

(1) Hypothesis (*pratijñā*): That mountain is fire-possessing.
(2) Ground or reason (*hetu*): Because it is smoke-possessing.
(3) Corroboration (*dṛṣṭanta*): Whatever is smoke-possessing is fire-possessing, like kitchen, unlike lake.
(4) Application (*upanaya*): That mountain, since it possesses smoke, is fire-possessing.
(5) Conclusion (*nigamana*): Therefore that mountain is fire-possessing.

This is a full-scale version of what later comes to be called an 'inference for others' (*parārthānumāna*), in other words, reasoning for convincing another. The Buddhists and others argued that this schema includes redundant elements, but over the centuries Nyāya steadfastly insisted that all five parts are necessary for an argument used to convince others. In actual philosophical polemics, however, Naiyāyikas tend to use a briefer form:

(1) Hypothesis: That mountain is fire-possessing.
(2) Reason: Because that mountain is smoke-possessing.
(3) Examples: (a) like kitchen (b) unlike lake.

Both the five- and three-membered forms, however, set out all five terms involved in an inference: (1) the *pakṣa* or subject of the inference (*that mountain*); (2) the *sādhya* or property that qualifies the *pakṣa* (*fire-possessing*); (3) the *hetu* or that other property which is related in an appropriate way to the *sādhya* (*smoke-possessing*); and the two kinds of examples, (4) positive (*sapakṣa*) and (5) negative (*vipakṣa*).

It is important to understand that each of the five Sanskrit terms italicized above is not to be understood as just a linguistic expression: instead, the Indians think of inference as being not about words, but about the things to which words refer. This ties in with their insistence on presenting examples: in the stock argument above, of things that are both smoky and fiery (*kitchen*) and neither smoky nor fiery (*lake*). These examples guarantee that the major premise 'Whatever is smoke-possessing is fire-possessing' has existential import. The Western notion of a formally valid inference with false premises and a false conclusion is alien to Indian logic.

The Indian logicians discussed various rules of inference, the violation of which would involve mistakes in reasoning. Perhaps the most important of these is the rule of the *sādhya*-pervaded *hetu*. This requires that the *hetu* must fall completely within the *sādhya*. For early Nyāya the pervasion relation is a relation among particulars; for later Nyāya what is meant is co-occurrence of properties, that is, a relation between universals. Either way though, *A* pervades *B* just in case wherever *B* occurs, *A* occurs. With appropriate caveats, this relation of pervasion or universal concomitance (*vyāpti*) can thus be reformulated as the major premise of a Western syllogism: for example, 'All smoke-possessing things are fire-possessing things.'

The logic here is deductive, but the premises are arrived at inductively. Crucial to this schema (which some scholars have called the Indian 'syllogism') is the notion of the inference-warranting pervasion relation (*vyāpti*) appealed to in the third member of the full-scale inference. Naiyāyikas are fallibilists about our knowledge of pervasions and hence inferential reasoning is defeasible: that is, reasoning based on an assumption of a *vyāpti* can in principle be defeated. Not all reasonings, then, are genuine inferences. It is significant here, however, what word Nyāya uses for such erroneous reasoning: *hetvābhāsa* or 'pseudo-inferences'. In other words, such erroneous reasonings are not really inferences at all, because inference is a *pramāṇa* and hence a reliable source of knowledge that cannot lead us astray.

Fallacies, debate and dialectics

The *Nyāyasūtra* contains a list of five classes of fallacious reasons (*hetvābhāsa*), all of which fail to possess the characteristics of the true reason (*hetu*), plus warnings about various kinds of debating tricks. The classes of five fallacies were elaborated upon by later commentators, but as Indian logic developed, much more attention was given to the formalization of the canonical inferential schema.

Nyāyasūtra 1.2.4–9 lists five classes of fallacious reasons: (1) a reason which is indecisive; (2) a reason that contradicts accepted tenets; (3) a reason intended to produce something but which only produces doubt; (4) a reason that is as much in need of proof as the thing to be proved; and (5) a reason that is mistimed. This list of five classes of fallacy provided the basis of elaborated classifications by later writers. Note that these are not 'formal' fallacies in the Western sense of being violations of the logical form of an argument. Rather, they are factors that prevent the inferential cognition from arising.

The *Nyāyasūtra* also has quite a lot to say about other kinds of logical faults. Thus it divides controversy (*kathā*) into three kinds (*Nyāyasūtra* 1.2.1–3): (1) discussion (*vāda*), which involves presenting two opposing views in five-membered arguments, proving correct conclusions by appeal to instruments of knowledge (*pramāṇas*) and indirect reasoning (*tarka*); (2) sophistry (*jalpa*), which is like a discussion but is aimed at victory (*vijaya*), not truth, and involves supporting and condemning arguments through quibbling, futile rejoinders and censure of all kinds; and (3) cavil (*vitaṇḍā*), which is sophistry without even trying to establish anything.

Quibbling or equivocation (*chala*) is defined as controverting a proposition by giving it a different meaning. Futile rejoinders (*jati*) are objections based on irrelevant similarities and differences. Ways of losing an argument (*nigrahasthāna*) are ways the arguer can spoil his case with dialectical shortcomings. The fifth and final book of the *Nyāyasūtra* deals with the latter two elements of the theory of debate in more detail, providing a list of twenty-four futile rejoinders and twenty-two ways of losing an argument. This supplements the discussion of the fallacies of the reason so that the combined account covers the various ways in which inferences can fail.

Later authors are sometimes a little disparaging about early Nyāya's fascination with the theory of debate, and after Dignāga the theory of fallacies certainly becomes more formal in character and much more tied to the theory of the syllogism. But if we were to adopt a dialogical approach to argument – as do many contemporary informal logicians, for example – then the crux of the theory of argument are the implicit rules that govern various kinds of dialogical exchange. We can then regard fallacies, not as a theoretically distinct notion, but as deviations from these rules. This approach leaves room for fallacies but makes an account of dialogical exchange, not fallacies, the basis of our account of argument. Indian logic, however, took a different direction. Although it grew out of a theory of debate, it eventually repudiated its origins – arguably moving closer to an ideal of a formal, deductive logic (see further Hamblin 1970, Oetke 1996, Taber 2004).

Medieval Buddhist logic

Medieval Indian logic was dominated by the Buddhist logicians Dignāga and Dharmakīrti, though there were also important contributions made by the Jainas. Dignāga (fifth century) built upon and systematized earlier Buddhist work in logic, setting out the framework within which later Buddhist thinkers addressed questions of inference and debate.

The Buddhist formulation of the standard inference schema is simpler than the Nyāya version:

Thesis (*pakṣa*): *p* has *s*.
Reason (*hetu*): *p* has *h*.
Pervasion (*vyāpti*): Whatever has *h* has *s*.

(Where *p* is the *pakṣa* or subject of the inference, *s* is the *sādhya* or property that qualifies *p*, and *h* is the *hetu* or that other property which is related in an appropriate way to *s*.)

Dignāga made three major contributions. First, he centred his account of inference around the distinction between inference for oneself (*svārthānumāna*) and inference for others (*parārthānumāna*). Second, he more precisely formulated the requirement that the *hetu* of a satisfactory inference must satisfy three conditions (*trairūpyahetu*): (i) it should occur in the case under consideration; (ii) it should be present in a similar case; and (iii) it should not be present in any dissimilar case. Pervasion is then defined in terms of the last two of these conditions. Third, he devised his 'wheel of reasons' (*hetucakra*), a matrix to classify pseudo-reasons in terms of the last two forms of the *trairūpyahetu*. A few words on each of these three innovations are in order.

The distinction between inference for oneself (*svārthānumāna*) and inference for others (*parārthānumāna*) was already implicit in earlier Indian logic, but Dignāga made it explicit: 'The inferential process is of two kinds: that which is for one's own sake, and that which is for the sake of other people. Inference for oneself consists in discerning an object through a sign that has three characteristics' (*Pramāṇasammucaya* 2.1; Hayes 1988a: 231). His leading idea here is the correlativity of the notions of *inference* (the cognitive process that generates knowledge) and *argument* (the techniques of persuasion). An inference for others, however, is meant to persuade other people and hence has to be laid out much more fully and explicitly than an inference for oneself. It is what takes place when one demonstrates to others the conclusion one has drawn through an inference for one's own sake.

Dignāga's claim that a properly formulated inference for oneself must satisfy the 'three marks' (*trairūpya*) is problematic for at least two reasons. First, because the second criterion seems redundant from a logical viewpoint (though perhaps not from an epistemological one). Second, and more importantly, because to know that the third criterion is satisfied we would have to know that all future instances will conform to all past ones. But obviously we cannot perceive this; nor can we infer it, on pain of an infinite regress. And yet a valid inference is supposed to deliver certainty (*niścaya*), or absence of doubt as to whether what is inferred is true. This latter problem with Dignāga's theory of inference is one that his successor Dharmakīrti tries to address.

Lastly, Dignāga's 'wheel of reasons' (*hetucakra*) is an ingenious way of classifying fallacies by showing the proper and improper relations between the *hetu* and the examples (the *sapakṣa* and the *vipakṣa*). He considers the nine possible ways in which the *sapakṣa* and *vipakṣa* can be related to the *hetu*, depending on whether the *hetu* is present in all, some or none of the *sapakṣa* and *vipakṣa*. These nine possibilities can be represented as a matrix (Matilal 1998: 8) (see figure 3.1).

Of these nine possibilities, only two (numbers 2 and 8) are valid inferences according to Dignāga, for only they satisfy all of the 'three marks'.

The most influential Buddhist logician was Dharmakīrti (seventh century), who built upon Dignāga's work and introduced two particularly important innovations. First, in the second chapter of his *Nyāyabindu* (Gangopadhyaya 1971; Stcherbatsky 1962), Dharmakīrti claimed that there is a kind of necessity to the *vyāpti* relation, a necessity that is grounded either in causation (*tadutpatti*) or in identity (*tādātmya*). This is the basis of his proposed answer to the question for Dignāga raised earlier: 'How can we ever come to know that a pervasion relation obtains?' In the case of causation, the idea is that if *x* is the

1. + *vipakṣa* + *sapakṣa*	2. − *vipakṣa* + *sapakṣa*	3. ± *vipakṣa* + *sapakṣa*
4. + *vipakṣa* − *sapakṣa*	5. − *vipakṣa* − *sapakṣa*	6. ± *vipakṣa* − *sapakṣa*
7. + *vipakṣa* ± *sapakṣa*	8. − *vipakṣa* ± *sapakṣa*	9. ± *vipakṣa* ± *sapakṣa*

+ = all; ± = some; − = none

Figure 3.1 Dignāga's 'wheel of reasons' (*hetucakra*)

cause of *y*, then knowing *y* has occurred allows us to infer that *x* must have occurred too. In the case of identity, Dharmakīrti has in mind an inference like 'This is a tree because it is a oak', which he takes to be a situation of identity because it is one where the truth-maker for a tree's being both an oak and a tree is in fact just one and the same unique particular.

Secondly, Dharmakīrti brought within the scope of inference a knowledge of absences, or negative facts. Although he rejected the Nyāya view that absences are real, he does affirm that we can have knowledge of something's absence through inference. Thus I infer the absence of an elephant in my room now because what I see before me is incompatible with what I would have seen had there been an elephant here.

It is unclear, however, that these innovations do in the end solve the problem of how can we ever come to know with certainty that a pervasion relation obtains (see Gillon 1991). After all, appeal to causation will not do the job here, for Dharmakīrti holds that our knowledge of causation is acquired by mere observation of sequences of events, even though such observations clearly cannot discriminate between genuine causal connections and spurious correlations. Neither will an appeal to identity succeed, for knowledge of the identity relation cannot be inferential or there would have to be an infinite regress of inferences to establish even one instance of it. Finally, as we shall soon see, a similar regress also threatens Dharmakīrti's account of our knowledge of absences.

Navya-Nyāya logic

The modern period of Indian logic is the period of Navya-Nyāya ('New Logic'). The most influential work of this school is certainly Gaṅgeśa's prodigious *Tattvacintāmaṇi* (fourteenth century). The next most eminent Navya-Naiyāyika is Raghunātha Śiromaṇi (sixteenth century), who further refined the analytical tools of Navya-Nyāya and introduced a number of ontological innovations. The Navya-Naiyāyika philosophers developed a powerful technical language which became the language of all serious discourse, an intentional logic of cognitions (*jñāna*) increasingly construed by most Indian philosophers as being independent of the realist metaphysics of Nyāya-Vaiśeṣika.

Arguably, Gaṅgeśa's key innovation is his treatment of cognition (*jñāna*) and hence it is that Navya-Nyāya logic is correspondingly a logic of cognitions. A cognition is a short-lived, episodic mental event. Cognitions are intentional: they are always *of* something. The object of a qualificative or determinate cognition is a relational complex of the form *aRb*, which Navya-Nyāya interprets as the cognition *of a in b by R*. Here *a* is the qualificandum (*viśesya*), *R* is the qualificative relation (*saṃsarga*), and *b* is the qualifier (*prakāra* or *viśeṣaṇa*). Qualification is a relational abstract that obtains in the world, but it is used to talk about cognitions. This *aRb* schema of analysis, then, is used by Navya-Nyāya to bridge the gap between the theory of cognition and ontology. A veridical awareness is a qualificative cognition of a particular as related to its properties, not a cognition of a representation.

This method of analysis is applied by Gaṅgeśa to the case of inferential knowledge. What he takes to underlie occurrences of inferential knowledge episodes is a relation that links instances of one kind of thing with instances of another kind of thing. This relation is, of course, pervasion (*vyāpti*). But Gaṅgeśa feels that the pervasion relation needs to be much more clearly and abstractly characterized than has been done hitherto.

Gaṅgeśa begins this task with the following definition:

> Inferential knowledge is cognition generated by cognition of a property-belonging-to-a-locus-and-qualified-by-a-pervasion. (Phillips 1995: 356)

The hyphens in the translation here indicate that the content of the relevant cognition is all of what is hyphenated. And it is this cognition that Gaṅgeśa takes to be the instrumental cause of an inferential knowing.

To fill out this definition, however, we need to be much clearer about what pervasion is. Gaṅgeśa first eliminates five definitions of pervasion in terms of non-deviation (*avyabhicāritatva*) of the *hetu* (*h*) from the *sādhya* (*s*):

> But now, in [that] knowledge of a pervasion which is the cause of an inference, what is pervasion? It is not simply nondeviation [of *h* with respect to *s*], for it is not that [nondeviation defined as] (1) 'nonoccurrent$_1$ [of *h*] to the locus of absence of *s*' nor [that defined as] (2) 'nonoccurrent$_1$ [of *h*] to the locus of that absence of *s* [which absence occurs] in what is different from a locus of *s*' nor (3) '[*h*'s] having a different locus from that of a mutual absence whose counterpositive is a locus of *s*,' nor (4) '[*h*'s] being the counterpositive of an absence which resides in all loci of absence of *s*,' nor (5) 'nonoccurent$_1$ [of *h*] to what is other than the locus of *s*,' since it is not any of these where *s* is universal-positive. (Ingalls 1951: 86)

He then goes on to consider and reject a total of twenty-nine attempted definitions of pervasion, the final eight of which he finds acceptable.

Obviously, it is impossible here to offer a proper introduction to the intricacies of Navya-Nyāya language and techniques (the interested reader should refer instead to the suggested readings at the end of this chapter). Even in translation, however, the very famous passage from the *Tattvacintāmaṇi* quoted above gives us a little of the flavour of Navya-Nyāya writing in Sanskrit: tersely scholastic and highly technical, but also clearly striving for increased precision and rigour. The original Sanskrit used is a non-symbolic language designed to describe a cognized structure in terms of the Navya-Nyāya theory, making heavy use of new concepts and terminology, like 'limitor' (*avacchedaka*) to denote the *mode* of cognition of an object.

The eight definitions of pervasion that Gaṅgeśa finds acceptable, however, simply tell us what pervasion consists in, in other words, what we would have to know in order to know that *s* pervades *h*. They do not tell us how to know whether *s* really does pervades *h*. How *is* pervasion known then? One very radical Indian answer to that question is: it never really is!

Pervasion and the problem of induction

One of the many interesting parallels between Indian and Western philosophy is the way in which the problem of induction arises in both. The sceptical position that in the West is associated with the name of David Hume in the eighteenth century was in India associated with the Cārvāka materialists. The problem arose in Indian philosophy in the context of the inter-school debates about the number and status of the *pramāṇas* or valid means of knowledge. Except for the Cārvāka, all the schools accepted at least perception (*pratyakṣa*) and inference (*anumāna*) as valid means of knowledge, although there was considerable dispute as to the ultimate status of these *pramāṇas*. The Cārvākas, however, are reported to have denied the validity of inference and only accepted perception as a *pramāṇa*. The reasons offered for this stand are fundamentally concerned with the supposed impossibility of justifying the inductive relation that is the basis of Indian inference forms.

We have already noted that the focus of concern in Indian logic was the ascertainment of the truth of the universal proposition of an inference form and hence the establishment of the validity of the given inference. This is the import of the rule of the *sādhya*-pervaded *hetu*, as can be illustrated by considering the following argument:

Hypothesis: That mountain is smoke-possessing.

Reason: Because that mountain is fire-possessing.

Examples: (a) like kitchen (b) unlike lake.

This argument is invalid because the *hetu* (fiery things) is not completely included within the *sādhya* (smoky things). It is possible to give examples of things that are members of the first class but not of the second. Here the standard instance adduced by Indian logicians is a red-hot iron ball, which is fiery but not smoky. This type of contrary instance is called an *upādhi* in Indian logic (see further Phillips and Tatacharya 2002). Discovering an *upādhi* amounts to a denial of the relation of universal concomitance (*vyāpti*) that must obtain between the *hetu* and *sādhya* of an Indian inference in order for it to be a valid inference.

But now the question arises as to what happens if we do not find any contrary instances. Can we then assume invariable concomitance? It is in this manner that the problem of justifying induction arose for Indian philosophers. When the whole validity of inductive inference rests on the relation of invariable concomitance, how can we be certain that this relation actually obtains? The problem here was conceived as being twofold. First, how to justify a generalization about the universal concomitance of *A*s and *B*s when we have not seen all past instances of *A*s and *B*s, let alone established that all non-*Bs* are also non-*As*. Second, how to justify the projection of past concomitance of *As* and *Bs* into the future when we have not seen any future instances of *As* and *Bs*.

The problem thus posed bears obvious and striking resemblances to what in Western philosophy has been viewed as the problem of justifying induction, a problem originally posed in the West by David Hume's analysis of causation in the eighteenth century. In India the problem arose much earlier, though in a different context. However, the general question of how to justify induction was considered seriously by Indian philosophers and various responses were elicited. We shall briefly examine four of these Indian responses: namely, the sceptical Cārvāka response, the Naiyāyika appeal to *sāmānyalakṣaṇa* perception, the Advaitin use of non-falsification (*abādhitva*), and the reply of the Buddhist logicians.

Cārvāka scepticism about inference

First of all, a word of caution about the nature of our historical knowledge of the Cārvāka school is appropriate. Most of what we know about Cārvāka doctrines and arguments is to be found in the reports of their views in the texts of their opponents, and correspondingly is likely to be open to polemical distortion (for further details, see Chattopadhyaya and Gangopadhyaya 1994; Bhattacharya 2002, 2010). Notwithstanding both this and the fact that Cārvāka seems to have been a fairly short-lived minority view, the standard representation of the Cārvāka position on inference continued to enjoy a polemical longevity in the works of their later Indian opponents, who obviously felt obliged to respond to what they took to be a serious challenge to epistemological orthodoxy.

The standard Indian representation of the Cārvāka response to the problem of justifying the inductive *vyāpti* relation was that they simply denied that inference really is a *pramāṇa*. For the Cārvāka, there is only one valid means of knowledge: namely, perception (*pratyakṣa*). According to the summary of their views in Mādhava's *Sarvadarśanasaṃgraha* (fourteenth century), they argued somewhat as follows (Radhakrishnan and Moore 1957: 231–3). Inference is dependent on universal concomitance (*vyāpti*). For inference to be a valid means of knowledge this relation of universal concomitance must be able to be known by one of the other *pramāṇas*. However, it cannot be known by any of the *pramāṇas*, as an examination of each of them shows. Thus perception (internal and external) cannot establish such a universal relation, since we never perceive all past particulars and no future ones are ever perceived. Neither can inference establish the universal proposition, since it is obvious that to appeal to inference to justify inference itself is to enter into a vicious regress. Testimony (*śabda*) is also rejected as the means of knowledge of the universal proposition, since it ultimately depends on perception or inference. Finally, comparison (*upamāna*) is ruled out too because it can only establish a quite different relation, namely, the relation of a name to the object named. These four categories are the four kinds of *pramāṇas* recognized by the Nyāya school and, although the Vedāntins recognize two more (*anupalabdhi* and *arthāpatti*), these cover the valid means of knowledge admitted by almost all the Indian schools. Hence the Cārvākas conclude that since *vyāpti* cannot be known by means of any of the *pramāṇas*, it must be the case that inference is not a valid means of knowledge.

However, the Cārvākas do offer an alternative account of inference. They claim that it is either based on a former perception, or that it is a mistake. The fact that it is sometimes followed by successful results is just an accidental coincidence. In other words, inference is a *psychological* process, not a logical one, and our reliance on such reasoning is due to psychological conditioning. It is sometimes accidentally successful, but there is no *logical* connection because, the Cārvāka argues, it has been established that we can never really know the *vyāpti* on which inference is based. (The resemblance to Hume is quite striking here, for he also concluded that induction cannot be epistemologically justified at all because it is not really a process of reasoning but rather a *habit* of expecting what has previously occurred in certain given circumstances to reoccur in similar circumstances.)

Of course, one difficulty with the Cārvāka explanation here is that the rate of accidental coincidence seems inordinately high. However, their opponents did not pursue this line of objection, which might easily have given rise to the types of discussion about probability theory that have so engrossed Western philosophers working on the problem of induction. Rather, the other Indian schools were more concerned to press home a charge of self-contradiction. They accused the Cārvākas of a self-contradictory use of inference to deny the validity of inference. It is not clear how far this charge is justified. If we invoke a distinction not present in Indian logic, the distinction between deductive and inductive argument, then it is possible to represent the Cārvāka argument as a valid deductive argument. Thus, the Cārvāka argues that if inference is a *pramāṇa*, then *vyāpti* must be knowable. But *vyāpti* cannot be known. Therefore, inference is not a *pramāṇa*. This is an instance of *modus tollens*: 'If *p* then *q*; not-*q*; therefore, not-*p*'. In other words, the Cārvākas were using a valid *deductive* argument to establish the invalidity of *inductive* arguments. Because they were not using an inductive argument themselves, it seems that the charge of self-contradiction has no basis.

How far the Cārvākas thought their strictures against inference were supposed to extend is now extremely unclear. There is some evidence that they were only concerned to attack inferences that moved from the material to the non-material. This would naturally eliminate theological inferences as exemplified, for example, in the Naiyāyika arguments for the existence of God, and this kind of criticism would seem in keeping with their reported anti-religious tone. They may also have been willing to allow inference a certain practical usefulness while still denying its status as a *pramāṇa*. Nevertheless, even given these modifications, the Cārvāka scepticism about the possibility of inference represented a serious challenge to the theoretical assumptions of the other schools. Moreover, it was a challenge they could not afford to ignore because the scepticism of the Cārvākas raises doubts as to whether there exists any form of universal regularity in the world, or whether such apparent regularities are merely projections of our own psychological conditioning.

This scepticism naturally calls into question the very possibility of achieving liberation (*mokṣa*), the avowed goal of the other schools of Indian philosophy. If we have reason to believe there is no regular connection between events and actions, then we have reason to believe that it is impossible for a person to enter into the course of events as a conscious causal agent whose decisions and activities have predictable consequences. Karma is a fiction since it can only be established by inference, which is not a *pramāṇa* if the Cārvākas are right. Thus, since it is not at all clear whether the attainment of *mokṣa* is even possible, it is obviously a waste of time engaging in religious activities and practising asceticism. Rather, the Cārvākas advocated a policy of hedonism and the pursuit of worldly pleasures. According to the *Sarvasiddhāntasaṃgraha*, they held that 'The enjoyment of health lies in eating delicious food, keeping company of young women, using fine clothes, perfumes, garlands, sandal paste, etc.' (Radhakrishnan and Moore 1957: 235). Faced with such a challenge, it was inevitably incumbent upon the *mokṣa*-oriented philosophers to defend inference as a valid means of knowledge, and we shall now examine some of these attempts.

The Nyāya defence of induction

The Nyāya response to this challenge was built upon their realist epistemology and ontology. They claimed that we can actually perceive (non-sensuously) the *vyāpti* relation. Jayanta Bhaṭṭa (tenth century) presents the Naiyāyika view in his *Nyāyamañjarī* thus:

> A man perceives that smoke and fire co-exist in the same locus. He comprehends by means of the method of difference that smoke is not present in the locus where fire does not exist. Then he synthesizes the results obtained by the joint method of agreement and difference and frames a judgment by means of the internal organ that smoke is the invariable concomitant of fire . . . The relation of concomitance obtaining between the middle term and the major term may be determined by means of the universals inhering in them (these two terms). The relation of concomitance holding between smoke and fire amounts to that of concomitance subsisting between the universals of smoke and fire. The positive aspect of the relation may be grasped by extraordinary perception acknowledged by the Naiyāyikas. But the negative aspect of the relation should also be grasped in order to grasp its invariable character. Therefore, we should also know that smoke does not exist where fire does not exist. (Bhattacharyya 1978: 252–3)

In other words, their account of the method of inductive generalization is as follows. First, we observe a uniform agreement in presence (*anvaya*) between two things *A* and *B*; that is, whenever *A* is present *B* also is present. Second, we observe that there is a uniform agreement in absence (*vyatireka*) between *A* and *B*; that is, whenever *B* is absent *A* also is absent. Third, we do not observe any contrary instance in which *A* is present without *B* being present, or vice versa. Given these conditions we conclude that there is a relation of invariable concomitance between *A* and *B*.

However, we still have to establish that this relation is independent of any *upādhi*. Thus, in addition to the method of sampling by observation of agreement and difference, the Naiyāyikas also utilize the method of indirect proof (*tarka*). The idea here is that we can indirectly prove a universal proposition like 'All smoke-possessing things are fire-possessing things' by disproving its contradictory proposition. In other words, if the universal proposition is false, then its contradictory 'Some smoke-possessing things are not fire-possessing things' must be true. But this would be to claim that there could be smoke without fire, a conclusion that is absurd because it denies the well-known causal relation between fire and smoke. Hence we can conclude that since 'Some smoke-possessing things are not fire-possessing things' is obviously false, then it must be the case that its contradictory 'All smoke-possessing things are fire-possessing things' is true.

The Naiyāyika method for establishing *vyāpti* as outlined to this point is basically simple enumeration supported by *tarka*. But, of course, this is not a sufficient reply to Cārvāka scepticism at all. In an induction by simple enumeration we move from some observed cases of *As* and *Bs* to a generalization about all *As* and *Bs*. It is precisely this move that the Cārvāka challenges. The real question is how it is possible for us to know from the observation of some *As* as related to some *Bs* that all *As* are related to *Bs*. The Nyāya reply here makes use of their doctrine of *sāmānyalakṣaṇa* perception: that is, the perception of a universal characterizing all members of a class, one of whose members is presented.

As we have already seen, Jayanta refers to this kind of 'extraordinary' perception in the *Nyāyamañjarī*. However, it is in the Navya-Nyāya that we encounter the fuller account of *sāmānyalakṣaṇa-pratyakṣa* where it is classified as one of three kinds of extraordinary (*alaukika*) perception. (The other two are yogic perception and *jñānalakṣaṇa-pratyakṣa*, or the perception of the features of something previously known as here and now presented.) Viśvanātha (seventeenth century) presents the Navya-Naiyāyika position thus:

> [W]here smoke or the like is connected with the [sense] organ, and the knowledge that it is smoke has arisen, with smoke as its substantive, in that knowledge smokehood is a feature. And through that smokehood as the connection, there arises the knowledge 'cases of smoke' comprising all smoke. (*Siddhāntamuktāvalī* 63; Mādhavānanda 1977: 100)

In other words, when we perceive particular smokes and fires we also perceive the universals smokeness and fireness inhering in them. Through this sense contact with smokeness and fireness, which are generic properties equally shared by all cases of smoke and of fire, we can in turn (nonsensuously) perceive all cases of smoke and of fire. Thus the concomitance of smoke and fire is established through an 'extraordinary' perception of the whole class of smoke-possessing things as related to fire. The objection that this alleged kind of perception would entail omniscience is forestalled by the claim that, although we could perceive all objects of knowledge comprehended under a generic character, they would still not be known in detail and we could not perceive their mutual differences.

Of course, this answer did not satisfy the Cārvākas at all. In the first place they simply replied that it is not true that we perceive universals and through them general classes. We only perceive particulars and only those particulars available to our ordinary perception. The Naiyāyikas object:

> So how can there be knowledge of all smoke as smoke and of all fire as fire, without the help of the connection based on a common feature? (*Siddhāntamuktāvalī* 65; Mādhavānanda 1977: 103)

But the Cārvāka answers that this begs the question, for we do not in fact perceive all smokes and all fires. Moreover, the particular smokes and fires that we do perceive exhibit no common feature and hence even less so would the innumerable members of the class of all smokes and the class of all fires.

In the second place we have the Cārvāka argument recorded in Mādhava's *Sarvadarśanasaṃgraha*:

> Nor may you maintain that this knowledge of the universal proposition has the general class as its object, because, if so, there might arise a doubt as to the existence of the invariable connection in this particular case [as, for instance, in this particular smoke as implying fire]. (Radhakrishnan and Moore 1957: 231)

This question of doubt occasions an important and ingenious Navya-Nyāya counterargument to the effect that without the admission of *sāmānyalakṣaṇa* perception the arising of the doubt whether smoke is the concomitant of fire cannot be accounted for. This follows from their definition of doubt (*saṃśaya*):

> Doubt is a knowledge of contradictory features, viz. presence and absence, with regard to the same substantive . . . The cause of doubt is the knowledge of attributes that are common to two things. (*Siddhāntamuktāvalī* 130; Mādhavānanda 1977: 215)

Hence the argument runs:

> For since the relation of fire to the smoke that is being perceived is already known, and no other smoke is known (at the time), the doubt whether smoke is the concomitant of fire or not is inexplicable. (*Siddhāntamuktāvalī* 65; Mādhavānanda 1977: 103)

The idea here is that the sceptic claims to have doubts about whether smoke is always accompanied by fire. But such a doubt is not about observed cases of smoke, for they have all been observed to be accompanied by fire. So the doubt must be about cases of smoke that are distant in time or space, and these cannot be perceived through the ordinary means of perception. If they are unperceived altogether, then such cases cannot be the source of the sceptic's doubt, given that doubt (*saṃśaya*) requires a wavering between two (previously perceived) characterizations of a given object. Hence only if the distant cases of smoke are perceived through *sāmānyalakṣaṇa* perception can we explain how the sceptic's doubt arises: the distant cases of smoke are perceived through the universal smokeness without thereby acquiring specific information about which of them is conjoined with fire, whereas the cases ordinarily present are perceived to be conjoined with fire.

The Cārvāka finds this argument uncompelling, however, since to have force it requires prior acceptance of Naiyāyika analyses of doubt and allied concepts (see further Mohanty 1993: 101–21). Cārvāka scepticism requires only the logical possibility of things being otherwise. Because it is only contingently the case that smoke is accompanied by fire, the concomitance of all smokes with fire is doubtful. The Nyāya logic, unconcerned with this kind of philosophical doubt, which the Naiyāyikas pragmatically dismiss as empty of content, cannot adequately answer the Cārvāka scepticism using the terms framed by its very different conception of enquiry.

All in all, the Cārvāka position here is clearly summed up in Jayarāśi's *Tattvopaplavasiṃha* (eighth century):

> There is another reason why the knowledge of an invariable relation cannot be established. Is it the cognition of a relation between two universals, or between two particulars, or between a universal and a particular? If it be the cognition of a relation between two universals, then that is incorrect, for the universal itself is not demonstrated (*anupapatti*)... Nor is it possible to conceive of such a relation subsisting between a universal and a particular object because of the indemonstrability [or impossibility, *asaṁbhavāt*] of universals.
>
> Nor is it [possible to think of] such a relation between two particulars for there are innumerable cases of particular fires and particular smokes, and also because... no common element exists among the many particulars. (Radhakrishnan and Moore 1957: 237)

The Advaitin defence of induction

The Advaitin answer to the Cārvāka challenge – classically presented in Dharmarāja's *Vedāntaparibhāṣā* (seventeenth century) – is somewhat different from that of the Nyāya school, although there are important similarities. The criterion of validity in Advaita Vedānta is unfalsifiedness (*abādhitva*). Thus concomitance can be affirmed on the basis of a single instance, and the Naiyāyika method of agreement and difference is unnecessary. This concept of non-falsification ties in closely with the Advaitin theory of the two levels of truth. Hence ordinary knowledge remains knowledge until falsified, but this falsification can take place in two ways. First, within the realm of ordinary knowledge there can be falsification through a negative instance. Second, the whole world appearance can be seen as illusion in the experience of *mokṣa*.

In common with the Naiyāyikas, the Advaitins hold that agreement in presence (*anvaya*) and non-observance of any exception are necessary conditions for establishing a *vyāpti* relation. However, they reject the Naiyāyika insistence on agreement in absence (*vyatireka*). They also reject the method of hypothetical argument (*tarka*) on the grounds that it is no use trying to test the validity of a *vyāpti* with the aid of a *tarka*, because a *tarka* itself involves another *vyāpti* which also requires proving, and so on. The third important difference between Nyāya and Advaita Vedānta with regard to inference is to be found in their respective positions on the question of the perceptual knowledge of a *vyāpti*. The problem under consideration is how to justify an inference that moves from the observation of a limited number of *A*s accompanied by *B*s to the conclusion that all *A*s are accompanied by *B*s. The Navya-Nyāya answer was that the perception of a particular involved the perception of a universal inhering in it, and hence the perception of all members of the class characterized by the perceived universal. Thus *vyāpti* is supposed to be established through (extraordinary) perception. The Advaitins, however, reject this account and argue in a somewhat different way. They claim that a general proposition like 'All smoke-possessing things are fire-possessing things' is justified because by perceiving particular instances of smoke and fire we are enabled to establish a relation between the two universals smokeness and fireness. It is only this relation that can supply the foundation of a general relation between all smoke-possessing things and all fire-possessing things, just insofar as they are respectively constituted by the universals smokeness and fireness.

The Advaitins hold, then, that a single observation can supply knowledge of a universal concomitance, provided that no exception is known of. That is, under certain optimum conditions a single observation can provide knowledge of a connection between two universals (for example, smokeness and fireness), and this is sufficient to justify the inference. One objection that the Advaitins did try to deal with was the apparent way in which a universal proposition like 'All cases of smoke are cases of fire' seems to state a relation obtaining between individual smokes and individual fires. Here the Advaitins reply that a universal proposition like 'All cases of smoke are cases of fire' is actually reached by a deductive inference from the *vyāpti* between smokeness and fireness. Upon the observation of only one case of such a concomitance between universals we can thereby argue that all other past and future smoke is accompanied by fire by virtue of its possessing the characteristic smokeness.

Of course, this account is completely unsatisfactory to the Cārvākas, who simply deny the existence of universals. Furthermore, some aspects of the Advaitin epistemological position were equally unacceptable to the other philosophers. In particular, their position on inference strongly reflects their belief that truth is to be identified with non-falsification (*abādhitva*). In Advaita Vedānta all knowledge gained through the *pramāṇas* is valid so long as it is unfalsified by experience, yet none of it is ultimately 'true' in that all the contents of the *pramāṇas* are in principle falsifiable. Only knowledge of *Brahman* is non-falsifiable.

Against this view the Dvaitin philosopher Madhva (thirteenth century) argued forcefully that a *pramāṇa* is supposed to give us knowledge of the world as it is. Hence it is nonsense to talk of a valid means of knowledge being ultimately falsified, which is what the Advaitin two-level theory of truth entails. Thus Madhva argues that in the case of perception, 'It would be contradictory to impose any temporal limit on the validity of perception and restrict it to the "present" moment of perception. If perception is to be invalidated later, how could it have any validity even now?' (*Anuvyākhyāna* 33; Sharma 1997: 59). Similarly, the Advaitin use of non-falsification in reply to Cārvāka scepticism about inference just misconceives the whole problem of establishing the *vyāpti* relation and hence the status of inference as a *pramāṇa*. By a universal relation (*vyāpti*) is understood a relation of concomitance independent of all conditions (*upādhi*). To talk of the contents of the *pramāṇa* inference as being ultimately falsified is simply to admit that the *vyāpti* relation is not independent of all *upādhis* and thus that inference is not a *pramāṇa*.

But this is precisely what the Cārvākas assert and what the Advaitin use of non-falsification was supposed to deny!

The Buddhist defence of induction

In his *Pramāṇavārttika* Dharmakīrti presents the Buddhist reply to Cārvāka-style scepticism thus:

> Experience, positive and negative, can never produce (a knowledge) of the strict necessity of inseparable connection. This always reposes either on the law of Causality or on the law of Identity. (Stcherbatsky 1962: I, 260)

And in the *Nyāyabindu* he reaffirms:

> Because, as regards (ultimate) reality, (the entity underlying the logical reason) is either just the same as the entity (underlying) the predicate, or it is causally derived from it. (Stcherbatsky 1962: II, 73)

Thus, according to this first line of defence, the Buddhists admit only two kinds of legitimate universal propositions. First, the *vyāpti* associated with causation is valid. Hence it is legitimate to assert an invariable association of smoke with fire because smoke is caused by fire and the law of causality is a universal law. The *pañcakāraṇī* test is used to determine whether two objects *A* and *B* are causally related or not. In brief: if it is the case (other things being equal) that the appearance of a given phenomenon *A* is immediately succeeded by the appearance of another phenomenon *B*, and the disappearance of *A* is immediately succeeded by the disappearance of *B*, then *A* and *B* are related as cause and effect. Once we know that *A* and *B* are causally related then we can assume that they are universally related. Second, the Buddhists also admit the *vyāpti* associated with identity as a legitimate universal relation. Thus to know that something is a *śiṃśapa* (a variety of tree) is to know that it is a tree because to deny the invariable concomitance associated with the genus–species relation is absurd.

Against this line of defence the Buddhists faced opposition on all fronts. On the one hand, both the Naiyāyikas and the Advaitins argued that there were other kinds of valid universal concomitances than just those based on the principles of causality and identity. For example, there is a universal relation of succession between day and night or between the seasons. On the other hand, the Cārvākas remain unsatisfied that the original problem has been solved. True, the Buddhists deny that inference has anything to do with ultimate and unrelated reality. However, even if the Buddhists analyze the cause–effect relation in terms of the belief that two things are causally connected, the original question still arises. That is, how can we be sure about this causal connection in all past instances and all future ones? If the Buddhists reply that they are only talking about the way in which our minds order data – that is, that the cause–effect relation is simply a human ordering of perceptual data – then the Cārvākas answer that it still has not been shown how it is that we can be sure that our minds will continue to order the data in the future as they have in the past.

Pragmatic defences

This leads us to the second and final line of defence used by the Buddhists: roughly, an appeal to the absurdity of practical alternatives. Doubting must have an end when it results in conceptual contradictions or pragmatic absurdities. This line of defence is reinforced by Dharmakīrti's general view that the test of practicality is the test by means of which we can separate accurate judgments from inaccurate ones. Thus in the end an inference is to be judged accurate only if it ultimately leads to successful action, and any general scepticism about inference would not pass that test. This Buddhist appeal to successful action is unpersuasive, however, since it just assumes what is in dispute: namely, whether we are *epistemically* justified in trusting that what has worked in the past will work in the future. At best, it would only show that we have *non-epistemic* reasons for believing in inductive inference.

Although Dharmakīrti's kind of pragmatic defence is in harmony with a strongly pragmatic strand within Buddhist thought generally, it is not entirely exclusive to the Buddhists. Thus Jayanta in the *Nyāyamañjarī* dismisses the Cārvāka challenge in this way:

> They cannot confute the validity of inference per se since its validity has been universally accepted.
>
> A woman, a child, a cow-herd, a cultivator and such other persons know another object (lying beyond the ken of their sense-organs) by means of its sure mark with absolute certainty.
>
> If validity is denied to inference then all worldly transactions cannot be conducted with the mere help of perception. All the people of the world should remain motionless as if they are painted in a picture. (Bhattacharyya 1978: 250)

And his fellow Naiyāyika philosopher Udayana argues in his *Nyāyakusumāñjali* (3.7) that 'doubt is permissible only so long as there is no contradiction'. This is to propose a behaviouristic criterion of doubt. If someone claims to doubt the existence of a *vyāpti* between smoke and fire, then why does he light a fire when he wants to produce smoke? His own activity indicates that his doubt is not real.

Here is the Navya-Naiyāika Gaṅgeśa making the same point in his *Tattvacintāmaṇi*, only this time not so much directly against the Cārvākas but against the Advaitin dialectician Śrīharṣa and his Cārvāka-influenced scepticism about the knowability of the pervasion relation:

> Were a person P, who has ascertained thoroughgoing positive correlations (*x* wherever *y*) and negative correlations (wherever no *y*, no *x*) to doubt that an effect might arise without a cause, then – to take up the example of smoke and fire – why should P, as he does, resort to fire for smoke (in the case, say, of a desire to get rid of mosquitoes)? (Similarly,) to food to allay hunger, and to speech to communicate to another person? (Phillips 1995: 161)

The point here seems to be that the sceptic about induction is insincere, as shown by his behaviour.

Of course, the obvious Cārvāka answer at this point will be that we may be so constituted psychologically that we come to expect a uniform regularity between instances of fire and instances of smoke, although there is no logical justification for such an expectation. The fact of such an expectation would not show that inductive inference is epistemically justified, nor that the sceptic is insincere about their scepticism.

Nor is the Navya-Nyāya use of cognitive blockers (*pratibandhaka*) to exclude the possibility of doubt uncontroversial. Their claim is that doubt about smoke being caused by fire is blocked from occurring by an awareness of a uniform agreement in the presence and absence of smoke and fire. This claim apparently requires it to be a cognitive law that there is such a relation between cognitions as determined by their objects: that is, that Navya-Nyāya's psychologistic theory of inference as being a logic of cognitions is sound. It also requires the tendentious assumption that a subject generally has only one cognition at a time.

It is, of course, well known that the problem of justifying induction has for centuries proved resistant to the efforts of Western philosophers to find a universally accepted solution. It seems too, that much the same can be said of the efforts of classical Indian philosophers to find a universally accepted solution to their own version of the problem of induction.

The scope of inference: *anumāna, upamāna, arthāpatti* and *anupalabdhi*

Distinct from the question of whether or not inference (*anumāna*) is ultimately justifiable as a *pramāṇa* is another issue much discussed by the Indian philosophers: namely, whether analogy (*upamāna*), presumption (*arthāpatti*) and non-apprehension (*anupalabdhi*) are all distinct *pramāṇas*, or just varieties of *anumāna*. Nyāya (but not Vaiśeṣika) admitted analogy as a distinct *pramāṇa*, but not presumption or non-apprehension. Prābhākara Mīmāṃsā allowed both analogy and presumption, but not non-apprehension. And Bhāṭṭa Mīmāṃsā and Advaita Vedānta admitted analogy, presumption and non-apprehension as all being distinct *pramāṇas*. A few words about each of these three disputed *pramāṇas* are in order here.

(1) By *upamāna* or analogy the Indians meant cases of coming to know of the following kind. Someone who does not know what a *gavaya* (a wild ox) is might be told that it is an animal like a cow. Subsequently encountering a *gavaya* in the forest, he then comes to know the animal before him is a *gavaya* in virtue of its similarity to a cow.

The developed Nyāya account of *upamāna* is that it is the process of reasoning by which we come to know, on the basis of a recognized similarity, that a word denotes a class of objects (*Bhāṣāpariccheda* 79–80). While both Mīmāṃsā and Advaita also accept *upamāna* as an independent *pramāṇa*, they give a different account of its nature. According to them, the fact that the word *gavaya* denotes the class of objects similar to the cow can be known either through verbal testimony or through inference. Instead what *upamāna* is needed to account for is our knowledge of the likeness of things (including the likeness between the *gavaya* and the cow). Nyāya replies that such knowledge can be adequately explained in terms of inference: we perceive that the *gavaya* is like the cow and then infer that the cow is like the *gavaya* using the general rule that if *A* is like *B*, then *B* is like *A*.

The Buddhist logicians interject that *upamāna* might still be a valid source of knowledge without being an independent one: our knowledge of the similarity between two classes of things is due to perception and our knowledge of the denotations of words is due to verbal testimony. Nyāya replies that while the similarity of things may be perceived and the class concept may be given by testimony, neither of these can account for the *application* of a concept to a particular class of things – which is what happens when we recognize a previously unknown object as belonging to a class signified by a class concept because it fits a given description. Moreover, knowledge of the referent of a word need not involve knowledge of a *vyāpti* – unlike the case of inference.

(2) By *arthāpatti* or presumption the Advaitins mean 'the postulation, by a cognition which has to be made intelligible, of what will make [that] intelligible' (*Vedāntaparibhāṣā* v.1). A standard example is explaining the fatness of one who fasts during the day by postulating that he eats at night. But *arthāpatti* is not to be confused with abduction: it is not just a hypothesis or an inference to the best explanation. An *arthāpatti* is a not a tentative supposition that awaits verification, but a supposition of the *only possible fact* that could explain the phenomenon in question and it carries with it absolute certainty. The Mīmāṃsaka philosopher Kumārila's definition of *arthāpatti* perhaps makes this feature clearer:

> When a fact ascertained by any of the six means of cognition [*pramāṇa*] is found to be inexplicable except on the basis of a fact not so ascertained, – the assumption of this latter fact is what constitutes [*arthāpatti*]. (*Ślokavārttika* 8.1; Jha 1964: 140)

Advocates of *arthāpatti* argue that it cannot be reduced to inference because (unlike *anumāna*) it is independent of the prior knowledge of *vyāpti*. This is because whereas the conclusion of an inference is the result of applying a general rule to a particular case, in the case of the fat man who fasts by day *arthāpatti* is the means of knowing the general rule. Moreover, the phenomenology of *arthāpatti* is such that it just does not *feel* in such cases as if we are inferring from premises, but rather that we are *supposing* something unknown to resolve a tension.

Although presumption is thus held for such reasons to be irreducible to inference, might inference be reducible to presumption? This is a possibility that was entertained by some Mīmāṃsakas, but mostly rejected on the grounds that our knowledge of a universal proposition like 'Wherever there is smoke there is fire' needs to be explained by appeal to inference.

(3) By *anupalabdhi* or non-apprehension Bhāṭṭas and Advaitins mean what they take to be the source of our primary knowledge of non-existence. Looking around my room now, I can truly say that I know both that there is no elephant here and that there is a cup before me on the table. But if sense perception requires contact between the senses and a sense-object, I cannot *perceive* the non-existence of the elephant in the way I perceive the existence of the cup. The Bhāṭṭas and Advaitins thus claim that it is the *pramāṇa* of non-apprehension (*anupalabdhi*) that makes known to us the non-existence of particular objects (like the elephant in my room).

Nyāya replies instead that the sense is related to the positive locus of non-existence (in this case, my room) and through that to the non-existence that is a characteristic of that locus. My room is presently qualified by the absence of an elephant, so when I perceive (directly) the room I perceive (indirectly) the absence of the elephant in it. But this theory is rejected by the Bhāṭṭas and Advaitins as being plausible only if the qualities of an object are all perceptible – and how can non-existence be a perceptible quality?

The Buddhist logician Dharmakīrti argues instead that when I truly report that there is presently no elephant in my room what I know is not a negative fact, and nor do I know it by perception. Rather, what I know is a simple positive fact and I know it by inference (*Pramāṇavārttikka* 3.3–6; Hayes and Gillon 1991). My inferential reasoning in this case can be reconstructed as roughly counterfactual in form:

(1) The causal conditions of perception known to me are such that, if there were an elephant presently in my room, I would know it.

(2) I do not know that there is presently an elephant in my room.

(3) Therefore, an elephant is not presently in my room.

The trouble with this attempt to reduce non-apprehension to inference, however, is that it does not answer the question of how I know (2). According to Dharmakīrti, I cannot *perceive* it to be true. But neither, presumably, can I *infer* it to be true unless I infer it from some other claim I know to be true – and so on *ad infinitum*. In other words, the Buddhist attempt to reduce non-apprehension to inference founders upon an infinite regress of inferences.

The Buddhist tetralemma (*catuṣkoṭi*)

Contrary to what is still too popularly believed, the overwhelming majority of classical Indian philosophers accepted the principle of non-contradiction: that is, not (*p* and not-*p*). Not only was the importance of avoiding contradiction (*virodha*) implicitly affirmed in Indian philosophical practice as displayed in the vast body of argumentation that the Sanskrit literature records, it was also explicitly affirmed in various authoritative works. Here are some examples of the latter: the Buddhist dialectician Nāgārjuna (second century) rejects an opponent's views 'for how can the real and the unreal, which are mutually contradictory, be one?' (*Mūlamadhyamakakārikā* 8.7); the later Mādhyamika Candrakīrti (seventh century) concurs that 'since being and non-being are mutually contradictory, they cannot exist in the same place' (*Prasannapāda* 532 on *Mūlamadhyamakakārikā* 25.14); the great Advaitin Śaṃkara (eighth century) opposes Jainism on the grounds that 'it is impossible that contradictory attributes like being and non-being should at the same time belong to one and the same thing' (*Brahmasūtrabhāṣya* II.2.33); and the Naiyāyika Udayana (eleventh century) clearly states that 'there cannot also be unity of two contradictories, for the mere statements of them will cancel each other' (*Nyāyakusumāñjali* 3.8).

Notwithstanding all this, there are two famous Indian logical doctrines that have sometimes been taken by some to imply minority positions that are more permissive of contradictions than the majority consensus would allow. The first of these doctrines is the Buddhist tetralemma (*catuṣkoṭi*); the second is the Jaina doctrine of sevenfold predication (*saptabhaṅgi*). Let us begin with the Buddhist tetralemma.

The early Pali texts report the Buddha as having sometimes responded to certain types of questions – the undetermined (*avyākatāni*) questions – in such a way as to set them aside as unanswerable because wrongly posed or inapplicable. Thus in the *Brahmajāla Suttanta* (*Dīgha Nikāya* 1), when the Buddha is asked about what happens to an enlightened being (a *tathāgata*) after death, he refuses to affirm any of the following options:

1. The *tathāgata* exists after death.
2. The *tathāgata* does not exist after death.
3. The *tathāgata* both exists and does not exist after death.
4. The *tathāgata* neither exists nor does not exist after death.

Exactly why the Buddha refused to affirm any of these possibilities has long been a matter of controversy. Any or all of the following might be the answer. Perhaps he thought such metaphysical speculation simply not conducive to the attainment of freedom from suffering, as is made explicit in another context (the famous poisoned arrow parable of *Majjhima Nikāya* 63). Perhaps he wished to indicate the ineffability of the ultimate truth about reality. Or perhaps he wished to set aside an improper presupposition of the question, as when he compared it to the question 'Which direction does a fire go when it goes out?' (*Majjhima Nikāya* 72). There he says that none of the four options 'fits the case' and so it is appropriate to deny all of the following claims: 'The flame goes north', 'The flame does not go north', 'The flame both goes north and does not go north', and 'The flame neither goes north nor does not go north'. Finally, there is scriptural evidence that some recluses at the time of the Buddha affirmed conjunctions like: 'There is another world, there is not, there both is and is not, there neither is nor is not' (*Dīgha Nikāya* 2). Such recluses were repudiated by the Buddha as 'eel-wrigglers', concerned only with evasive quibbling. The use of the fourfold negation thus contrasts the teaching of the Buddha with such unworthy evasions.

Be that as it may, the fourfold negation of the original *catuṣkoṭi* takes on a rather different cast in later Madhyamaka Buddhism, with both negative and positive versions of the *catuṣkoṭi* being employed. While it is uncontroversial that the central Madhyamaka teaching is that everything is empty (*śūnya*) of inherent existence (*svabhāva*), we find Nāgārjuna writing:

> 'It is empty' is not to be said, nor 'It is non-empty', nor that it is both, nor that it is neither; ['empty'] is said only for the sake of instruction. (*Mūlamadhyamakakārikā* 22.12)

And Nāgarjuna's direct disciple Āryadeva generalizes this conception of the tetralemma thus:

> Being, non-being, [both] being and non-being, neither being nor non-being; such is the method that the wise should always use with regard to identity and all other [theses]. (*Catuḥśataka* 14.21)

The Madhyamaka method of employing the negative version of the tetralemma here, then, seems to be to arrive at ultimate truth through the refutation of all four possible alternatives, irrespective of the propositions to which they apply.

These four negations, however, are problematic to represent in Western classical logic. An obvious first pass would be to take the Madhyamaka to be negating all of the following four statements:

(1) p

(2) $\sim p$

(3) $p \mathbin{\&} \sim p$

(4) $\sim(p \vee \sim p)$

But on this construal the four options would not be exhaustive in the way that they are supposed to be: (3) would entail both (1) and (2), and – assuming De Morgan's Laws and Double Negation – option (4) is equivalent to (3). Furthermore, the conjunction of the negations of (1)–(4) would obviously generate various contradictions.

Elsewhere, however, Nāgārjuna employs instead a positive version of the tetralemma:

> All is real, all is unreal, all is both real and unreal,
>
> All is neither unreal nor real; this is the [graded] teaching of the Buddha. (*Mūlamadhyamakakārikā* 18.8)

Here the suggestion seems to be that the Madhyamaka *affirms* all four options. But then once again the Madhyamaka would clearly be committed to denying the principle of non-contradiction.

In fact the commentarial tradition of Indian Madhyamaka did not interpret either Nāgārjuna's negative or positive versions of the *catuṣkoṭi* as licensing a rejection of the principle of non-contradiction. One commentarial response to the appearance of contradiction was instead to suggest that what it shows is that ultimate reality is inexpressible. This is how Buddhapālita (sixth century) interprets the tetralemma, so that the ultimate truth is that nothing is true or not true because reality is incommunicable, unconceptualizable and non-discursive (Lindtner 1981: 208–9). The obvious worry with this, of course, is that it seems that the very claim that ultimate reality is indescribable is itself a description of ultimate reality. Not so, says Bhāviveka (sixth century): while all conceptualization falsifies reality, some (negative) statements come closer to representing it correctly – namely those rejecting false superimpositions.

Another commentarial response was *parameterization*: that is, to introduce implicit qualifying terms (parameters) into seemingly contradictory statements in such a way as to remove the apparent contradiction. Thus, faced with an apparent contradiction of the form p & $\sim p$, we try to find some ambiguity in p such that we can plausibly argue that what is really meant by p & $\sim p$ is the (consistent) conjoint assertion of both p (in a certain respect) and $\sim p$ (in a different respect).

Such parameterization of the *catuṣkoṭi* can take various forms. One version appeals to the supposed context of the utterance. Thus Candrakīrti (seventh century) appeals to the notion of the Buddha's 'graded teaching' (*anuśāsana*), whereby apparently conflicting teachings are to be understood as each appropriate for different audiences but all reconcilable as leading towards some single end. This notion of there being a hierarchy of teachings involved here is also present in the interpretation offered in the *Akutobhayā* (a commentary traditionally – but now contestedly – attributed to Nāgārjuna himself). There it is said that 'all is real' affirms the conventional truth of the Abhidharma doctrines, 'all is unreal' denies their ultimate truth, 'all is both real and unreal' asserts both their conventional truth and ultimate falsity, and 'all is neither real nor unreal' expresses the insight of the *yogins* free of all falsifying conceptions.

Finally, we might take our lead from these Indian commentators and also – when appealing to the Buddhist distinction between ultimate and conventional truth – follow the commentary on the *Mūlamadhyamakakārikā* of the great fourteenth-century Tibetan Mādhyamika Tsongkhapa (Samten and Garfield 2006: 448) in effectively treating 'ultimately' and 'conventionally' as modal qualifiers. Then we can read the positive *catuṣkoṭi* as the assertion that everything is real (conventionally), is not real (ultimately), both is real (conventionally) and not real (ultimately), and is neither real (ultimately) nor not real (conventionally). And this interpretation of the tetralemma, of course, renders it entirely compatible with the principle of non-contradiction (albeit at the cost of a little stylistic inelegance, insofar as it obliges us to add extra words to illuminate Nāgārjuna's darkly gnomic original text).

Jaina logic

The other Indian logical doctrine that has sometimes been taken to imply a rejection of the principle of non-contradiction is the Jaina doctrine of sevenfold predication (*saptabhaṅgi-naya*). For the Jainas, *saptabhaṅgi* is a logical tool for the teaching of the central metaphysical doctrine of Jainism: *anekāntavāda*, literally 'the doctrine of non-onesidedness'. *Anekāntavāda* implies that while the Jaina view of reality is authoritative, rival philosophical doctrines are only wrong on account of their onesidedness. Hence, from the proper perspective, they may be integrated into the Jaina system. In other words, wrong views are best seen as *nayas*, viewpoints that are partial expressions of truth. For example, an existent may be both eternal (as a substance) and non-eternal (as modes). Philosophical claims need, then, to be properly parameterized through the use of conditional assertion (*syādvāda*).

Syādvāda (literally 'the doctrine of *syāt*') maintains that every statement is made from some perspective and accordingly really ought to be prefaced with the conditional operator *syat*. In ordinary Sanskrit the word means 'may be' or 'perhaps', but the Jaina logicians give it a technical usage better translatable as something more like 'in some respect', 'from a certain viewpoint', or 'conditionally'.

Consider, for example, the statement 'The pot exists'. The *saptabhaṅgi* doctrine tells us that any entity (including the pot) can be described with respect to just seven predicates, each of which expresses one aspect of the truth about the entity under description:

(1) Conditionally, the pot exists (*syāt ghaṭah asti eva*).

(2) Conditionally, the pot does not exist (*syāt ghaṭah na asti eva*).

(3) Conditionally, the pot exists; conditionally, the pot does not exist (*syāt ghaṭah asti eva syāt ghaṭah na asti eva*).

(4) Conditionally, the pot is inexpressible (*syāt ghaṭah avaktavyam eva*).

(5) Conditionally, the pot exists; conditionally, the pot is inexpressible (*syāt ghaṭah asti eva, syāt ghaṭah avaktavyam eva*).

(6) Conditionally, the pot does not exist; conditionally, the pot is inexpressible (*syāt ghaṭah na asti eva, syāt ghaṭah avaktavyam eva*).

(7) Conditionally, the pot exists; conditionally, the pot does not exist; conditionally, the pot is inexpressible (*syāt ghaṭah asti eva, syāt ghaṭah na asti eva, syāt ghaṭah avaktavyam eva*).

Why just seven predications? Because, as the Jaina logician Malliṣeṇa (thirteenth century) explains, the seven predications are the three simple ones – (1), (2) and (4) – plus all possible combinations of those three: 'And freedom from contradiction of the whole seven-mode doctrine is understood from this triad of modes called non-existence, existence, and indescribability, because these three alone are the chief modes and the remaining modes are included in these through combinations' (*Syādvādamañjarī* 24; Radhakrishnan and Moore 1957: 266). Note Malliṣeṇa's firm insistence that the *saptabhaṅgi* is free from contradiction. Yet over the centuries the Indian opponents of the Jainas repeatedly presented variants of the charge that *anekāntavāda* and its associated logical doctrine of *saptabhaṅgi* were in fact mired in contradiction. Why so?

One reason for the charge is that in some earlier Jaina writings the third predication is instead presented as:

(3*) Conditionally, the pot exists and does not exist (*syāt ghataḥ asti na asti eva*).

This would indeed be contradictory, but many later Jaina logicians – including Vādideva Sūri, Hemacandra and Malliṣeṇa – explicitly corrected this early misrepresentation. The third predication is instead formed by combining the first two in a sequential (*krama*) order.

Another reason for the charge of contradiction is the failure to grasp the way that *syāt* functions as a conditionalizing operator. It is true, of course, that 'The pot exists' and 'The pot does not exist' are contradictories and hence their combination as 'The pot exists and does not exist' is a contradiction. But once we prefix the first two of these statements with *syāt* we get instead:

(1*) Conditionally (= under a certain condition C_1), the pot exists.
(2*) Conditionally (= under a certain condition C_2), the pot does not exist.

These two statements are not contradictories and so their conjunction as (3) is not a contradiction.

What, though, of the fourth predication? Consider Malliṣeṇa's explanation of what it involves: 'When one wishes to designate a single entity with the two modifications, existence and non- existence, emphasized as primary simultaneously, the entity... is indescribable [*avaktavyam*] because of the lack of an adequate word' (*Syādvādamañjarī* 23; Radhakrishnan and Moore 1957: 265). Does this mean that the claim that the pot is inexpressible is self-refuting, since it describes what is claimed to be indescribable? Not so, replies Malliṣeṇa: 'But it is not indescribable in every way, because [if it were] it would be inexpressible even by the word "indescribable".'

Malliṣeṇa's explanation of the fourth predication, however, does suggest that the Jainas associate it with the simultaneous assertion and denial of the pot's existence: that is, a contradiction. And yet it is also clear that Malliṣeṇa explicitly says that, in the case of the third predication, 'indescribability in the form of affirmation and negation is not contradictory, one to the other' (*Syādvādamañjarī* 24; Radhakrishnan and Moore 1957: 266).

This leaves us with at least two interpretive possibilities. The first is that the fourth predication introduces a third truth value: *both true and false*. On this view, Jaina logic does permit some contradictions, but not those where things are contradictory in the sense of being unable to obtain together (Priest 2008). The other possibility is that the third truth value introduced by the fourth predication is instead *neither true nor false*, in which case Jaina logic does not permit contradictions, just as they have always asserted (Ganeri 2002). There is clearly a sense in which the Jainas regard the fourth predication as neutral, and the first and second predications as, respectively, positive and negative (Matilal 1981: 54). What the interpretive choice between *both true and false* and *neither true nor false* effectively amounts to is a choice between two different kinds of neutrality.

Conclusion

It should be apparent by now that the Indian philosophers not only reasoned, but reasoned extensively about reasoning. There are, though, at least four features of Indian logic that are worth highlighting as interestingly different from Western logic. Firstly, there is the importance to the Indians of justifying inductive reasoning because of its centrality to the Indian 'syllogism'. Secondly, there is the epistemological focus of Indian logic, given that inference is taken to be a *pramāṇa* or reliable means of knowledge. Thirdly, there is the marked presence of psychologistic elements in Indian logic – particularly in Navya-Nyāya, where we find a conception of logic according to which the study of connections between mental events and the justification of inferentially acquired knowledge episodes is central. And finally, there is the historical fact that while in the West it was the model of mathematics that shaped logic, in India it was instead the model of (Sanskrit) grammar. This last feature means that it should come as no surprise that the Indian philosophers also had much to say about the philosophy of language – the focus of the next chapter.

Suggestions for further reading

For introductions to the varieties of rationality and reasoning in Indian philosophy, see Chakrabarti 1997b and Potter 1963. For an extended study of the place of reason in Indian philosophy, see Ganeri 2001b. On the history of Indian logic, see further Matilal 1998, 1985, Ganeri 2004 and Vidyabhusana 1978. On the history of Western interpretations of Indian logic, see Ganeri 2001a. On the ancient Nyāya syllogism, see further Potter 1977 and Chakrabarti 1977. On fallacies, debate and dialectics, see Solomon 1976. On medieval Buddhist logic, see further Matilal and Evans 1986, Hayes 1988a, Hayes and Gillon 1991, Tillemans 2000 and Stcherbatsky 1962. On Navya-Nyāya logic, see Sen and Chatterjee 2011, Ingalls 1951, Matilal 1968, Bhattacharyya 1990 and Potter and Bhattacharyya 1992. On the problem of induction in Indian philosophy (with particular reference to the Nyāya viewpoint), see Chakrabarti 2010. For more on the Indian debates about the relations of inference to analogy, postulation and non-apprehension, see Chatterjee 1950, Datta 1960 and Bhatt 1989. On the Buddhist tetralemma see Ruegg 1977, Tillemans 1999 and Priest 2010. On Jaina logic, see Matilal 1981, Ganeri 2001b, 2002 and Priest 2008.

4 Word

Introduction

Indian philosophical concerns with language were very much connected with the early development of Sanskrit linguistics. Indeed, the Sanskrit grammar of Pāṇini (fifth century BCE) became a methodological paradigm for Indian philosophers in a way comparable to that in which Euclid's mathematical *Elements* became one for Western philosophers (see Staal 1988). Accordingly, some of the concerns of classical Indian philosophy of language are closely wedded to the peculiarities of the Sanskrit language. But Indian philosophers (and linguists) also concerned themselves with more general issues, particularly theories of meaning and the problem of universals. The very different metaphysical commitments of the different Indian philosophers meant that they espoused a wide range of views on topics like reference and existence, the relations between word-meaning and sentence-meaning, literal and metaphorical meaning, common nouns and universals, ineffability and the nature of the signification relation, and identity statements.

In Western philosophy two issues have traditionally been central to the philosophy of language. One is the relation between ourselves and our language; the other is the relation between our language and the world. The former topic is usually called *pragmatics* and the latter *semantics* (though the boundaries between the two are often blurred). Very roughly, pragmatics is concerned with the way in which context contributes to meaning, whereas semantics is concerned with the relation between signifiers (like words or sentences) and what they stand for. Indian philosophers addressed both topics, often in ways that are interestingly different from Western philosophers.

Relevant to pragmatics were the theories of linguistic understanding (*śābdabodha*) developed by the Indian philosophers, which specified the conditions for the understanding of the meaning of a sentence. These included knowledge of the speaker's intention (*tātparyajñāna*), which was agreed to be of special importance for the comprehension of meaning in cases where the expression used is ambiguous.

With respect to semantics, the Indian philosophers were unanimously direct referentialists about meaning: that is, they all thought of meanings as entities (*artha*) and identified the meaning of a linguistic expression with the external object denoted by the expression. (In other words, they did not posit sense as a component of the meaning of an expression in addition to its reference.) This general agreement, however, did not preclude vigorous debate about what sort of entity meanings should be identified with: particulars, generic properties, or both together. Similarly, a common commitment to direct referentialism also did not preclude keen debate about whether word-meaning or sentence-meaning is primary for semantics.

At least two familiar difficulties for direct referentialism about meaning were explicitly addressed by the Indian philosophers: the problem of empty terms and the problem of informative identity statements. The former problem is generated by the fact that while it seems we can talk meaningfully of non-existent entities, presumably there is nothing there we can *refer* to. How can this be so if meaning is just direct reference? The other problem is to explain how identity statements of the form '*A* is *B*' can be genuinely informative, since if meaning is just reference such statements should be no more informative than '*A* is *A*'.

Finally, in discussing the meaning of general terms Indian philosophers disagreed about the need to postulate universals as the referents of such terms. Accordingly, there was a lively Indian debate about the problem of universals, with realists of various kinds on one side lined up against the Buddhist nominalists on the other side.

Word-meaning

Indian theories of meaning dealt with a variety of issues, at least some of which intersect with the concerns of Western theories of meaning. Among these are the following questions: What are the meanings of words, and of sentences? How are such meanings established? And how do such meanings become known?

Let us begin with theories of word-meaning. Although Indian philosophers of language generally agreed that the primary function of a word is to stand for an object and hence the meaning (*artha*) of a word is the object it stands for, there was disagreement about whether words or sentences are the principal bearers of meanings. Some theorists (including Nyāya-Vaiśeṣika and Bhāṭṭa Mīmāṃsā) held word-meaning to be more fundamental in that the meaning of a sentence is a function of the meanings of the words in that sentence. Prābhākara Mīmāṃsā, in contrast, held that the individual words do not express any meaning until they are united in a sentence. All of these theorists, however, still conceded that words are real constituents of language. The important exception to that consensus is the Grammarian philosopher Bhartṛhari (fifth century), for whom words are only the artificial constructions of the grammarian and are in fact unreal (*asatya*).

Among those philosophers who held that words do have meanings we find a variety of candidates proposed as being the kind of object that a word can stand for. A minority view, associated with Sāṃkhya, is that it is just a particular, for it is only particulars we have experience of and it is always some particular cow, not the class of cows, that we mean when we say 'The cow is white'.

This view is criticized by the Jainas on the grounds that the word 'cow' does not mean a particular cow, but the generic form or shape (*ākṛti*) of cows. This Jaina view, however, is in turn accused by Naiyāyikas (*Nyāyabhāṣya* II.2.63) of failing to account for cases where there is similarity of shape but not identity of meaning (as in the case of a clay cow), or difference of shape but identity of meaning (as in the case of gold, which remains the same substance in spite of assuming different shapes). The moral apparently to be drawn is that the *ākṛti* is just the ordered collection of parts and it is not this that is the meaning of a word, for we apply a word to a thing we know to be characterized by a universal property and the *ākṛti* is not characterized by a universal property.

The Bhāṭṭa Mīmāṃsā view is that the meaning of a word is this universal property, which they take to be just the essential quality common to the members of a class. In the *Tantravārttika* (I.3.33), Kumārila argues that if the primary meaning of the word 'cow' was a particular cow, then the order 'Bring a cow' could not be what it so clearly is: namely, an order to bring – not a specific cow, or all cows – but just an animal belonging to the species cow. The Naiyāyika response is that this Bhāṭṭa concentration solely on the bare universal fails to explain how upon hearing the word 'cow' any particular cows can present themselves to the hearer's mind.

Instead early Nyāya (*Nyāyabhāṣya* II.2.66) held that the primary meaning of a word is a particular (*vyakti*) characterized by a universal (*jāti*) and a form (*ākṛti*).

This is obviously an amalgamation of all the other views so far considered and as such was considered by their opponents to be nothing but an unstable compromise. Hence the developed Nyāya-Vaiśeṣika view of word-meaning is more commonly that the meaning of a word is just 'a particular as characterized by a universal (*jātiviśiṣṭavyakti*)' (Annaṃbhaṭṭa's *Tarkasaṃgraha-dīpikā*, 66): for example, the meaning of 'cow' is a particular cow as characterized by the universal cowness. The theory that a word means only a particular is rejected for much the same reasons as those given by the Mīmāṃsā, but the Mīmāṃsā theory that a word means only a universal is rejected as failing to appreciate that it is only through our encounters with particulars that we can understand universals.

In contrast the Buddhist logicians, who did not accept the reality of universals and who held that particulars are all momentary, developed a very different account of word-meaning. Their theory, known as 'exclusion theory' (*apohavāda*), maintains that to say of a particular that it is a cow is just to say that it does not belong to the class of things that are non-cows. Prima facie it might seem that this account is hopelessly circular, since the meaning of the term 'non-cow' can be understood only if we already understand the term 'cow'. But the Buddhists have quite a bit more to say about *apoha* and its nominalistic implications, as we shall see later in this chapter.

All the theories mentioned so far identify the meaning of a word with some non-linguistic entity: a particular, a shape, a universal, a combination of one or more of these, or an exclusion function. A different approach is to identify meaning with a partless linguistic symbol that the Grammarian philosophers call a *sphoṭa*. The fullest treatment of this concept is to be found in the work of Bhartṛhari, who we have already mentioned as believing in the unreality of words (and hence word-meanings), though not of sentences. So let us now turn to the issue of sentence-meaning.

Sentence-meaning

As we have already noted, Nyāya-Vaiśeṣika and Bhāṭṭa Mīmāṃsā held word-meaning to be more fundamental in that the meaning of a sentence is a function of the meanings of the words in that sentence. Prābhākara Mīmāṃsā, on the other hand, held that the individual words do not express any meaning until they are united in a sentence. But all these theorists still conceded that words are real constituents of language. In contrast, Bhartṛhari believed that words are only the artificial constructions of the grammarian and are in fact unreal, advocating a semantic holism according to which only sentences are meaning bearers.

In his *Vākyapadīya*, Bhartṛhari defends this idiosyncratic theory with considerable ingenuity. Consider, for example, his response to the objection that his theory fails to fit with our experience of sentences containing an unfamiliar word, where it seems that 'the meaning of the familiar word (or words) is conveyed and the question "What is it?" is asked about words . . . which are not familiar' (II.72; Pillai 1971: 53). Bhartṛhari boldly replies that instead such a case is better described as our failing to be able to assign a word-meaning to the unfamiliar word because we have failed to understand the sentence (II.92). A sentence is in reality a single undivided utterance that conveys a single undivided meaning, but the ignorant imagine that 'sentences which are . . . integral wholes are similar to each other in certain parts and dissimilar from each other in certain other parts' (II.94). Sentence-meaning, then, is to be grasped as a unity, and the *sphoṭa* is the indivisible symbol expressing this meaning.

The term *sphoṭa* is derived from the Sankrit root *sphuṭ*, 'to burst'. In the Grammarian tradition it is effectively identified with the linguistic sign as meaning bearer, that from which the meaning 'bursts forth'. Note that on Bhartṛhari's theory, too, the meaning (*artha*) is still the referent: the *sphoṭa* theory is a theory about the nature of the meaning bearer, a kind of hypostatization of meaning that is supposed to help explain how meanings are made known. For Bhartṛhari the meaning of a sentence, which is integral and indivisible, is grasped by an instantaneous flash of insight (*pratibhā*) (II.143).

Bhartṛhari's theory came in for vigorous criticism from most other Indian philosophers, who opposed his sentence holism in favour of some form of atomism. It is clear, however, that all these philosophers were (in different ways) addressing a serious problem in the philosophy of language: namely, the problem of sentential unity.

The problem of sentential unity

The problem of sentential unity is the problem of the relation of our understanding of the meaning of a sentence to our understanding of the meanings of the words that compose it. If words have meanings, why is the meaning of a sentence not just the meaning of a list of words? The problem is sharpened by considering two principles often associated in Western philosophy with the name of Frege:

The Context Principle: A word has meaning only in the context of a sentence.

The Composition Principle: The meaning of a sentence is a function of its constituent words.

Prima facie, each principle articulates a compelling linguistic intuition, but jointly the principles seem in conflict.

In the history of philosophy we can distinguish at least four competing accounts of the relation between word-meaning and sentence-meaning, each of which gives differing weights to the two principles above (see further Siderits 1991):

(1) Only sentences, not words, have meanings and the meanings of sentences themselves are indivisible wholes.

(2) All words have complete meanings and the meanings of words in a sentence are fused into a whole by some syncategorematic device.

(3) Some terms are semantically complete (or 'saturated') while others are not, and unified sentential meaning is provided by the concatenation of saturated and unsaturated expressions.

(4) All words are semantically incomplete and sentential unity is provided through a process of mutual assistance between all the words of a sentence.

Position (1) asserts the primacy of sentence-meaning over word-meaning and is known in Western philosophy as essentially Quine's view (Quine 1960). It is also, as Quine acknowledges and as we have already seen, prefigured in the writings of Bhartṛhari. According to this kind of sentence holism, sentences are wholes and they are the unanalyzable units of meaningful discourse. Word-meaning is just a theoretical construction of grammar. Words stand semantically to sentences much as phonemes stand semantically to words. True, we need to cognize the words of a sentence in order to understand it, but so too do we have to cognize the phonemes of a word in order to understand it. To suppose that the meaning of the sentence 'Socrates is wise' is therefore a function of the meanings of its independently meaningful constituent words is as foolish as supposing that the 'rat' in 'Socrates' and the 'is' in 'wise' are independently meaningful. Effectively, position (1) affirms the Context Principle and denies the Composition Principle.

Position (2) is the traditional Aristotelian approach, according to which all words are semantically complete and sentential unity is achieved through syncategorematic devices like the copula which provide the 'glue' that holds the word-meanings of a sentence together. This was the dominant view in the Western philosophical tradition until Frege introduced (3), which is now widely accepted. It is also a view that was prominent in the Indian philosophical tradition, with versions of it being advocated by the Nyāya and Bhāṭṭa Mīmāṃsā schools. Effectively, position (2) affirms the Composition Principle and denies the Context Principle.

Position (3) is the Fregean theory, according to which some terms (names) are semantically complete or 'saturated' and others (predicates) are incomplete or 'unsaturated'. Unified sentential meaning is provided by the concatenation of saturated and unsaturated expressions, with the incompleteness of predicative expressions providing the semantic 'glue' that binds the individual components into a unified sentential meaning. Effectively, position (3) seeks to acknowledge both the Context and Composition Principles insofar as 'in the order *of explanation* the sense of a sentence is primary, but in the order *of recognition* the sense of a word is primary' (Dummett 1981: 4).

Position (4) holds that *all* words are semantically incomplete and require the assistance of other words to complete their semantic role. Sentential unity is provided through a process of mutual assistance between all the words of a sentence. William James made some suggestive remarks, perhaps interpretable along these lines, about how our understanding of the meaning or 'idea' of a spoken sentence is related to our consciousness of the uttered words (James 1950: I.281). And Frank Ramsey flirted with such a theory when he entertained the view that all the constituents of a sentence are alike incomplete, names no less than predicates (Ramsey 1931). But for a developed version of the theory of uniform semantic incompleteness we need to turn again to the Indian philosophical tradition and to the 'related designation' (*anvitābhidhāna*) theory of the Prābhākara Mīmaṃsā school. Effectively, position (4) also seeks to acknowledge both the Context and Composition Principles. In accord with the Context Principle, it affirms that words do not have meaning in isolation but only when used in sentences. In accord with the Composition Principle, it affirms that words do nevertheless have meanings and that the meaning of a sentence is determined by the *related* meanings of its component words.

The sentence holism of (1) seems implausible. It is vulnerable to the standard 'infinite capacity, finite resources' argument employed in favour of the Composition Principle: sentences are innumerable, but the word lexicon is finite. Our ability to understand novel sentences is best explained on the supposition that we do so via our prior understanding of the meanings of their component words together with the rules of syntax. Sentence mastery increases in proportion to growth of vocabulary at a rate that is more than merely arithmetical. Moreover, the sentence holist has no explanation of the semantic relation between a sentence and its negation.

The word atomism of (2) is also unsatisfactory. It fails to do justice to a central feature of sentence-meaning, namely the fact that the meaning of a sentence is a unified relational complex. If the words that make up a sentence have meaning in isolation from any sentential context, then how can they constitute such a unity? Or as the Indian philosopher Jayanta (ninth century) puts it, how can a row of discrete stakes merge to form a continuous line? There is surely an enormous difference between a sentence and a mere list of names.

The Fregean theory of (3) can account for the requisite sentential unity by appealing to the existence of unsaturated subsentential predicative expressions that, when joined with saturated names, supply the semantic 'glue'. However, crucial to the theory is a strong asymmetry thesis: predicates are semantically incomplete, but both sentences and names are semantically complete in the same or comparable senses. This thesis is certainly disputable. Ramsey, for instance, expressed scepticism about the existence of any essential distinction between the subject and predicate of a sentence, and hence too about any fundamental classification of things based upon the subject–predicate distinction. The sentence 'Socrates is wise', he suggested, is just as much 'about' wisdom as 'about' Socrates; indeed we could express the very same point by saying instead 'Wisdom is a characteristic of Socrates'.

The 'related designation' theory of (4) proposes instead a uniform semantic incompleteness for all subsentential expressions. Names are just as unsaturated as predicates; no word is semantically complete except in the context of a sentence. This proposal certainly gives due weight to the Context Principle. But if no word can specify a determinable meaning except in the context of a sentence, how can the meaning of a sentence ever be computed in the way the Composition Principle implies? More particularly, how can we explain our prompt understanding of the meanings of novel sentences?

The Prābhākara philosophers who developed the related designation theory respond as follows. True, no words are semantically complete except in the context of a sentence, and thus complete meaning can only be determined in a sentential context, through relation to the meanings of the other words involved. However, while this correctly describes the situation with respect to the *complete* meaning of a word, part of the meaning of a word remains invariant over the different sentences in which it occurs, and this common core provides the basic material necessary for the compositional process.

This notion of a common core is also used to reply to a different objection pressed by Indian opponents of the theory. Suppose all word-meanings are context-sensitive in the way the related designation theory proposes. Now consider the two-word sentence 'XY', meaning a connected unity. According to the theory, the meaning of a subsentential word contains within itself, implicitly, the whole sentence-meaning. In other words, 'X' conveys the unitary meaning of 'XY' itself – as also does 'Y'. But this seems tantamount to the claim that the meaning of a word is nothing but the meaning of the sentence it is a part of: in other words, sentence holism. On the other hand, if we reject sentence holism in favour of the view that sentences are made of parts which are words, but also hold onto the Prābhākara claim that the meaning of one part contains the meaning of the whole, then the other part of the sentence seems redundant. In other words, the related designation theory faces a dilemma: either it reduces to sentence holism, or it involves redundancy.

The Prābhākara reply is that although 'X' in the example is only completely meaningful in relation to the sentence 'XY', nevertheless we also must admit an invariant core meaning of 'X': roughly, 'X in relation to ___', where the blank is to be filled with either an individual or a relational complex. Even if a word does not have an invariant meaning, there can still be an invariant component of the meaning of a word which is common to each of the sentences in which the word occurs. Thus the word 'X' introduces into a sentence an incomplete core meaning ('X in relation to ___', minus its correlate). Sentential unity requires the mutual saturation of such incomplete terms. Hence the meaning of 'X' in the sentence 'XY' is just that word's core meaning in relation to the other word in the sentence.

Obviously much more needs to be said if the related designation theory explaining sentential unity is to be defended as clearly superior to its rivals, especially the Fregean theory. But perhaps enough has been said to suggest that the theory looks a promising and too little appreciated approach to the problem of sentential unity. It forms an interesting and potentially fruitful compromise between relatively uniform incompleteness and Fregean compositionality, giving due weight both to the intuition that sentential context adds information with respect to each of the subsentential parts involved and to the intuition that functional composition on fixed initial resources is necessary to compute meaning.

How are meanings established?

The main issue here for the Indian philosophers was a dispute about the role of conventions in establishing a relation between words and the objects meant by them. Thus on the one hand, we find Nyāya-Vaiśeṣika and the Buddhists holding that meaning relations are conventional; on the other hand, we find Mīmaṃsā and Advaita Vedānta holding that meanings are eternal and inherent in the very nature of words.

That meaning relations are conventional will likely seem obvious to most modern readers. Like the early Buddhists, they will be inclined to point out that is an implication of the way in which the same word arbitrarily has different meanings in different languages. Nyāya presents the argument thus:

> Word-object relations are not natural but conventional, for words designate objects according to the desires of [name-introducers, such as] the seer (*ṛṣi*), the noble (*ārya*) and the foreigner (*mleccha*). If word-object relations were natural, words could not be used in accordance with their desires, any more than light has the capacity to reveal different colours to different groups of people. (*Nyāyabhāsya* 2.1.56; Ganeri 2006: 89)

The conventionalist has to concede, however, that within a linguistic community the word–object connection cannot be easily flouted by individuals. Thus Nyāya introduces an appeal to authoritative mandates that fix meaning relations in a way that individual members of a linguistic community cannot alter. The first user of the language wills that a particular word designates some object and later users of the language learn this convention as part of learning the language. After a time the linguistic community typically forgets the originators of such conventions, but still remembers the conventions. According to some Naiyāyikas, the most important of such conventions have a divine origin and authority: it is God (*Īśvara*) who ordains that a particular word designates an object. (Indeed, Udayana (eleventh century) utilizes the purported need for an authoritative fixer of word–object conventions as a premise in one of the series of proofs for the existence of God he presents in the fifth chapter of his *Nyāyakusumañjali*.)

Both Mīmaṃsā and Advaita Vedānta hold instead that meanings are eternal and natural; in other words, the relation between word and object is not conventional. In contrast to conventionalism, this is likely to seem a very odd theory to the modern reader, and it will need a little explanation. The key idea here is that for Mīmāṃsā (the originators of the theory) the relation of word and meaning is not merely already established in the sense that current language users did not create it but merely received it from their elders, but truly eternal in the sense that no one ever established it: it is natural (*autpattika*) and authorless (*apauruṣeya*).

The fullest defence of this theory is to be found in the *Ślokavārttika* of Kumārila Bhaṭṭa (seventh century). Kumārila's argumentative strategy is basically negative: he tries to show that there is no way the designative capacity of words could have been brought into existence, leaving the fact that it is beginningless as the only alternative. His main focus, then, is on criticizing theories that attribute the designative capacity of words to the establishing of conventions. Kumārila argues that, when we examine the notion of a linguistic convention more closely, we can see that it is attended by all kinds of difficulties. In brief, his leading idea is that any convention that might be purported to establish meaning relations would in fact have to be established *within* language, not *prior to* language in the way that the conventionalist theory requires.

In order to address the scenario of forming a convention supposed to fix word meaning, Kumārila begins by setting these four possibilities:

> Is this 'conventional rule' made in accordance with the requirements of each individual mortal being, or of each utterance (of the word)? Or is it made once for all, at the beginning of creation, by some one person? And does the relation differ with each (different person or utterance), or is it one only? (*Ślokavārttika* 16.13–14; Jha 1983: 349–50)

As a Mīmāṃsaka atheist, Kumārila firmly rejects as epistemically unsupported the possibility that God ordained the convention at the beginning of the world, and elsewhere in his texts he offers independent arguments for this rejection. Instead he is more concerned here with the possibility that the convention is made for each person. This possibility, however, permits of two alternatives: (i) that everyone makes the same meaning assignment, or (ii) that it varies from person to person. Kumārila briskly dismisses the first alternative, apparently deeming it wildly implausible that all persons would coincidentally converge on the same meaning assignment in the absence of a previously established relation. The more interesting alternative, so far as he is concerned, is the second, which he criticizes in some detail (16.15–22).

Against the claim that there is one convention per person, Kumārila points out that in ordinary usage there is no awareness of this among members of a common linguistic community, though presumably there should be if the theory is correct. Moreover, if each person understood words according to their own conventions, then communication would be impossible. We would all be speaking and understanding different languages and no one would understand one another.

Kumārila locates what he takes to be the fundamental weakness of the conventionalist theory thus:

> In order to point out a relation (for the sake of) the hearer, what relation could the speaker have recourse to? If it be the one which he has already known, then the speaker cannot be said to point it out to him (because he already knows it); and if he points out an altogether new relation, then this latter not having ever been known by the hearer to lead to the comprehension of any meaning (he could never comprehend the word used). (6.22–3, Jha 1983: 351)

In other words, any convention to establish meaning relations would in fact have to be established *within* language, not *prior to* language in the way that the conventionalist theory requires.

Nor does the Buddhist observation that the same word can have different meanings in different languages entail conventionalism. Kumārila believed that any meaning is inherently capable of being expressed by more than one word, in other words, that the eternal relation between word and meaning is not one-to-one.

A modern reader will probably still be unconvinced by Mīmāṃsā anti-conventionalism. After all, are there not developed modern game-theoretical and evolutionary accounts of conventions (including linguistic conventions) emerging in a way that does not presuppose any explicit or tacit agreement (see, for instance, Lewis 1969 and Skyrms 1996)? Perhaps. But if such accounts of the emergence of conventions require that there be at least pre-existing thought, and thought requires language (as the Mīmāṃsakas and many others have believed), then it may be that semantic anti-conventionalism has not yet been laid to rest.

How do meanings become known?

What conditions have to be fulfilled in order for the meaning of a sentence to be understood? According to most Indian philosophers of language, to answer this question is to specify the normal conditions for *śābdabodha*, and these conditions are mutual expectancy (*ākāṅkṣā*), semantical appropriateness (*yogyatā*), contiguity (*āsatti*), and – at least for some theorists – intention (*tātparya*).

Mutual expectancy or *ākāṅkṣā* occurs when a word is unable to convey a complete sense in the absence of another word and hence occasions the hearer's desire to know the other words that will complete the sense of the speaker's utterance. For the Mīmāṃsakas this is a psychological expectancy, but for the Naiyāyikas and the Grammarians it is a syntactical expectancy (i.e., the need for syntactical completeness of the sentence).

Semantical appropriateness or *yogyatā* is the congruity of the words in a sentence for mutual association. A standard Indian example contrasts the sentence 'He wets it with water', which has *yogyatā* because wetting is usually done with a liquid like water, with the sentence 'He wets it with fire', which lacks *yogyatā* because wetting cannot be (non-metaphorically) done with fire.

Contiguity or *āsatti* (also referred to as *saṃnidhi*) is the condition that the words in an uttered sentence should be temporally contiguous so as to permit an uninterrupted utterance.

Finally, intention or *tātparya* refers to the meaning intended to be conveyed by an utterance, and it can be viewed as the meaning intended by the speaker or as the purport of the utterance. There was a broad consensus among Indian philosophers of language about both the role of contextual factors in deciding this *tātparya* and its importance in deciding the meaning of a sentence. There was, however, no similar consensus as to the exact role played by *tātparya* in verbal comprehension.

According to the theory of *śābdabodha*, then, in order to understand the meaning of a sentence the hearer must understand the meanings of the words of the sentence, recognize their syntactical and semantical appropriateness, be able to synthesize the word-meanings into a single related meaning, and be able (where appropriate) to disambiguate by reference to the speaker's intention. (From the way the four conditions are presented it should be obvious that the Indian philosophers were concerned firstly with spoken sentences, and then – by extension – with written texts.)

It is the *tātparya* condition on *śābdabodha* that is the only controversial one of the four outlined above, and so the one that merits further discussion. The Indian grammatical tradition recognized from an early date the importance of contextual factors in determining the meaning of an expression, including an appeal to the speaker's intention to resolve ambiguities. Moreover, as we have already seen, both the Bhāṭṭa Mīmāṃsakas and the Naiyāyikas take the sentence to be a concatenation of the individual words it contains. Unsurprisingly, then, they both appeal to the power of *tātparya* to explain how a connected meaning is comprehended from a sentence. This is because although each word in a sentence gives its own isolated meaning, a string of unconnected meaningful words cannot produce by itself a unified sentential meaning. But from the use of words in juxtaposition it is also to be assumed that the speaker has uttered them with the intention of conveying a connected sense.

Nevertheless there are important differences in the way *tātparya* was understood by Nyāya-Vaiśeṣika on the one hand, and by Bhāṭṭa Mīmāṃsā (and Advaita Vedānta) on the other. For the Naiyāyikas *tātparya* is the meaning intended by the speaker. The speaker's intentions cannot, however, overturn the primary meanings of the words, as fixed by divinely ordained conventions. Instead it is only in cases of ambiguity or metaphor that it is appropriate to appeal to contextual factors to determine the speaker's intention. A standard Nyāya example here is the sentence 'Bring the *saindhava*', where the word *saindhava* in Sanskrit can mean either salt or a kind of horse. Knowledge of the speaker's intention gleaned from contextual clues is necessary to disambiguate the speaker's utterance and understand its meaning (*Siddhāntamuktāvalī* 84; Mādhavānanda 1977: 171).

The Mīmāṃsakas and the Advaitins view *tātparya* differently from the Naiyāyikas. The *Vedāntaparibhāṣā*, a seventeenth-century Advaitin manual, explains it thus:

> Intention [*tātparya*] is not the utterance (of words) with the object of producing a cognition of a particular thing, for then Vedic texts uttered by a person who does not know their meaning would not be intelligible... It cannot be urged [in such a case that] verbal comprehension takes place from a

> knowledge of God's intention, for we find that even a person who does not believe in God understands the meaning of the Vedic passages... Intention is the capacity to produce cognition of a particular thing. The sentence 'There is a jar in the house' is capable of producing a cognition of the relation of a jar, and not that of a cloth, to the house. (*Vedāntaparibhāṣā* iv.38–9)

Two important Nyāya claims are effectively being denied here. Firstly, that knowledge of the speaker's intention is a necessary condition for verbal comprehension: after all, even a sentence recited by a parrot might be comprehensible to an audience, though they have no inclination to attribute any semantic intentions to the parrot. Secondly, that intention is separable and distinct from meaning: instead the intentionality of a sentence is intrinsic to it in much the same way that meanings are intrinsic to words according to the Mīmāṃsā theory of language we have already encountered. Thus just as every word has an inherent capacity to express its meaning, so too a sentence has a natural capacity to produce a unified cognition of its meaning. Since a sentence's intentionality is in this fashion not distinct from its meaning, the *tātparya* or intent of a sentence can be determined without reference to the psychological state of the speaker.

Empty subject terms

A familiar challenge for a referentialist theory of meaning is our apparent ability to speak meaningfully of the non-existent. To use an Indian example: when we say 'The rabbit horn does not exist' we apparently say something both meaningful and true. But on a referentialist theory of meaning this sentence can only be meaningful if the subject term denotes something. So it looks like we have to assume the existence of something (the rabbit horn) in order to deny its existence: an obvious contradiction!

In twentieth-century Western philosophy one of the most popular responses to this difficulty was to try to analyze it away by paraphrasing the offending sentence so as to separate its logical structure from its grammatical structure. Thus ordinary proper names are treated as disguised descriptions and descriptions are analyzed in the spirit of Russell's theory of definite descriptions. For example: parsing the sentence 'Pegasus does not exist' in this Russellian fashion we get something like 'It is not the case that there is exactly one *x* which is a flying horse of Greek mythology', a sentence which does not lead to any contradiction.

In India a comparable strategy of paraphrasing sentences with empty subject terms was adopted by Nyāya-Vaiśeṣika (Matilal 1985). Naiyāyikas are fond of a slogan, 'Whatever exists is knowable and nameable' (*'astitvaṃ jñeyatvam abhidheyatvam'*). Prima facie this thesis seems especially implausible when we consider the case of nameability. First, it seems we can readily name entities that do not exist (e.g., Pegasus, rabbit horns). Second, we can apparently at least imagine there may be unnameable entities. But in doing so we name these entities 'unnameable'. Thus, since they are nameable, they must exist, but since they are both nameable and unnameable they also cannot exist – a contradiction.

To these objections Nyāya responds by distinguishing between empty referring expressions and non-empty referring expressions. Briefly, the Nyāya strategy is to treat empty referring expressions as complex and their simple parts as standing for real elements. Sentences like 'The rabbit horn does not exist', which apparently refer to non-existent entities, are translated into sentences like 'There is no relation between the rabbit and a horn', which refer only to entities (including relations) that are reals according to Nyāya metaphysics. 'Nameable' means, then, nameable in the ideal language of the Nyāya system wherein all genuine names refer to reals admitted by Nyāya ontology. No such real is either unnameable or unknowable.

The Nyāya analysis of negation reinforces this programme of paraphrase. For Nyāya, an absence or negation must be an absence of something. This something is called the counterpositive (*pratiyogin*) of the absence in question. Thus Uddyotakara (seventh century) appeals to this doctrine in his *Nyāyavārttika* in order to reject the Buddhist denial of the self (*ātman*) as self-refuting:

> By using the (referring) expression 'The self' we speak of the being (of the self) whereas by saying 'does not exist' we go on to deny the same. A certain object which is denied in a certain locus must be existent in some place other than that locus; thus when (the predicate) '. . . does not exist' is applied to an object to which the term 'The jar' is also applied, the application of the term 'The jar' in such a context (in an identifying manner) does not allow us to assert the absolute nonexistence of the jar, but only permits us to assert that it is absent from a certain place or at a certain time – by the words 'The jar does not exist'. (Chakrabarti 1982: 228–9)

But, the argument continues, the self is not located in time or space and hence cannot be significantly denied in this way. In contrast to the term 'the rabbit horn', which refers to a relation rather than an unreal entity, the term 'the self' refers to a named particular, a metaphysical simple.

Naturally, much of this seemed unacceptably tendentious to the Buddhists, who certainly wanted to be able to assert that many things their opponents believed in – including selves and non-momentary entities – do not exist.

The Buddhist logicians on non-existent entities

Now the Nyāya position is that an unreal entity cannot be the subject term of a meaningful statement because subject terms must refer to something real. But then, the Buddhist rejoins, the assertion of this claim would be self-refuting because 'an unreal entity' is the subject of the statement making the claim. Interestingly, Udayana (eleventh century) actually concedes in his *Ātmatattvaviveka* that the Nyāya assertion of the principle that nothing can be affirmed or denied of an unreal entity violates that very principle:

> In order to avoid a self-contradictory object not established by any means of knowledge, you [i.e., the Buddhists] have conceded that one can make statements about the non-existent. Similarly, in order not to allow any statement about the non-entities in our discourse on the means of knowledge, we concede that a self-contradictory statement (prohibiting the use of non-entities) is possible, although it is not supported by any means of knowledge. If you treated both the cases in the same manner, we would not have said anything about non-entities. (We have made the above self-contradictory statement because you first raised the question.) (Matilal 1985: 104)

In other words, Udayana prefers to embrace a 'superficial' self-contradiction rather than abandon the more deeply entrenched commitment to realism. To follow the Buddhist logicians and allow fictitious entities as subject terms threatens to collapse the crucial distinction between actual and fictitious entities.

The Buddhist logicians from Dignāga (fifth century) onwards have no such qualms. Dignāga himself, however, actually seems to have entertained two quite different ways of dealing with the problem of empty subject terms in Buddhist refutations of the pseudo-entities accepted by their opponents (Tillemans 1999, Yao 2009). The first way is just to paraphrase the reasoning in question so that the subject is understood in ways acceptable to the Buddhist.

Dignāga's other way with empty subject terms is to take the subject in non-existence proofs to be just a *conceptual representation* of the entity in question and not the entity itself. It is this second, more radical, approach that was taken up by Dharmakīrti (seventh century) and later Buddhist logicians like Jñānaśrīmita (tenth century) and Ratnakīrti (eleventh century).

Broadly speaking, these Buddhist philosophers shared a common philosophical framework, even if their views sometimes diverged. They all held that ultimately the only reals are momentary particulars (*svalakṣaṇa*) and that the universals (*sāmānyalakṣaṇa*) known by the mind are but conceptual constructions. Such conceptual constructions are explained in terms of *apoha* theory, which claims that a concept that has no real referent is established through the exclusion of other concepts. Thus the empty term 'rabbit horn' is ontologically on a par with a non-empty term like 'cow', in that both just refer to certain verbal objects (*śabdārtha*). But although there is no difference between empty and non-empty subject terms insofar as all of them are just conceptual constructions, some objects have causal efficacy (*arthākriya*). Those that have no such causal efficiency, such as the rabbit horns, are not real existents. This allows us to assert without inconsistency, 'Rabbit horns exist as imagined concepts but are not real existents'. Unreal entities like rabbit horns, then, can be described coherently as having properties.

The approach of the Buddhist logicians, then, is a kind of 'pan-fictionalism' that places all intentional objects on the same level. That this might involve a drift towards idealism did not faze them, since they were all sympathetic to Yogācāra idealism as a final ontology.

Two types of negation

Since the Indian context for the issue of empty terms primarily involved the subjects of negative existential statements, the Buddhist philosophers also thought it important to stress the relevance to the problem of a distinction between two types of negation: implicative negation (*paryudāsa-pratiṣedha*) and non-implicative negation (*prasajya-pratiṣedha*). This distinction, first introduced into Indian thought by the Grammarians, is (very roughly) analogous to the distinction between term negation and predicate negation in Western traditional logic. So in the case of implicative negation we implicitly affirm a property while negating another: for example, 'The glass is not-red' (which implies that the glass is some other colour). In contrast, non-implicative negation is a simple negation that does not imply any affirmation: for example, 'The glass is not red' (which does not imply that the glass is any colour).

The Buddhists appeal to the relevance of this distinction for the problem of empty subject terms by claiming that when they deny that some pseudo-entity has a property (e.g., 'The rabbit horn does not exist') the negation involved is non-implicative and no positive assertion of any other property is implied at all. In contrast, statements with implicative negation such as 'The rabbit horn is not-sharp' (which implies the affirmation of its bluntness) are fallacious.

The most popular Buddhist approach to the problem of empty subject terms, then, was not to abandon commitment to a referential theory of meaning, but instead to combine an appeal to the two types of negation together with the method of conceptual subjects.

Identity statements

Another familiar difficulty for a referentialist theory of meaning is how to account for informative identity statements. The 'paradox of identity' at issue here is succinctly summed up by Wittgenstein: 'Roughly speaking, to say of *two* things that they are identical is nonsense, and to say of *one* thing that it is identical with itself is to say nothing at all' (*Tractatus Logico-Philosophicus*, 5.5303). If identity is a relation, then it obtains either between two distinct things, or between a thing and itself. On the one hand, it is clearly false to say that *A* is identical with *B*, if *A* and *B* are distinct things; on the other hand, it is just tautologous to say that *A* is the same as itself. And yet the sentence 'The morning star is identical with the evening star' expresses not a linguistic tautology, but an astronomical discovery.

In Western philosophy Frege famously dealt with this paradox by distinguishing between the *sense* and *reference* of an expression (Frege 1960). The reference of an expression is the object to which it refers (as the planet Venus is the reference of 'the morning star'), while the sense of an expression is the particular mode in which a sign presents what it designates. 'The evening star' differs in sense from 'the morning star' even though it has been discovered that both expressions refer to Venus. Frege says that an identity statement will be true and informative if the sign of identity is flanked by two names with the same reference but different senses.

This kind of solution to the problem was not available to the Indian philosophers of language because, as already mentioned, the Indian semanticists were unanimously direct referentialists about meaning: in other words, they all thought of meanings as entities (*artha*) and identified the meaning of a linguistic expression with the external object denoted by the expression. Generally speaking, then, they did not posit sense as a component of the meaning of an expression in addition to its reference – even if it may be arguable (see Siderits 1991, Ganeri 2006) that certain sense-like elements nevertheless crept into the tradition.

The existence of informative identity statements, however, was certainly not unknown to the Indian philosophers. Indeed, for Advaita Vedānta, there is a major issue at stake there, for they claim that the essence of the Vedas can be known through understanding a single sentence: the famous 'That art thou' ('*tat tvam asi*') of the *Chāndogya Upaniṣad* (6.8–16). What does this sentence mean according to Advaita? In the context of the Upaniṣadic dialogue between Uddālaka and his son Śvetaketu, *tat* is taken to refer to *Brahman*, *tvam* to refer to Śvetaketu's self, and *asi* means that the words *tat* and *tvam* have the same referent.

In his commentary on *Chāndogya Upaniṣad* 6.16, Śaṃkara explicitly denies that '*tat tvam asi*' is just a figurative identification meaning the self is like *Brahman*. This is because figurative language requires that the speaker knows that the things identified are really different – as when a courageous man is spoken of as a lion. Instead the sentence 'That art thou' is taken to be an identity statement: '"That thou art" . . . asserts, without the slightest restraint, that the "Thou" is absolutely and entirely the same as Being, the Self' (Jha 1942: 363). Moreover, this is not merely an uninformative tautology, since a proper understanding of the sentence conveys enlightenment.

There might seem to be a bit of difficulty, though, about squaring all this with the Advaitin insistence that *Brahman* is ineffable and cannot be denoted directly by words. If 'that' means *Brahman*, it also must mean it indirectly. And this is why many post-Śaṃkara Advaitins understood '*tat tvam asi*' as involving a kind of *lakṣaṇā* or secondary meaning. Whereas the primary meaning (*abhidhā*) is the direct relation between a word and its meaning, such that knowledge of the word leads immediately to knowledge of its relation to that meaning, the secondary meaning (*lakṣaṇā*) of a word is the indirect or implied meaning we understand when its primary meaning is contextually inappropriate. *Lakṣaṇā* involves a kind of transfer of meaning by using a word to denote a referent other than its normal one, but in some way intimately related to it.

Sadānanda (fifteenth century) summarizes the protracted Advaitin debate on the secondary meaning of *tat tvam asi* thus:

> This dictum is a proposition conveying identity, by virtue of the three relations of its terms, viz. 'Thou art that'... [These three are] the relation between two words having the same substratum;... the relation between two words qualifying each other (so as to signify a common object); and... the relation between two words and an identical thing implied by them (here the Inner Self). (*Vedāntasāra* IV.148–9; Nikhilananda 2006: 86)

It is the third case that is taken to be the most salient here. This is the kind of meaning transfer, often called *jahad-ajahal-lakṣaṇā*, which preserves a part of the original meaning and rejects the rest. Hence in the sentence 'That art thou' the word 'thou' does not mean 'Śvetaketu as son of Uddālaka', a callow and ignorant youth. Instead it means him stripped of all such individual attributes, while 'that' means the universal Self. In other words, it is the pure consciousness in the individual self that is identified with that in the universal Self. This is a case where one part of the primary meaning of a sentence is given up and another part retained. Thus notwithstanding what Śaṃkara says in his *Chāndogya Upaniṣad* commentary, on Sadānanda's interpretation the sentence *tat tvam asi* does in one sense involve a kind of metaphor (*lakṣaṇā*), albeit not a purely qualitative one like 'The boy is a lion'.

Dharmarāja (seventeenth century), however, rejects this line of interpretation by 'the followers of tradition'. For him, the sentence 'That art thou' involves no *lakṣaṇā* at all:

> For, notwithstanding the fact that two qualified entities presented (to the mind) by significance [*śakti*] cannot be (logically) connected with each other to convey an identical meaning, there is no contradiction in connecting two substantives [*viśeṣya*], also presented with significance, so as to yield an identity of meaning. (*Vedāntaparibhāṣā* IV.27)

Hence when 'that' is said to be 'thou' only the identity of the substantives is involved, not their attributes, and words refer directly to substantives and not their attributes. It is just when words refer (indirectly) to attributes that *lakṣaṇā* is involved.

Dharmarāja reinforces his point here by offering what he takes to be a proper example of what the type of meaning transfer called *jahad-ajahal-lakṣaṇā* really involves (IV.29). Consider the sentence, 'Protect the curd from the crows'. Here the word 'crows' loses its express meaning and takes on an implied meaning 'spoilers of curd', for the sentence is to be understood as enjoining protection of the curd from any pest likely to spoil it (including parrots, dogs, and so on). In contrast, with the sentence 'That art thou' we do not find any such implication, and so it is not an example of this type of *lakṣaṇā*. Hence the claim of earlier Advaitin teachers that the sentence '*tat tvam asi*' involves *lakṣaṇā* is best understood as merely a tentative dialectical concession in the course of argument, rather than an expression of the final view of Advaita Vedānta.

Notwithstanding these intramural debates, all Advaitins would certainly at least agree that '*tat tvam asi*' is an informative identity statement, the proper understanding of which can effect liberation. And most would also agree that if one says 'That art thou' knowing the truth about the true Self, one is not directly denoting *Brahman*. Finally, they would all agree too that introducing the Fregean sense–reference distinction is ineffective here, for the sentence '*tat tvam asi*' does not mean that *tat* and *tvam* are just two names for the one Reality.

The problem of universals

As in Western philosophy, one important impetus for Indian philosophical debate about the problem of universals was semantic. In discussing the meaning of general terms, Indian philosophers disagreed about the need to postulate universals as the referents of such terms. Accordingly, there was a lively Indian debate about the problem of universals, with realists of various kinds on one side lined up against the Buddhist nominalists on the other side.

In the realist camp were Mīmaṃsā and Nyāya-Vaiśeṣika. Both schools admit the existence of universals corresponding to general terms, with these universals being conceived of as eternal entities existing independently of our minds. Both schools also hold that universals are essential for the justification of inference and the explanation of our experience of particulars sharing a common character. But there is a fundamental difference between the positions of the Naiyāyikas and the Bhāṭṭa Mīmaṃsakas about the relation between universal and particular. Nyāya (together with Prābhākara Mīmaṃsā) holds that a universal is different from a particular and yet not apprehended separately because a universal inheres in its various particulars. Bhāṭṭa Mīmaṃsā, however, rejects this relation of inherence (*samavāya*).

On the other side, in the nominalist camp were the Buddhist logicians, who defended the *apoha* theory. Given their metaphysics of universal flux, they are committed to denying the existence of universals and permanent substances. They urge a number of objections against the Indian realists' theories, but more important for their own error theory of universals is their positive theory, a version of nominalism. Very roughly, the Buddhist *apoha* theorists claim that when we use a general term like 'cow' we refer to every individual that is not a non-cow. The advantage of this theory for Buddhists is that it does not require any general essence that all pots have to share. Instead, the term 'cow' refers as the result of a double negation.

Nyāya-Vaiśeṣika realism about universals

Nyāya-Vaiśeṣika represents what is probably the most rigorously developed Indian version of realism about universals. We have already seen that Nyāya claims that the meaning of a word is a particular as characterized by a universal: for example, the meaning of 'cow' is a particular cow as characterized by the universal cowness. Unflinching metaphysical realists, Naiyāyikas accept that this semantic claim commits them to an ontology that includes at least particulars, universals and relations. Unflinching epistemological realists as well, Naiyāyikas accept that universals must be perceptible too.

Another (perhaps more fundamental) Nyāya argument for universals is from our experience of particulars sharing a common character. Universals are then invoked to ground our classifications of objects into natural kinds, classifications that would otherwise be just arbitrary and conventional (a possibility Naiyāyikas think deeply unlikely).

A universal (*sāmānya*) is defined as 'an entity that is eternal and inseparably present in many entities' (*Siddhāntamuktāvalī* 8). Such a universal is distinct from, and independent of, any particulars it (wholly) inheres in. But not everything that inheres in a particular is a universal: for example, colours are qualities (*guṇas*), non-repeatable tropes that inhere in particulars. Moreover, for Nyāya the particulars inhered in by universals are (*pace* Plato) just as real as the universals that inhere.

Not every general word, however, can correspond to a universal: this would violate the principle of *lāghava* (literally 'lightness'), the Indian equivalent of Ockham's Razor. We are only entitled to posit the minimum number of entities needed for our explanations of the phenomena. Hence Udayana (eleventh century) famously introduced in his *Kiraṇāvali* a set of six restrictive conditions for genuine universals (*jāti*) as opposed to 'surplus properties' (*upādhi*), where the former correspond to real natural kinds and the latter to seeming natural kinds:

(1) A universal cannot inhere in fewer than two things.

(2) No two universals can inhere in exactly the same things.

(3) No two universals are 'cross-cutting', partially overlapping one another.

(4) No universal can lead to an infinite regress.

(5) No universal can undermine the nature of the entity in which it inheres.

(6) No universal can be unable to be related to the things in which it purportedly inheres.

The first condition excludes uniquely instantiated properties (like *being Mahātma Gandhi*) from being universals. The second condition excludes co-extensive properties (like *being a cordate* and *being a renate*) from being universals. The third condition – the only one that is controversial among Naiyāyikas themselves – excludes the possibility of two universals inhering jointly in some things and individually in others. This excludes *being an element* and *being material* from both being universals because, within the Vaiśesika ontology, these two properties have *partially* overlapping instances. The fourth condition excludes a property like *universalhood* (the property common to both *potness* and *cowness*) from being a universal. The fifth condition excludes a property like *individuatorness* (the property common to all the haecceity-like ultimate individuators (*viśeṣa*) of Vaiśeṣika ontology) from being a universal. The sixth condition excludes a property like *inherenceness* from being a universal, for otherwise the relation (inherence) would inhere in one of its relata (inherences).

All the properties excluded by this set of conditions from being genuine universals (*jāti*) corresponding to natural kinds are classified as being 'surplus properties' (*upādhi*), in other words, potentially useful ontological placeholders awaiting further investigation. The precise status of these *upādhi* becomes a matter of lively debate in later Navya-Nyāya, but from what has been said so far it should be obvious that, whatever the ultimate merits of

Nyāya realism about universals, it certainly cannot be dismissed as just a naive hypostatization of general terms.

Bhāṭṭa Mīmāṃsa realism about universals

We have already seen that Mīmāṃsā believes in universals as the referents of words, so it is unsurprising to find them concurring with the Naiyāyikas on the existence of universals. However, as mentioned earlier, there is a fundamental difference between the positions of the Naiyāyikas and the Bhāṭṭa Mīmaṃsakas about the relation between universal and particular. Nyāya (together with Prābhākara Mīmaṃsā) holds that a universal is different from a particular and yet not apprehended separately because a universal inheres in its various particulars. Bhāṭṭa Mīmaṃsā, however, rejects this relation of inherence (*samavāya*).

Kumārila Bhaṭṭa's argument against inherence is in the form of a dilemma (*Ślokavārttika* 4.148–50; Jha 1983: 94). Is inherence different or non-different from the terms of the relation? On the first option, inherence requires another relation to be related to them, and so on *ad infinitum*. On the second option, inherence becomes superfluous. The latter possibility is apparently the one that Kumārila himself favours, since he thinks that the relation between universal and particular is one of identity-in-difference (*bhedābheda*).

The Naiyāyikas rejoin that the first horn of Kumārila's dilemma is flawed because inherence does not need another inherence relation to link the first inherence relation to its relata. They also complain that the Bhāṭṭa use of the notion of identity-in-difference is unacceptably obscure. A universal, according to Kumārila, is not entirely distinct from the particular it characterizes; it is not a separate entity that inheres in the latter. Instead universal and individual comprise a single entity that is both universal and particular in nature (*Ślokavārttika* 13.5–11; Jha 1983: 282–3). But the Bhāṭṭa argument for this is merely the claim that our experience is always of a unified cognition of universal and particular. In his *Nyāyakandalī*, Śrīdhara (tenth century) objects that if this purported cognition is a perception that universal and particular have the same form, then what we have is identity but not difference. On the other hand, if it is a perception that two things differ, then we have difference and not identity. Of course, it *is* true that we see that the universal and particular have different yet intimately related forms, but that is precisely what is explained by recourse to inherence!

Buddhist *apoha* nominalism

The Buddhists, of course, are uninterested in these family quarrels among realists, since they deny outright the existence of universals as being incompatible with their metaphysics of universal flux. Against the Indian realists' theories they urge a number of objections, mostly railing against the conceptual oddities implicit in the notion of an unproduced, partless universal that is distinct from, and yet wholly present in, all its associated particulars. It is clear that they find the whole idea of realism about universals intuitively bizarre. Thus the polemical jibe of Paṇḍita Aśoka (ninth century) in his *Sāmānyadūṣaṇa*: 'One can clearly see five fingers in one's own hand. One who commits himself to a sixth general entity fingerhood, side by side with the five fingers, might as well postulate horns on top of his head' (Siderits, Tillemans and Chakrabarti 2011: 11–12). Of course, the Buddhists do have one strong argument in favour of nominalism: its ontological 'lightness' relative to realism. But to capitalize on this advantage the Buddhists also need to offer a plausible rival positive account of our ability to use general terms without supposing that universals exist. This is what *apoha* theory is supposed to do. According to the ontology of the Buddhist logicians, the world consists of nothing but momentary particulars (*svalakṣaṇa*) and the universals (*sāmānyalakṣaṇa*) known by the mind are but conceptual constructions. Such conceptual constructions are explained in terms of *apoha* theory, which claims that a concept that has no real referent is established through the exclusion of other concepts.

A classic example to illustrate what the Buddhists mean here was provided by Dharmakīrti (seventh century) in his *Pramāṇavarttika* (I.73–4). Consider the property of *being fever-reducing*: while some herbs might be fever-reducing, these herbs might not have anything in common other than this property. There might not even be one particular way to reduce fever that all of these herbs share. Dharmakīrti argues that it would be obviously foolish to assert that there is a universal *fever-reducingness* or *anti-pyreticness* that inheres in all these herbs. Instead, it makes more sense to claim that the term 'fever-reducing' applies to them because they are not part of the 'exclusion class' of non-fever-reducing things. So the term 'fever-reducing' applies to particulars that are excluded from the exclusion class. And the same applies to any kind term according to the Buddhist logicians: it refers to the exclusion of its exclusion class.

A standard Indian objection to this was forcefully posed by Kumārila, considering the apparent circularity of the Buddhist claim that the general term 'cow' can be understood as referring to exclusion of its exclusion class 'not-cow':

> [If] you admit of the *cow* as an (independently) established entity, for the sake of having an object for your negation *apoha*, then the assumption of the *apoha* would become useless (inasmuch as the idea of *cow* is admitted to be established independently of it). And in the absence of an idea of the *cow* as an established entity, there can be no idea of *non-cow*; and as such how could you explain the idea of the *cow* to be based upon the idea of the *non-cow*? (*Ślokavarttika* 5.84–5; Jha 1983: 311)

The charge is that in order to form the first exclusion class 'non-cows', we already have to know what a cow is, and hence we have to have an idea that some particulars are cows. So we have to be able to refer to cows before being able to refer to 'non-cows'. But if that is true, then the negation of 'non-cows' as the referent for cows becomes obsolete: the term 'not non-cow' would be equivalent to the term 'cow'.

In reply the Buddhist logicians appeal to the distinction between two types of negation that we encountered earlier in this chapter: implicative negation (*paryudāsa-pratiṣedha*) and non-implicative negation (*prasajya-pratiṣedha*). The first type is analogous to sentential negation based on bivalence and the law of the excluded middle, so that any sentence *p* is true if and only if its negation, *not-p*, is false. This means that *not-not-p* is equivalent to *p*. The second type of negation, however, allows for a term like 'unkind' to be the negation of 'kind' without it being the case that someone has to be either kind or unkind. The *apoha* negation is taken to be of this latter type, so that *not non-p* is not the same as *p* and does not require the existence of universals. Instead *not non-p* supposedly is able to account for the meaning of *p* without collapsing into *p*.

Whatever the ultimate merits of this intriguing suggestion, it is perhaps appropriate to conclude our discussion by noting the existence of two types of *apoha* theory within the Buddhist logical tradition (see Tillemans 2011). The Buddhist logicians all agree that there is a sharp distinction to be drawn between the real particulars that comprise the world and the general concepts we use in talking about them. So how do word and world mesh? One approach to *apohavāda* is 'top-down': we begin with the resources of logic and language and try to show how these can enable us to pick out the pure particulars, notwithstanding their lack of generality. The other approach is 'bottom-up': we try to show how the pure particulars can generate felt resemblances and hence general concepts. Arguably, the 'top-down' approach originates with Dignāga (fifth century) and the 'bottom-up' approach with Dharmakīrti (seventh century). Whether these two approaches are in fact complementary or in conflict is an open question, but what is unquestionable is that – to date – it is the 'top-down' approach that has received the most attention, both in classical India and in the West. The detailed exploration of the ways in which the 'bottom-up' approach to *apoha* theory might account for our concept formation still awaits further development.

Conclusion

Although one important impetus for Indian philosophical debate about the problem of universals was semantic, the problem was also very much a metaphysical problem. That is, the Indians were not just concerned to explain what general terms refer to, but also what it is in the world that we experience when we experience a class of particulars as all being tokens of the same type. Does an explanatorily adequate ontology require, for instance, admitting repeatable properties as well as non-repeatable qualities, substances as well as bundles of property instances, and so on? In other words, to grapple with the problem of universals we need to shift from just investigating language and its relations to the world on to investigating the nature of the world itself. The fundamental nature of the world is, of course, the traditional domain of metaphysics, and hence it is that Indian metaphysics is the subject of the next chapter.

Suggestions for further reading

Two very useful overviews of Indian semantics are Staal 1969 and Houben 1997. More detailed studies of various topics in Indian philosophy of language include Raja 1969, Matilal 1990, Siderits 1991, Ganeri 1999, 2006, Coward and Raja 1990 and Scharf 1996. On word-meaning and sentence-meaning, see further Matilal and Sen 1988 and Mohanty 1992. For a lucid and sympathetic discussion of Mīmāṃsā anti-conventionalism about meaning, see Taber (forthcoming). On empty subject terms, see also Chakrabarti 1997a. For more on Advaitin treatments of the *mahāvākya* identity statements, see Murty 1974. On the problem of universals in Indian philosophy, see Dravid 1972. For the Nyāya-Vaiśeṣika account of universals, see further Chakrabarti 1975, Potter 1977, Phillips 1995, Halbfass 1992. On Buddhist *apoha* theory, see Siderits, Tillemans and Chakrabarti 2011.

5 World

Introduction

The complement to *pramāṇa* theory is *prameya* theory. Whereas the *pramāṇas* are the means of knowledge, the *prameyas* are the knowables, cognizable entities that constitute the world. With respect to the number and kinds of such entities, there was a very wide variety of opinion among classical Indian philosophers. Moreover, since according to most Indian systems knowledge of reality is at least a necessary condition for liberation, these metaphysical disputes were taken to be of practical as well as theoretical importance.

Ontology is an attempt to answer the question 'What is there?' But to answer that question we need to distinguish between two separate, though intertwined, questions: 'How many *entities* are there?' and 'How many *kinds* of entities are there?' In both cases the interesting answers are: 'One', 'Two', and 'Many' (i.e., monism, dualism and pluralism). Note, however, that a position about the number of kinds of entities that exist does not in itself entail any particular position about the number of entities that exist. Nor does a dualism or pluralism about the number of entities itself entail any particular position about the number of kinds of entities.

There were, correspondingly, quite a variety of Indian responses to the question 'What is there?', including variants of monism, dualism and pluralism about both entities and kinds. Advaita, for instance, holds that there is numerically only one entity (*Brahman/ātman*) and that all plurality is illusory. Viśiṣṭādvaita qualifies this monism and maintains that while there exists only one ontologically independent substance (God), there also exist other dependent entities (souls and material entities). Sautrāntika Buddhism, in contrast, holds that there are numerically many entities, but only one *kind* of thing: momentary particulars (*svalakṣaṇas*). Yogācāra Buddhism and Cārvāka also agree that there is only one kind of thing, but disagree about whether it is mental or material. Sāṃkhya-Yoga, on the other hand, asserts that reality consists of just two kinds of things but a plurality of entities: many selves (*puruṣas*) and a single evolving primal matter (*prakṛti*). Finally, Nyāya-Vaiśeṣika is pluralist about both entities and kinds: there are many kinds in the world, though there are only seven basic ontological categories (*padārtha*).

Underpinning these disagreements about the nature and number of reals are sometimes also important differences of opinion about the criterion of reality. According to the Buddhists, for instance, to be real is to be causally efficacious. For Advaita, however, the real is that which is never sublated (*abādha*) by any manner or means. Thus only *Brahman*, free from all limitations of space, time and individuality, is truly real.

In their systematic development of these differing ontologies, Indian philosophers mostly utilized a common methodology. Since even the most revisionary Indian metaphysicians usually took seriously the defeasible deliverances of common sense, they often conceived of their task as the construction of a philosophical system which permitted all objects recognized by common sense to be reduced to logical constructions out of the favoured primitive entities of the system. This general methodological stance is equally true, for example, of the Buddhist logicians (who favoured an event ontology of momentary particulars), of Nyāya-Vaiśeṣika (who favoured a rich ontology of universals, qualities and particulars), and of late Advaita (who favoured an entity monism). Indian metaphysical disputes were, then, less about the reductionist project per se (Madhyamaka Buddhism is a notable exception), than about the details of the attempted reductions: for example, do we really need to posit wholes as well as parts, substances as well as properties, selves as well as mental states, and so on.

Many metaphysical topics were debated in classical India. These included various abstract issues of fundamental ontology, some of which we will touch upon in a moment. They also included some perhaps more practically focused topics, two of the most important of which were causation (to be discussed later in this chapter) and the nature of the self (to be discussed in the next chapter).

Criteria of reality and two revisionary metaphysics

As already mentioned, underpinning the Indian disagreements about the nature and number of reals are sometimes important differences of opinion about the criterion of reality. Indian metaphysicians (like their Western counterparts) typically conceived of *prameya* metaphysics as the study of ultimate reality. Accordingly, they presupposed that there is a fundamental distinction between appearance and reality, between what merely appears to be the case and the reality that ultimately lies behind all appearances. But what marks this gap? A proposed criterion of reality addresses this question by specifying a condition that must be met in order for an object to qualify for inclusion in the class of ultimate reals.

Two prominent Indian versions of such criteria of reality are that of the Buddhist logicians, for whom to be real is to be causally efficacious, and that of the Advaitins, for whom the real is that which is never sublated (*abādhita*) by any manner or means. In each case the relevant criterion of reality was utilized as a premise in an interesting argument for a particular revisionary metaphysics. Let us begin with the case of Advaita Vedānta.

Advaita Vedānta and the ultimately real

The central idea of Advaita Vedānta is that the ultimate reality is the Self (*ātman*), which is one though appearing as many, and that this one Self is identical with the Absolute (*Brahman*). The world and the apparent diversity of individuals in it are not real. The world appearance is like the appearance of a rope as a snake, or mother-of-pearl as silver. Liberation means coming to see the whole world appearance as an illusion, much as the snake and the silver are sublated in the correction of ordinary perceptual illusions. Only the experience of *Brahman* can never be sublated and hence only *Brahman* is ultimately real.

The basic ontology of Advaita is thus famously and pithily summarized in a single line from the *Bālabodhinī* (traditionally, though disputably, attributed to Śaṃkara): '*Brahman* is real, the world is false, the individual soul is only *Brahman*, nothing else (*brahma satyaṁ jagan mithyā jīvo brahmaiva nāparaḥ*)'.

What, however, does it mean to be 'real' (*sat*)? Later Advaitins distinguish the 'real' from both the 'unreal' (*asat*) and the 'false' (*mithyā*). Only illusory and imaginary objects are unreal, whereas the apparent world is false. The mark of the real is unsublatability through the three times (i.e., past, present and future). Or as Madhusūdana Sarasvatī (sixteenth century) puts it in his *Advaitasiddhi*: 'Unreality is not the contradictory of reality, whose nature is unsublatability in the three times, but rather is what never forms the object of cognition as reality in any substratum whatever (*trikālādhyatvarūpasattvavyatireko nāsattvam, kiṁtu kvacid apy upādau sattvena pratīyamānatvānadhikaraṇtvam*)' (Madhusūdana Sarasvatī 1937: 50–1). Thus we have the real (*sat*) as what is unsublatable in the three times, the unreal (*asat*) as what is completely uninstanced, and the false (*mithyā*) as whatever is left over, in other words, whatever is neither real nor unreal, including both the practically real and the illusory.

In his *Khaṇḍanakhaṇḍakhādya* the twelfth-century Advaitin philosopher Śrīharṣa also accepts the unsublatability criterion of reality, which he formulates as 'that for which there is no contradiction at any time or place for anyone at all is to be admitted to exist' (Granoff 1978: 83). Utilizing it, he then goes on to develop an intriguing explicit argument for scripture being the source of our knowledge of the unique ultimate reality of the non-dual *Brahman*. Roughly, the argument goes something like this (Phillips 1995: 83–8; Granoff 1978: 147–60):

(1) Scripture allows us to cognize *Brahman* as self-conscious, all-inclusive and non-differentiated.
(2) What is cognized is to be accepted unless the cognition is defeasible.
(3) The nature of *Brahman* precludes any defeat.
(4) Therefore *Brahman* is real.

Clearly, this argument includes several controversial premises. One such premise is the epistemological thesis about self-certification (*svataḥprāmāṇyavāda*) that Advaita shares with Mīmāṃsā and which we encountered in Chapter 2: namely, the thesis that a cognition is to be accepted as veridical unless challenged and eliminated. Another disputed premise is that the nature of *Brahman*-cognition as self-conscious, all-inclusive and non-differentiated uniquely precludes any defeat. But it is a third premise that is most relevant to our present discussion: that is, the claim that what is never defeated is real.

Arguably, this latter claim is vulnerable to a devastating counterexample due to the Viśiṣṭādvaitin philosopher Rāmānuja. Rāmānuja vigorously defends the realist's bedrock conviction that ultimate reality could conceivably transcend all our epistemic evidence and hence that a cognition could be both undefeated and yet false. He supports his point with the following striking counterexample (*Śrībhāṣya* I.1.10):

> Let us imagine a race of men afflicted with a certain special defect of vision, without being aware of this their defect, dwelling in some remote mountain caves inaccessible to all other men provided with sound eyes. As we assume all of these cave dwellers to be afflicted with the same defect of vision, they, all of them, will equally see and judge bright things, e.g. the moon, to be double. Now in the case of these people there never arises a subsequent cognition sublating their primitive cognition; but the latter is false all the same, and its object, viz., the doubleness of the moon, is false likewise; the defect of vision being the cause of a cognition not corresponding to reality. (Thibaut 1971: 74–5)

The Buddhist causal criterion

The Buddhist logicians favour instead a different criterion of reality: for them the mark of reality is causal efficacy (*arthakriyākāritva*, 'the power of making become'). Their reasoning in favour of such a criterion of existence is basically twofold: metaphysically, the quest for ultimate reality is the quest for the causes that ultimately produce effects; epistemologically, nothing can be known which is not capable of producing a change in the knower. Thus causal efficacy is the test of the real.

This criterion is, of course, a version of a familiar test that entities must pass in order to gain admission to many philosophers' ontologies.

> *The Causal Criterion*: An entity is to be counted real if and only if it has causal powers.

The criterion here is an epistemologically motivated one, with the leading idea being that there is no good reason to postulate entities that have no causal power. Perhaps such entities are logically possible, but we can never have any reason to think them actualities.

This idea also has a venerable history in Western philosophy. Thus, for example, we find the following passage in Plato's *Sophist*, where the Eleatic Stranger suggests that causal power is the mark of being:

> I suggest that anything has real being, that is so constituted as to possess any sort of power either to affect anything else or to be affected, in however small a degree, by the most insignificant agent, though it be only once. I am proposing as a mark to distinguish real things, that they are nothing but power. (247d–e)

The Master Argument for Buddhist Momentariness

Now combining this kind of criterion of reality with a commitment to the existence of metaphysical simples (i.e., a set of fundamental impartite objects or *dharmas* out of which all partite objects are composed), Buddhist philosophers of the Sautrāntika school conclude that reality is ultimately composed of causally efficacious but momentary simples. The only further premise required is a version of the Principle of Sufficient Reason: there must be an explanation for an event occurring at the time it does occur, rather than at some other time.

Given these assumptions, the eleventh-century philosopher Ratnakīrti offers an explicit and ingenious argument for the Buddhist theory of the momentariness of simples (McDermott 1969: 41–3, 71–2). With a little licence, the argument can be reconstructed as a tree diagram (Figure 5.1): beginning from the assumption that some simple *X* exists, every branch of the tree terminates either in the proposition that *X* is momentary, or that (contrary to assumption) *X* does not exist.

Ratnakīrti's reasoning is roughly as follows. If a simple *X* exists then it must have causal powers and be causally efficacious. But then there must be an explanation as to why *X* is causally efficacious at one time rather than another. And insofar as *X* is a simple whose causal powers are part of its essence or nature, that explanation must be in terms of the properties of *X* alone. But all of this can be true just in case X is a momentary existent. After all, the intrinsic causal potency of a non-momentary entity could not be held in abeyance: if a simple does not discharge its causal potency in the first moment of its existence, then there could be no explanation in terms of its inherent nature why *X* was causally efficacious at a later time rather than an earlier time.

To be persuasive the argument needs setting out in a bit more detail. So let us now present more formally the *Master Argument for Momentariness* diagrammed in Figure 5.1. Begin by supposing of any simple *X* that it exists. Obviously enough, it must be that *X* either exists for only a moment, or it exists for more than a moment. If the first option is the case and *X* exists for only a moment, then clearly the doctrine of momentariness is true. If, on the other hand, the second option is the case and *X* exists for more than a moment, then either *X* produces all its effects in the first moment of its existence, or it produces its effects successively over time.

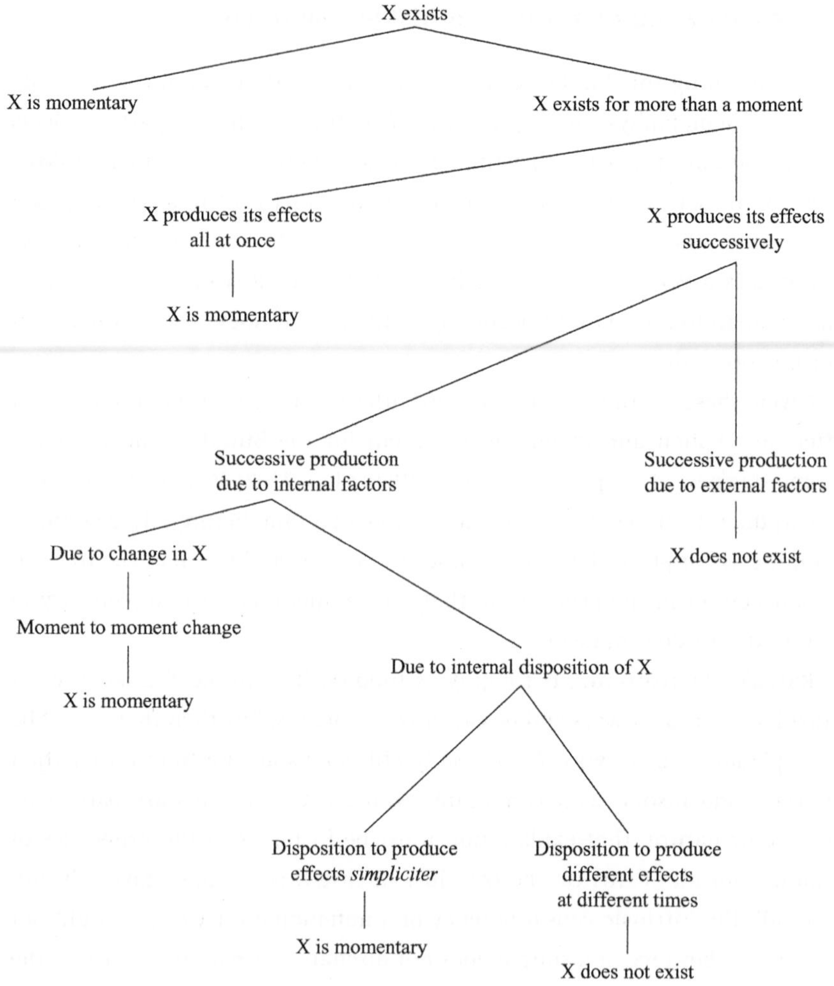

Figure 5.1 The Master Argument for Momentariness

Suppose that *X* produces all its effects in the first moment of its existence. Then because existence is causal efficacy, *X* exists only for that first moment: in other words, *X* is momentary.

Suppose instead that *X* produces its effects successively over time. Then there are just two possibilities: either *X*'s successive production of its effects is due to factors internal to itself, or it is due to external factors.

We cannot coherently suppose it is due to external factors, for *ex hypothesi* *X* is a simple and its causal powers are intrinsic to it. Thus if the external factors are a cause of the effect, *X* itself is not the cause and hence it lacks causal powers and so does not exist.

We must suppose, then, that the successive production of effects might be due to factors internal to the simple *X* that is the cause. But the internal factors for successive production must either be due to a change in *X* itself, or due to an internal disposition within *X*. The first option would mean that *X* would have to change from moment to moment (since existence is pragmatically equivalent to causal efficacy). But then each moment would produce a different effect and hence at each moment *X* would have to be a different entity. In other words, *X* would once again have to be momentary.

The only available alternative option is to suppose that the internal factors for successive production must be due to an internal disposition within *X*. This route in turn leaves us with just two possibilities: either there is an internal disposition to produce the effects *simpliciter*, or else there is an internal disposition to produce different effects at different times. The former option would mean that all effects would be produced in the first moment and therefore once again there would be momentariness.

The latter option, on the other hand, is incoherent. *Ex hypothesi*, *X* is a simple and its causal powers are intrinsic to it. Hence as a unitary permanent entity, *X* must have a capacity to produce its effects *simpliciter* – in which case we have momentariness. The only alternative is to suppose that *X* has no such capacity, in which case the cause could not exist at all. In other words, there is no sense to be made of the claim that a unitary cause produces effects all by itself *at different times*.

It may seem tempting to object that successive production might be due to *both* internal and external factors. But this also is not really an option open to us here, for we are supposed to be considering only simples possessed of intrinsic causal powers. Thus if there is an internal disposition in the cause to produce effects successively, it is in the *nature* of the cause to do so. And this cannot be the case if the production of the effects will not occur without a series of further extraneous factors.

Thus the intended upshot of the Master Argument for Momentariness is that any simple possessed of intrinsic causal powers must be a momentary entity. Of course, we might instead read the argument as pointing towards a *reductio* of the notion of a simple, at least insofar as this is understood as the notion of an impartite entity possessed of intrinsic causal powers.

Interestingly, this is roughly the moral that the rival Madhyamaka tradition of Buddhist philosophy draws. Following the lead of the first chapter of Nāgārjuna's *Mūlamadhyamakakārikā*, they argue that if a simple is supposed to be a momentary entity or phenomenon capable of bringing about another by virtue of a causal power that is essentially part of its nature, then there are no such metaphysical ultimates. Causation is just regularity and the project of metaphysical foundationalism that is supposed to terminate in simples is just a search for a philosophical chimera. We shall discuss Madhyamaka metaphysics more fully later in this chapter, but first a word or two about the alternative Nyāya-Vaiśeṣika approach to ontology through the construction of a descriptive metaphysics.

Nyāya-Vaiśeṣika realism

The Nyāya-Vaiśeṣika realists' approach to ontology is rather different from that of those Indian revisionary metaphysicians just discussed. Thus Naiyāyikas invoke no single criterion of reality that implies much of our ordinary experience is deluded. Instead they favour a kind of descriptive metaphysics predicated on the premise that all knowledge points to an existing object beyond it and independent of it. There are, then, a plurality of reals, all characterized by 'is-ness' (*astitva*), nameability (*abhideyatva*) and knowability (*jñeyatva*). And all of these various existents are in turn divisible into certain fundamental categories (*padārtha*). The fully developed version of the Nyāya-Vaiśeṣika classificatory system recognizes seven such categories: substance (*dravya*), quality (*guṇa*), motion or action (*karma*), universal (*sāmānya*), particularity (*viśeṣa*), inherence (*samavāya*) and absence (*abhāva*). Moreover, most of these classes are themselves further divisible into subclasses: nine types of substance, twenty-four types of quality, five types of motion, and so on.

Since etymologically the term '*padārtha*' is the meaning (*artha*) of a word (*pada*), it is not unnatural to see the Nyāya-Vaiśeṣika categories as intended to be metaphysical correlates of linguistic structures. This would enable Naiyāyikas to attempt to justify their categorical schema through an argument to the best explanation: just these hypothesized categories best explain certain features of our linguistic practices.

In his *Lakṣaṇāvalī* (Tachikawa 1981) the eleventh-century Naiyāyika Udayana offers an original and influential ordering of the traditional Vaiśeṣika categories. He begins by defining *padārtha* as that which can be named. Nameable entities are then divided into two kinds: positive presences (*bhāva*) and negative absences (*abhāva*). Within the first group he then distinguishes between: (i) things that have others inhering in them but do not inhere in others (i.e., substances, qualities and motions), and (ii) things that do not have others inhering in them but inhere in others (i.e., universals, individuators and inherence). Absences, in contrast, do not have others inhering in them and do not inhere in others.

Two of these categories merit special attention. The first is inherence (*samavāya*), a category that does a lot of work in Nyāya-Vaiśeṣika metaphysics. Inherence is the relationship that obtains between entities that cannot occur separately. It relates qualities, motions, universals and individuators to substances. It also relates universals to qualities and to motions. Finally, it relates wholes to the parts that are their cause. In short, inherence is the principle that restores unity to concrete things after their categorical decomposition.

The other category worth special mention is absence (*abhāva*), a later addition to the Vaiśeṣika categorical scheme. The standard Naiyāyika arguments for its inclusion are semantic and epistemological. The semantic argument is that true denials of existence require absences as truth-makers. Thus when we deny truly that there is an elephant present in the room, what makes this true is that there is an absence of an elephant there. The epistemological argument is that we experience such absences: looking for the elephant in the room, I *see* directly its absence (i.e., the negative fact that the elephant is not there). And since all knowledge points to an object beyond it and independent of it, in this case the object must be an absence.

Absences are of four types: (1) prior absences (as of a pot before it is produced), (2) destructional absences (as of a pot after it is destroyed), (3) absolute absences (as of colour in air), and (4) mutual absences (as between a pot and a cloth). All of these absences, however, must have an absentee (*pratiyogin*), that which the absence is an absence *of*. There is no absence which has an unreal absentee.

Faced with the objection that it seems we can name entities that do not exist (e.g., Pegasus, rabbit horns), Naiyāyikas respond by distinguishing between empty referring expressions and non-empty referring expressions. Briefly, their strategy is to treat empty referring terms as complex and their simple parts as standing for real elements. Sentences like 'The rabbit horn does not exist', which apparently refer to non-existent entities, are translated into sentences like 'There is no relation between the rabbit and a horn',

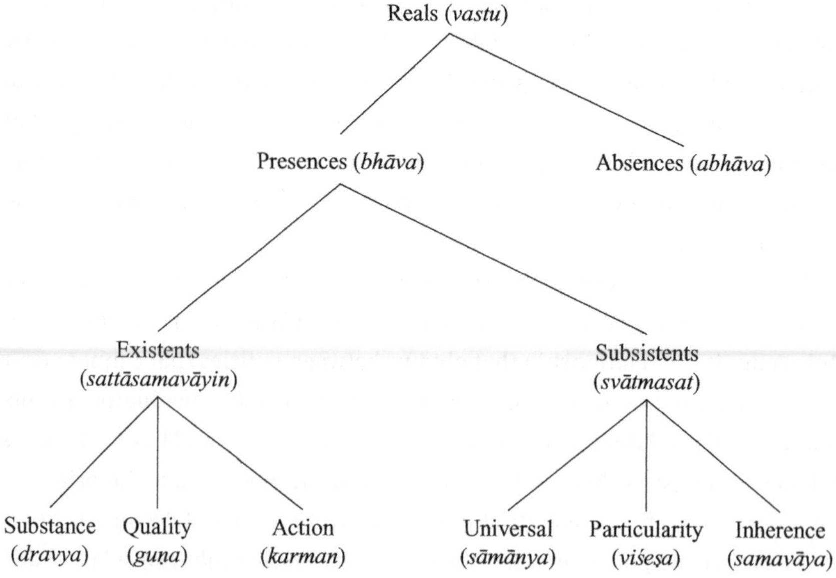

Figure 5.2 The Nyāya-Vaiśeṣika categories

which refer only to entities (including relations) that are reals according to Nyāya-Vaiśeṣika metaphysics. 'Nameable' means, in other words, nameable in the ideal language of the Nyāya system wherein all genuine names refer to the reals admitted by Nyāya ontology. No such real is either unnameable or unknowable.

The developed Nyāya-Vaiśeṣika categorical scheme, then, can be diagrammed as in Figure 5.2. We begin with the general class of the reals (*vastu*), which is divisible into presences (*bhāva*) and absences (*abhāva*). The presences are further divisible into two subclasses: the existents (*sattāsamavāyin*) and the subsistents (*svātmasat*). The former exist in virtue of having the highest universal, being (*sattā*), attached to them; the latter exist in their own right. Substance, quality and action are all existents; universals, particularity and inherence are all subsistents. Anything outside of all these categories is unreal, like the son of a barren woman.

Madhyamaka metaphysics

Madhyamaka Buddhism is famously centred on the doctrine of emptiness (*śūnyatā*), that is, the claim that all entities are empty of *svabhāva* or essence.

Who, in contrast, is supposed to be committed to the error of affirming the existence of *svabhāva*? According to the later developed Prāsaṅgika-Madhyamaka tradition, the answer to that question is: not only all philosophical schools except the Prāsaṅgikas, but all unenlightened beings. The primary target of Nāgārjuna's critique in his *Mūlamadhyamakakārikā*, however, is the Buddhist Abhidharma tradition.

Probably the most influential of the various Indian Abhidharma schools was the Sarvāstivāda (or Vaibhāṣika) school. And undoubtedly the most influential text of that school was Vasubandhu's *Abhidharmakośa* (Pruden 1991), composed in the fourth century.

Like all Buddhist philosophers in the various Abhidharma traditions, the Sarvāstivādins espoused some type of bundle theory according to which the concrete particulars of our ordinary experience (tables and chairs, cats and dogs, and so on) are reducible to bundles of momentary impartite simples called *dharmas*. Among the Indian Ābhidharmikas there were competing classifications of these *dharmas*. The Sarvāstivāda list recognizes 75 types of *dharmas*: 47 mental *dharmas*; 11 physical *dharmas*; 14 *dharmas* that are neither mental nor physical; and 3 unconditioned *dharmas*. The fundamental constituents of the world, then, are these *dharmas*, definable in terms of their intrinsic natures (*svabhāva*). These *dharmas* are called the primary existents (*dravyasat*) and the composite entities constructed out of primary existents are secondary or 'conceptual' existents (*prajñaptisat*). It is important to understand, however, that for the Sarvāstivādins both primary and secondary existents *exist*, but in different ways insofar as the former *ground* the latter.

Another way the Sarvāstivādins describe this situation is to say that only *dharmas* are ultimately real (*paramārthasat*), though wholes constructed out of *dharmas* are conventionally real (*saṃvṛtisat*). The distinction is explained by reference to the way in which things that are ultimately real resist analysis in a fashion that things that are conventionally real do not:

> If the idea of a thing disappears when this thing is broken into pieces, then this thing has relative existence (*saṃvṛtisat*); for example, a jug: the idea of a jug disappears when it is reduced to pieces. If the idea of a thing disappears when this thing is dissipated, or broken to pieces, by the mind, then this thing should be regarded as having relative existence . . . If when a thing is broken to pieces or dissipated by the mind, the idea of this thing continues, then this thing has absolute existence (*paramārthasat*). (*Abhidharmakośa* VI.4)

Finally, it is also important to recognize that the seemingly dry Abhidharma project of observational analysis and categorization of the fundamental existents that comprise the world was in fact conceived by the Sarvāstivādins to be of absolutely crucial soteriological importance: 'Apart from the discernment of the *dharmas*, there is no means to extinguish the defilements, and it is by means of the defilements that the world wanders in the ocean of existence. So it is with a view to this discernment that the Abhidharma has, they say, been spoken by [the Buddha]' (*Abhidharmakośa* I.3). Proper analytical knowledge of the nature of the existents that comprise the world is thus a necessary condition for the extinction of the defiling passions and hence too for liberation from suffering (i.e., the attainment of *nirvāṇa*). In other words, metaphysics really matters!

Since for the Ābhidharmikas a *dharma* has but a single nature and has that nature intrinsically, then a *dharma* could not lack that nature and still exist: in other words, a *dharma* possesses its *svabhāva* essentially. Hence to deny, as Mādhyamikas do, that anything has *svabhāva* is tantamount to denying that anything has an essence. This is why the doctrine of emptiness is often glossed as the view that there are no essences.

On what grounds do Mādhyamikas deny that anything has an essence? There is no single master argument for emptiness. Instead Nāgārjuna and other Mādhyamikas give a variety of arguments on different topics (causation, motion, the self, *nirvāṇa*, etc.). These arguments do all share a common form, though: they are *prasaṅga* or *reductio ad absurdum* arguments that start by assuming there are entities that have essences and then derive unacceptable consequences from that assumption (unacceptable, that is, to the opponent).

It is a matter of modern scholarly dispute whether Nāgārjuna's *prasaṅga* refutations really are successful, or whether they smuggle in illegitimate assumptions (see, for instance, Robinson 1972 and Hayes 1994). But let us put aside that question here to focus instead on a different one: namely, what sort of metaphysics is Nāgārjuna engaged in? After all, even though he is sometimes interpreted as avoiding metaphysical theses, he does seem to affirm at least one fundamental metaphysical truth: namely, that all things are empty or essenceless (including emptiness itself).

Nāgārjuna is a notoriously difficult philosopher to interpret, arguably because his texts so often seriously underdetermine precise readings. Thus over the centuries he has been read in many different ways: as a nihilist, a relativist, an absolutist, a mystic, a sceptic, a deconstructionist, and so on. Let us consider here just one currently popular interpretation: Nāgārjuna as anti-realist (see, for instance, Siderits 2003 and Westerhoff 2009). According to this reading, Nāgārjuna's metaphysical position is best understood as a variety of something like modern anti-realism.

The majority of traditional philosophers, both in India and in the West, have been *realists* in the following sense of that multivalent term: they have believed that there is an objective reality about which we form beliefs and make claims; that such beliefs and claims are true in virtue of corresponding to that reality; and that this correspondence obtains or not quite independently of our ability to determine whether this is so. (All of this characterization of realism is, of course, entirely compatible with vigorous intramural disagreements among realists as to the specific nature of objective reality.) *Anti-realists*, in contrast, deny the existence of any such 'objective reality' and hold that what we call 'reality' is constructed in part by our conceptual activities or by the conceptual tools we employ in our enquiry. Hence ontological anti-realism is sometimes glossed as the view that there are many different ontological frameworks, holding that different sets of entities exist, and that while some frameworks may be more useful than others for certain purposes, there is no fact of the matter as to which framework is correct.

Now it is certainly understandable that some interpreters might take Madhyamaka to be a kind of anti-realism insofar as Mādhyamikas would seem to be unfriendly to the notion of a mind-independent entity to which beliefs, when true, must correspond. Moreover, if realism is construed as a view committed to the existence of intrinsically existent truth-makers, then naturally Mādhyamikas will seem to be anti-realists: they are indeed committed to denying that there are any such independently existing things that ground ordinary knowledge and practice. For Mādhyamikas the ultimate truth is that there is no ultimate truth *in the sense that the Ābhidharmikas understand that term* (i.e., as involving primary existents that are resistant to analysis): this is what the *prasaṅga* arguments are supposed to show.

But perhaps the anachronistic label 'anti-realism' is nevertheless not the most perspicuous way to represent Madhyamaka metaphysics. After all, Nāgārjuna does seem to think that there is a fact of the matter about emptiness: it is *true* that all things are empty. But from a Madhyamaka point of view it cannot be that the truth-maker for that claim about emptiness is some sort of intrinsically existent entity. So just what is the content of that truth?

As already mentioned, the central Madhyamaka doctrine of emptiness is often glossed as a doctrine of essencelessness. What is an essence? That is a large and controversial question, but consider the following suggestion: think of an object's essential properties as those that underlie and explain the object's other properties. Essences are not merely those properties that an object has necessarily, but those that *ground* all its other properties. Exactly what 'ground' means here is obviously open to further debate, but the leading idea is this: metaphysics is not about what exists, but about what grounds what. In other words, it is about what is *fundamental*.

We have already noted that for the Ābhidharmikas, who are Nāgārjuna's primary targets in the *Mūlamadhyamakakārikā*, the fundamental constituents of the world are *dharmas* definable in terms of their intrinsic natures (*svabhāva*). These *dharmas* are the primary existents (*dravyasat*) and the composite entities constructed out of primary existents are secondary or 'conceptual' existents (*prajñaptisat*). Both exist, but the former ground the latter. The logical structure of other Indian metaphysical systems is not so dissimilar, which is why Mādhyamikas thought their original critique of Abhidharma to be generalizable to include non-Buddhist ontologies. To be sure, the other Indian metaphysicians disagree on the nature and number of fundamental entities, but they all believe some fundamental entities ground others. (And, of course, much the same is true of most Western metaphysical systems.) Madhyamaka, in contrast, famously rejects this whole project of searching for grounds. This is why emptiness is said to be itself empty and why we are warned not to grasp at emptiness itself as grounding things, an error as dangerous as grasping a snake wrongly (*Mūlamadhyamakakārikā* 24.11).

Madhyamaka, then, is a kind of metaphysical anti-foundationalism. Of course, such a metaphysical understanding of emptiness will certainly run counter to the grounding project common to most Indian and Western metaphysicians. But then, as Nāgārjuna reminds us (*Ratnavālī* 1.79): 'Beyond good and evil, profound and liberating, this [doctrine of emptiness] has not been tasted by those who fear what is entirely groundless.' Historically, however, Madhyamaka had relatively little influence on Indian philosophy (notwithstanding its modern popularity): indeed, for the three centuries after Nāgārjuna's death there do not even seem to have been any Mādhyamikas active in India. From an Ābhidharmika point of view, of course, this is easy enough to explain. Nāgārjuna's central claim that all entities are empty of any intrinsic nature seemed to them tantamount to the claim that there are no primary existents (*dravyasat*), and hence only secondary or 'conceptualized' existents (*prajñaptisat*). But that in turn seems to imply that all things are constructs and yet there is nothing for them to be constructed out of! Hence the Ābhidharmikas felt that, notwithstanding Nāgārjuna's protests to the contrary, Madhyamaka was effectively just a kind of nihilism.

Causation: the context of the Indian theories

Unsurprisingly, the sorts of disputes about abstract issues of fundamental ontology that we have been considering so far in this chapter had significant implications too for the shape of Indian debates about some more practically oriented metaphysical issues. Two of the most important of these issues were the nature of causation and the nature of the self. We shall discuss the former in what remains of this chapter and the latter in the chapter that follows.

Causation was acknowledged as one of the central metaphysical problems in Indian philosophy. The classical Indian philosophers' concern with the problem basically arose from two sources: first, the cosmogonic speculations of the Vedas and Upaniṣads, with their search for some simple unitary cause for the origin of this complex universe; and second, the Vedic concern with ritual action (*karman*) and the causal mechanisms by which such actions bring about their unseen, but purportedly cosmic, effects. Once the goal of liberation (*mokṣa*) came to be accepted as the highest value, these two strands of thought entwined to generate intense interest in the notion of causation.

Indian philosophers extensively discussed a number of issues relating to causation, including the nature of the causal relation, the definitions of cause and effect, and classifications of kinds of causes. Typically they stressed the importance of the material cause, rather than (as in Western philosophy) the efficient cause. Only the materialistic Cārvākas denied the reality of causation, taking it to be subjective. This is unsurprising given that a concern with demonstrating the possibility of liberation motivated the theories of causation and only the Cārvākas denied this possibility.

The Indian theories of causation are traditionally classified by reference to the question of whether the effect is a mode of the cause. According to this taxonomy there are two principal theories of causation. One is the identity theory (*satkāryavāda*), which holds that the effect is identical with the cause, a manifestation of what is potential in the cause. The other is the non-identity theory (*asatkāryavāda*), which denies that the effect pre-exists in its cause and claims instead that the effect is an altogether new entity.

The commitment to the ideal of liberation provides the context for understanding the classical Indian philosophers' concern with causation in the following way. Typically the theoretical problem of Indian philosophy is to provide an account of the world which allows for the possibility of our successfully entering into it as agents set on liberation from suffering (*duḥkha*). In order to guarantee the feasibility of liberation we need to be assured that there are reliable causal connections between events and actions such that it is possible for a person to enter into the course of events as a conscious agent whose actions have predictable consequences. To do this the Indian philosophers sought to identify those causal chains relevant to liberation, and to analyze the nature of the causal relation as exhibited among the members of those chains.

A number of such causal chains were proposed. One of the oldest and best known is the Buddhist chain of dependent origination (*pratītyasamutpāda*). This twelvefold chain runs: ignorance; dispositions; consciousness; body and mind; the six sense fields; sense contact; sensation; desire; clinging; becoming; birth; old age and death. Each of these factors is both conditioning and conditioned. This is expressed in a traditional Buddhist formula characterizing the relation between the links:

> When this is, that is; this arising, that arises. When this is not, that is not; this ceasing, that ceases. (*Majjhima-nikāya* III.63)

The possibility of liberation (called *nirvāṇa* in Buddhism) requires that we be able to break the chain at certain points where the links are only necessary conditions for what follows. In Buddhism the favoured weak links are ignorance (*avidyā*) and desire (*tṛṣṇa*), which can be eliminated with (respectively) knowledge and non-attachment.

The alternative causal chains of the Jainas, of Nyāya-Vaiśeṣika and of Sāṃkhya-Yoga differ in their details. However, all include ignorance as a link and hence guarantee the possibility of liberation through the possibility of the elimination of ignorance by right knowledge. It is essential for the possibility of liberation that the causal chains which bind us to suffering are such that at least some of the members are necessary but not sufficient conditions for other members, otherwise we could not enter the chain and reverse our condition of bondage. On the other hand, the chain must not have gaps, for if there is no necessary connection between the links, then none of our actions can be relied upon to bring about the goal of liberation. Thus once we have identified the causal chain that leads to bondage, we also need to say something about the causal relation itself.

As already mentioned, two basic models dominate Indian thinking about the nature of the causal relation. One is the model favoured by the identity theory (*satkāryavāda*) of Sāṃkhya-Yoga. A standard illustration is the case of milk and curds: the milk is the cause and the curds are the effect. But the milk is the same stuff as the curds; one is merely transformed into the other. Generalizing from this kind of example leads to the view that the effect pre-exists in its cause. In fact a cause and its effect are not two separate, discrete entities but instead two states of the same enduring substance. The major apparent difficulty with this model (in both its Sāṃkhya and Advaitin versions) is that the causal relation threatens to be too strong. If nothing can become other than what it is already, how can we unenlightened beings ever achieve our own liberation?

The competing model of the causal relation is the one favoured by the non-identity theory (*asatkāryavāda*) of Nyāya-Vaiśeṣika and (some) Buddhists. A standard Naiyāyika illustration is the pot and its two halves: the two halves of the pot are its causes and the pot is the effect. (Indian potters make a pot by first making the two halves and then joining them.) According to this model the effect is not pre-existent in the cause. Effects are instead conceived of as wholes inhering in pre-existing parts that are their causes.

The Buddhist versions of the non-identity theory are rather different because Buddhism generally denies that there are any persisting substances at all; things are instead momentary. A standard illustration is the way in which whirling a flaming torch creates in watchers the impression of a persistent object: a circle of fire. Similarly, the momentary occurrences of things in certain patterns create the impression of persisting objects existing in the world.

Both versions of the non-identity theory claim to avoid the error of making the causal relation too strong, for effects are not identical with their pre-existing causes. They also both claim to avoid making the causal relation too weak, for both in their different fashions try to guarantee the regularity of causal relations. However, to vindicate the latter claim, each school has to develop a rather elaborate ontology and epistemology, the details of which come in for criticism from other schools.

A third position tries to occupy the middle ground between the identity theory and the non-identity theory. This is the stance taken by the Jaina theory of non-absolutism. According to this theory, there are a variety of aspects from which any entity can be viewed. Thus from one viewpoint the effect is pre-existent in the cause and from another viewpoint it is not. The theory attempts to provide a compromise account of the causal relation that is neither too strong (as the identity theory threatens to be), nor too weak (as the non-identity theory threatens to be).

Common to all these causal theories, however, is the assumption that causation is real and not merely subjective. This is natural enough, since all these theories accept the original problematic: how to analyze the nature of the causal chain so as to guarantee the feasibility of attaining liberation. The one exception to this in Indian philosophy is to be found in the views of the Cārvāka materialists. These philosophers were sceptics about both causation and the possibility of attaining liberation. They espoused an anti-religious materialism and a subjectivist account of causation as being merely observed conjunction of events.

We can arrange, then, the Indian theories of causation in the following sequence. First, we have Cārvāka scepticism about causation, with its attendant scepticism about the possibility of liberation. All the other theories can be represented as various defensive responses to this scepticism. Thus the identity theory seeks to guarantee the possibility of liberation with an account of causation that makes it a very strong relation. Two distinct versions of the theory were developed: the transformation theory of Sāṃkhya-Yoga and the appearance theory of Advaita Vedānta. The non-identity theory, on the other hand, tries to preserve the possibility of liberation while making causation a rather weaker relation. Again, two versions of the theory were developed: the Nyāya-Vaiśeṣika theory and the Buddhist theory of conditioned origination. The Jaina theory is an attempted synthesis of the identity and non-identity theories.

Cārvāka scepticism about causation

As anti-religious materialists, the Cārvāka had no interest in vindicating the possibility of liberation. And as strict empiricists in their epistemology, they refused to admit anything but perception as a valid means of knowledge. Accordingly, they refused to admit causation as an invariable and unconditional relation. All we can know is what we perceive and all we perceive are conjunctions of events, not a dependence relation between events. These conjunctions may be regarded as purely accidental: hence their views are sometimes known as accidentalism (*yadṛcchāvāda*). Rather than supposing that some things are effects dependent on other things which are causes, the Cārvāka held that it is more reasonable to suppose things occur because of their own natures (*svabhāva*): hence their views are sometimes called naturalism (*svabhāvavāda*).

This sceptical position was criticized by all the other schools. The most common criticism was of the overly restrictive epistemology that led to this sceptical result. Indeed, the Cārvāka position was often viewed as a *reductio ad absurdum* of its strict empiricist premises. Accordingly the response of the other schools was usually to try to develop from a less restrictive epistemology a more generous ontology which included causal relations.

Another common complaint, however, was that Cārvāka scepticism was self-refuting. One Naiyāyika version of this charge claims that the scepticism about causation is refuted by the sceptics' own behaviour: they purport to doubt the causal relation between fire and smoke, but light a fire when they want to produce smoke. Of course, the Cārvāka might just reply here that we are so constituted psychologically that we expect a uniform regularity between instances of fire and smoke. Notwithstanding this, there is no real justification for this expectation; it is just a habit of expecting what has previously occurred in certain circumstances to reoccur in similar circumstances. But for the liberation-oriented philosophers, the Cārvāka's philosophical anthropology here is far too pessimistic. The agent trapped in the patterns of habit is paradigmatically the unliberated being; liberation is freedom from such bondage and understanding the causal chains which lead to bondage also allows us to discover the route to freedom.

Sāṃkhya-Yoga and the transformation theory

Sāṃkhya-Yoga espouses the identity theory (*satkāryavāda*), so called because it holds that an effect (*kārya*) is already existent (*sat*) in its cause in a potential form. The Sāṃkhya version of the theory is also called transformation theory (*pariṇāmavāda*) because it holds that the cause undergoes a real transformation into its effect through the causal process.

The standard Sāṃkhya arguments for the identity theory presented in Īśvarakṛṣṇa's *Sāṃkhyakārikā* (verse 9) are basically that something cannot emerge out of nothing, that the effect must be of the same material as the cause, and that specific causes can only cause specific effects. In order to guarantee all of this the effect must pre-exist in the cause; it is a modification of what was already present. Thus according to the metaphysics of Sāṃkhya the manifest world must have an existing cause that the effect pre-exists in. This is nature (*prakṛti*), conceived of as a unitary principle underlying observable phenomena, which are transformations of this substance. The self (*puruṣa*) is merely the passive witness of the entirety of this.

The key Sāṃkhya examples of causation involve material causation: as when a seed grows into a plant; milk is transformed into curd; or oil seeds are transformed into oil. In these cases a cause and effect are plausibly just two states of a single continuing substance. The Naiyāyikas objected that the Sāṃkhya theory abolishes the distinction between material and efficient causes. But this is not quite true, for Sāṃkhya-Yoga also admits another type of cause: the efficient or instrumental cause (*nimittakāraṇa*). However, this is not supposed to act upon the material cause and transform it into an effect. Rather it simply removes the barriers which check the material cause (*prakṛti*) from transforming from a relatively unmanifested state to a more manifested state. The *Yogabhāṣya* (4.3) compares it to how a farmer allows water to flow from a filled bed to another just by removing the obstacles.

The transformation theory insists that there is a necessary relation between cause and effect. To this extent it responds to the Cārvāka sceptical challenge to the possibility of liberation: there is indeed an invariable concomitance between cause and effect, since the latter is just a manifested state of the former. But the theory threatens to make the causal relation too strong. Transformation theory holds causation to involve a real transformation of a common stuff. But then nothing can be other than what it already is and the presently unenlightened can never attain liberation. Sāṃkhya-Yoga responds to this objection by developing a radical dualism between nature (*prakṛti*) and self (*puruṣa*). The self is essentially unaffected by the causal transformation of *prakṛti*. As the *Sāṃkhyakārikā* (verse 62) puts it: 'No one, therefore, is bound; no one released, likewise no one transmigrates. Only *prakṛti* in its various forms transmigrates, is bound and is released' (Larson 1979: 274). Because the *puruṣa* is just pure, contentless consciousness it cannot be bound or liberated. Realizing the absolute separation of *prakṛti* and *puruṣa*, ceasing to misidentify ourselves with our bodies, we come to appreciate our true natures as pure consciousnesses. This realization leads to liberation (called *kaivalya* in Sāṃkhya-Yoga), a condition apart from all suffering. The difference between bondage and liberation, then, is not an ontological one, but an epistemological one. The removal of the epistemological condition of ignorance is sufficient for liberation.

Advaita Vedānta and the appearance theory

The Sāṃkhya epistemological model of the route to freedom has much in common with the Advaitin approach to the problem. However, the Advaitin view came to be called appearance theory (*vivartavāda*), for it differs importantly from the Sāṃkhya-Yoga version of the identity theory. In particular, the transformation theory views an effect such as the pot as a genuine transformation of the clay which constitutes it; both cause and effect are real. By contrast, the appearance theory views the effect (the pot) as not real, but only an appearance (*vivarta*). This is because Advaita espouses a radical monism: only the Absolute (*Brahman*) is real and the Self (*ātman*) is identical with *Brahman*. Accordingly, the Advaitin theory of causation is a version of the identity theory in that the effect (the illusory world around us) is in a sense not different from its cause (*Brahman/ātman*). However, the effect is ultimately unreal, though the cause is real (thus the theory is sometimes called *satkāraṇavāda*, 'existent-cause-theory').

It is only on the level of phenomenal reality, then, that the Advaitins are willing to defend the identity theory. The Advaitin philosopher Śaṃkara, for instance, endorses on this level the familiar Sāṃkhya arguments that otherwise anything might come of anything and that clearly nothing comes of nothing. He also adds others of his own, including the suggestion that since the perceptibility of cause and effect are not independent it is reasonable to suppose that they are identical (*Brahmasūtrabhāṣya* II.1.15).

Ultimately, however, when we consider the relation between the world and *Brahman*, the effect is merely an *apparent* effect. This is because the Advaitins accept both that *Brahman* is an eternal being and that an eternal being must have eternal effects. Yet since worldly phenomena are clearly not eternal, they conclude that they cannot be genuine effects of *Brahman*, but merely illusory or apparent effects. Insofar as *Brahman* underlies these appearances, however, it can be viewed as the material cause of the world. This is in accord with the Advaitin theory of perceptual error, according to which there must be something real that underlies a false appearance.

On the appearance theory, then, causality is an apparent relation between a (comparatively) unreal effect and a (comparatively) real cause, between a thought construction and that which grounds such a construction. The focus of the theory of causation thus shifts away from a concern with external relations between objects, and towards a concern with the epistemic or awareness relation involved in such constructions. Accordingly, liberation is conceived of epistemically as the realization of what one already essentially is: *Brahman*.

Clearly this theory of causation is only as plausible as the concept of *Brahman* as pure being upon which it rests. But this latter notion was vigorously rejected by many other Indian philosophers and the appearance theory thus requires a controversial monism to support it. Moreover, the identity theory's attempt to guarantee the causal relation, begun by Sāṃkhya and continued by Advaita, seems to end up with too strong an account of causation. The only way out of this difficulty seems to be to insist that, in some sense, we are already liberated but do not know it. Then liberation becomes an epistemological matter, not an ontological one. But with bondage no longer conceived in material terms, we have a corresponding drift both away from epistemological realism and towards metaphysical monism or dualism.

Nyāya-Vaiśeṣika and the non-identity theory

Nyāya-Vaiśeṣika represents a robust commitment to both epistemological realism and metaphysical pluralism. The Naiyāyikas define a cause as an invariable and independently necessary antecedent of an effect (*Bhāṣāpariccheda* 16). That is, the causal relation is a uniform temporal relation that is necessary in the sense that there can be no counter-instances (though the relation is not a logical one in the Western sense). Moreover, the constant conjunction involved is a relation between properties, rather than between particular events.

Nyāya recognizes three kinds of causal factor: inherent cause (*samavāyikāraṇa*); non-inherent cause (*asamavāyikāraṇa*); and instrumental cause (*nimittakāraṇa*). The inherent cause is that substance in which the effect abides by the relation of inherence. Thus the pot-halves or the threads are the inherent causes of the pot or the cloth because the latter effects inhere in the former causes. Note that for Nyāya the halves or the threads are not that out of which the pot or the cloth is composed. Rather the effects inhere in the causes so that, for instance, the cloth is not produced *out of* the threads, but subsists *in* the threads.

The non-inherent cause is a cause which (directly or indirectly) inheres in an inherent cause. For example, in the production of a pot, the pot-halves are the inherent cause of the pot and the contact between the pot-halves, which inheres in the pot-halves, is the non-inherent cause of the pot.

The first two kinds of causal factor are together necessary but not sufficient to produce an effect. The category of instrumental (or efficient) cause lumps together all the remaining causal factors. These include the agents of actions and other supporting factors.

The Nyāya theory takes the effect to be an absolutely new thing. The Sāṃkhya argument that a non-existent effect cannot be brought into existence is dismissed by Naiyāyikas as confusing an absolute non-entity (like the hare's horn, which is non-existent for all time) with what is merely non-existent before a particular time (like the pot before it is produced by the potter).

Nyāya also rejects the Sāṃkhya argument that since not just anything can produce anything, there must be a necessary relation between cause and effect requiring that they coexist contemporaneously. The Naiyāyikas claim that the relevant necessity is supplied by the fact that the relation is between universals and particulars.

Essential to the Nyāya theory is the notion of inherence (*samavāya*). Inherence is the relation that connects wholes and parts (like pots and pot-halves, threads and cloth); it also connects substances and their qualities. Inherence is defined as the relation between two inseparable things related as located to locus. Inherence explains the relation of the pot to the pot-halves which are its material cause without falling into the identity theory's mistake of identifying the effect with its cause (and hence being unable to explain why the effect does not come into existence as soon as the cause does). Moreover, inherence relates the self (*ātman*) to its qualities, including wrong notions. This allows for the wrong notions to be destroyed without thereby destroying the self, thus guaranteeing the possibility of liberation.

The most popular objection to the Nyāya theory is the infinite regress argument against inherence, apparently first presented by Dharmakīrti (*Sambandhaparīkṣā* 4):

> Since of two relata there is a connection through one, this one is a relation – well, then, if that is proposed, what is the relation of the two, the relation and the relata? There is an infinite regress, and therefore the idea of a relation does not hold. (Phillips 1995: 22–3)

In other words, if two entities *A* and *B* are to be related by the inherence relation *R*, which is itself a distinct entity, then it is also necessary that *A* and *R* be related by a different inherence relation *R**, itself a distinct entity. But then, of course, *A* and *R** have to be related by a yet different relation *R***, and so on *ad infinitum*.

The Naiyāyikas reply that there is no regress because there is no other relation to connect inherence to its relatum. Clearly they cannot mean that the relatum and its relation are identical, for then, by the transitivity of identity, *A* would not only be identical with *R*, but also with *B*! Instead the later school of Navya-Nyāya appeals to the notion of a self-linking connector (*svarūpasambandha*). The leading idea here is that while *A* requires the inherence relation *R* to connect it to *B*, *A* can be its own connector to *R*.

Buddhist theories

The Buddhists reject the Nyāya version of non-identity theory because it seems to them that inherence is too strong a relation for causation. This is because the Buddhist theory of momentariness (*kṣaṇikavāda*) implies that there can be no persisting relation between any two entities, nor any persisting entities. Instead they espouse an ontology of momentary events, each of which is causally efficacious, grouped into various patterns. Moreover, the theory of dependent origination is understood to imply that an effect is not the result of a single cause, but of many causes working together. The Buddhist schools attempted various classifications of this totality of causes and conditions.

Abhidharma Buddhism analyzes reality into elements (*dharmas*). A distinction is also admitted between a *dharma* and its characteristics (*lakṣaṇa*). But this distinction quickly leads to a quasi-substantialism in the Sarvāstivāda school, as the concept of a *dharma*'s enduring essence or 'own-nature' (*svabhāva*) is introduced as the bearer of a *dharma*'s 'own-characteristics' (*svalakṣaṇa*). The concept of *svabhāva* is utilized by the Sarvāstivādins to explain the continuity of phenomena, which are analyzed into momentary existences: one aspect of a *dharma* changes while another (the *svabhāva*) remains unchanged. This idea is used to explain the connection between cause and effect: a mango seed gives rise only to a mango tree because of the unchanging essence of 'mango-ness' that is in the seed and tree. Thus *svabhāva* is a kind of underlying substratum of change, a quasi-substance.

The Sautrāntikas rejected this theory as incompatible with the Buddha's doctrine of 'no-self', for to say that a thing arises from its 'own-nature' is just to say it arises from the self. Instead the Sautrāntikas held existence to be but a series of successive moments. A seed is just a series of such point-instants and the seed-series gives rise to the tree-series in the sense that the latter succeeds the former. Causality, then, is just contiguity or immediate succession. But what of the origin of the series themselves? The Sautrāntikas maintain that the seed-series, at one time non-existent, comes into existence: that is, the effect does not pre-exist.

Hence the Sarvāstivādins, with their appeal to a quasi-substantial essence, end up with a causal theory that threatens to become a Buddhist version of the Sāṃkhya identity theory. The Sautrāntikas, on the other hand, espouse a Buddhist version of the non-identity theory that fails to provide for any kind of necessity in the causal relation. Either way, the possibility of liberation is not guaranteed: the first account is too strong; the second too weak.

This situation provides the context for the Mahāyāna developments. The Yogācārin idealists give up the reality of the external object and join the drift away from epistemological realism. But the Mādhyamikas take a different line, exemplified in the celebrated critique of causation by the second-century Buddhist philosopher Nāgārjuna in his *Mūlamadhyamakakārikā* (Siderits and Katsura 2013). The first chapter of that text famously begins:

> Not from itself, not from another, not from both, nor without cause:
> Never in any way is there any existing thing that has arisen. (1.1)

Here Nāgārjuna refers to and rejects four types of causal theory: (i) self-causation; (ii) external causation; (iii) both (that is, a combination of self- and external causation); and (iv) non-causation. The first type of theory includes the Sāṃkhya identity theory; it also includes the Sarvāstivādin theory. The second type includes the Nyāya non-identity theory; it also includes the

Sautrāntika theory. The third is the Jaina theory. The fourth is the Cārvāka theory.

In a virtuoso dialectical display Nāgārjuna argues that the first option is absurd since it supposes that production of what already exists. The second option is absurd because the cause cannot be totally extraneous to its effect, or anything might cause anything. The third option is also untenable, since it just combines the first two options. The fourth option is unacceptable because it implies randomness and the inefficacy of action.

The last claim makes it clear that Nāgārjuna does not deny causation per se. Rather, causality is interdependence: that is, all things are on a par, dependent on one another. Accordingly, everything is empty (*śūnya*) of an independent essence. But all the causal theories criticized understand causation as an asymmetrical dependence relation with one relatum self-existent and hence more real. Instead the Buddha's teaching of dependent origination is that everything is interdependent, and this is equivalent to the truth of emptiness (*śūnyatā*), that nothing has any self-existence or essence. Liberation is the realization of this emptiness.

Jaina non-absolutism

The Jainas also agree that everything is interdependent. However, they insist too that it is still possible to distinguish the more real from the less real. Jaina non-absolutism (*anekāntavāda*) is the theory that everything in the world has various aspects that permit everything to be seen from various viewpoints. With respect to causation, this means that cause and effect are partly identical and partly non-identical. A cause has a power (*śakti*) to produce an effect and from this viewpoint the effect is pre-existent in the cause. But the effect is a new substance qua its form and from this viewpoint the effect is not pre-existent in its cause. This explains both why a particular effect can only be produced from a particular cause and why an extra effort is needed to bring about that effect. Thus a pot is pre-existent in the clay insofar as its matter is concerned, but not insofar as its shape is concerned. The potter's effort is required to shape the clay into a pot.

The Jaina view seeks, then, to combine the merits of both the identity and non-identity theories, while avoiding the difficulties of each. The theory is also very close to the identity-in-difference (*bhedābheda*) theories of certain theistic Vedāntins. The major difficulty with the theory from its opponents' point of view is that it just doubles the trouble by trying to have things both ways. To the extent that the Jaina theory of causation is a version of the identity theory, the causal relation is too strong to guarantee the possibility of liberation; to the extent that it is a version of the non-identity theory, the causal relation is too weak.

Conclusion

Causation is a concept that is about as central as any to our thinking about the world. Hence David Hume called it 'the cement of the universe', implying that it holds everything together. Moreover, causation plays this role not only with regard to the physical world, but also with regard to the mental and the social dimensions of reality. From our own internal points of view as conscious subjects, however, understanding our nature as selves can seem just as important to our thinking about the nature of reality. And so it was that the Indian philosophers also gave a great deal of attention to the metaphysics of the self, the topic of the next chapter.

Suggestions for further reading

On Advaita Vedānta, see Deutsch 1969, Deutsch and van Buitenen 1971, Potter 1981 and Phillips 1995. On Nyāya-Vaiśeṣika metaphysics, see Potter 1977, Bhaduri 1975, Halbfass 1992 and Phillips 1995. On Indian Buddhist metaphysics, see Siderits 2007. On the Abhidharma ontology, see also Williams 1981. On Nāgārjuna's Madhyamaka, see further Siderits and Katsura 2013, Garfield 1995, 2002, Westerhoff 2009 and Tillemans (forthcoming). On Indian theories of causation, see Potter 1963 and Bhartiya 1973. On Cārvāka, see Chattopadhyaya and Gangopadhyaya 1994. On Sāṃkhya, see Larson 1979 and Larson and Bhattacharya 1987. On Jaina non-absolutism, see Mookerjee 1995.

6 Self

Introduction

The classical Indian philosophers developed highly articulated theories of the self, often claiming a correct understanding of the nature of the self to be a necessary, or sometimes even a sufficient, condition for liberation. Indian theories of the self traditionally divide into two broad classes: those who explain our diachronic and synchronic identity by reference to an enduring substantial self (*ātmavādins*) and those who deny the existence of such a self, taking instead a 'modal' view of reality (*anātmavādins*). The orthodox Hindu philosophers and the Jainas all take the former view. Hence, though they disagree on the nature and number of such selves, they are all non-reductionists of some sort about our identity. Most Indian Buddhist philosophers (including the Theravādins, the Vaibhāṣikas, the Sautrāntikas, the Yogācārins and the Svātantrika-Mādhyamikas) take the latter view and hence are all plausibly classifiable as reductionists about our identity.

This chapter begins by introducing how the problem of the self arises in accounting for the nature and felt unity of our experiences, both at a time and over time. It then goes on to focus in particular on the dualistic theories of Nyāya-Vaiśeṣika and Sāṃkhya-Yoga, the non-dualism of Advaita Vedānta, and the Buddhist 'no-self' theory. Finally, it addresses the issue of the supposed normative implications of these rival Indian theories of the self.

The problem of the self

The problem of the self arose for the ancient Indian philosophers much as it did for Western philosophers. In both traditions one way into the problem is to take the self (*ātman*) to be whatever it is that is the referent of the term 'I' in sentences like 'I am now conscious', 'I cooked this rice', 'I remember attending my daughter's wedding', and so on. Minimally characterized in this way, the existence of the self seems indubitable. Hence the great Advaitin philosopher Śaṃkara (eighth century) claims that denial of the self is just straightforwardly self-refuting, appealing to a sort of *cogito* argument:

> Moreover the existence of Brahman is known on the ground of its being the Self of every one. For every one is conscious of (his) Self, and never thinks 'I am not'. If the existence of the Self were not known, every one would think 'I am not'. And this Self (of whose existence all are conscious) is Brahman. (*Brahmasūtrabhāṣya* I.1.1)

But Śaṃkara also immediately goes on to make it clear that, although the existence of the self in this minimal sense is indubitable, it still remains an open question what the nature of this indubitable self actually is: 'But if Brahman is known as the Self, there is no room for enquiry into it. Not so, for there is a conflict of opinions as to its special nature' (I.1.1). Among the various opinions about the nature of the self that Śaṃkara thinks have to be fought against are the Cārvāka identification of the self with the body, Buddhist 'no-self' theories, and the dualist theories of Nyāya-Vaiśeṣika and Sāṃkhya-Yoga.

Interestingly enough, the Naiyāyika philosopher Uddyotakara (seventh century) says something very similar about the minimal conception of the self in his *Nyāyavārtikka*, notwithstanding that his own developed theory of the self is very different from that of the Advaitins:

> No one actually disagrees about the existence of the self but disagrees only with this or that particular manner of determining its nature, e.g. (as to whether) the self is simply the body or it is the cognitive faculties like the Understanding, or it is a bundle of all these (mental and physical phenomena) or it is some (substance) other than all these. And that is a controversy regarding the specific nature of the self which could not be reasonably raised unless the existence of the self was taken for granted as established. (Chakrabarti 1982: 228)

The development of more detailed theories about the nature of the self is in turn constrained by what assumptions seem most reasonable in order to explain whatever it is that accounts for the truth of various sentences utilizing the term 'I'. For example, some true sentences (like 'I am less than two metres tall') seem to allow for the self to be entirely a physical entity, while others (like 'I am conscious') are not so obviously explicable in terms of an entirely physical self. Again, the truth of sentences like 'I am the very same person as the child in that old photograph' apparently requires that the self can retain its identity over time. Some philosophers claim that this means that the self must be a simple (partless), enduring thing; others claim that the self's diachronic identity is compatible with the self being nothing but a bundle of connected experiences.

The Cārvāka materialists held that the 'I' in sentences like 'I am fat' and 'I am conscious' refer to the very same entity: the body. But this was very much a minority opinion among the Indian philosophers – among other reasons, because it was incompatible with the widespread Indian belief in rebirth. The Buddhists held a 'no-self' (*anātman*) view, which denied that 'I' referred to any single entity at all. Instead persons were conceived of as just bundles of impermanent psycho-physical elements, linked over time by various causal relations. This is tantamount to a denial of the self (*ātman*) insofar as the *ātman* is 'thickly' conceived (as in most Hindu schools) to be an entity that is permanent, a controller, and not subject to suffering (*duḥkha*). The Buddhists argued that the psycho-physical aggregates that apparently compose a person over time clearly have none of these properties and, in the absence of any perceptual or inferential evidence for the existence of anything over and above the aggregates that does have such properties, it is most reasonable to deny the existence of any permanent and impartite self. Conventionally, however, there is no reason not to continue to use the reflexive pronoun, so long as we do not thereby mislead ourselves into thinking there is a permanent self for us to become attached to.

The Hindu philosophers, in contrast, typically defended various forms of self–body dualism according to which the self is a kind of immaterial simple. Nyāya-Vaiśeṣika, for instance, ascribed physical properties to the body and states of consciousness to the self, with the latter conceived of as an impartite non-physical substance. Sāṃkhya-Yoga also maintained a dualist position, but allowed that at least some states of consciousness are physical properties of the physical body.

Nyāya-Vaiśeṣika dualism

The central Nyāya-Vaiśeṣika argument for the existence of a permanent non-physical self is characteristically holistic in form, utilizing their categorical schema already outlined in the previous chapter. Thus Naiyāyikas begin from the implicit premise that not only does our mental life have both diachronic and synchronic unity, but that the best way to account for this is by an appeal to a 'unity of centre' (Broad 1927). In other words, the unity of the mind is to be explained in terms of a particular existent – a centre – that 'owns' the mental events as attributes. In principle, of course, such a centre could be a physical entity; but it seems rather difficult to isolate a plausible physical candidate for the role and the Naiyāyikas accordingly infer that the self, which is the centre that unifies our mental life, is in fact an enduring immaterial substance.

The Nyāya-Vaiśeṣika argumentative strategy for the existence of an enduring immaterial self is effectively an argument by elimination, couched in terms of their ontological categories. As already mentioned, they begin from the presupposition that our mental lives have both diachronic and synchronic unity and that this is best explained by an appeal to a 'unity of centre'. This is taken to be at least part of the moral of the cryptic maxim: 'Desire and hatred, wilful effort, pleasure and pain, and knowledge are the marks of the self' (*Nyāyasūtra* 1.1.10). The leading idea here seems to be that the existence of the continuously existing self can be inferred from the fact that mental states like desire, hatred and so on are directed towards objects that have been experienced to be pleasant or painful in the past. And this in turn is taken to imply that the subject of those present mental states is a single enduring entity that is the very same self as the subject of those past experiences.

What kind of entity, then, could this centre be in terms of the developed Nyāya-Vaiśeṣika sevenfold categorical schema? Naiyāyikas argue, firstly, that the mental events comprising our mental lives are impermanent and so cannot belong to the categories of universal, particularity or inherence, since these are all permanent entities. Secondly, since a mental event inheres in only a single substance, whereas a substance or an action inheres in many substances, mental events must by elimination be qualities. But qualities require a substance to serve as the substratum they inhere in (there are no 'free-floating' qualities in the Nyāya-Vaiśeṣika ontology). Finally, this substance must be indivisible, otherwise it cannot serve as a true 'unity of centre'. After all, if we were to allow that the unifying self has parts, then what unifies those parts in such a way as to make them all parts of the same self? A 'super-self'? On pain of regress, then, the self must be indivisible. This indivisibility, however, implies that the self cannot be the body, which is clearly divisible. Thus the Nyāya-Vaiśeṣika argument by elimination concludes that mental events must inhere in a simple, non-physical substance: an eternal self (*ātman*).

Of course, this argument by elimination will likely seem theory-bound to those not already committed to the Nyāya-Vaiśeṣika metaphysics, but a Naiyāyika would reply with a counter-challenge: show me a fully developed rival metaphysical theory that better explains the phenomena of our experience! If rival metaphysical theories have to be compared holistically relative to criteria like explanatory power, consistency and simplicity, then establishing that the Nyāya-Vaiśeṣika system is, all things considered, inferior to a rival system is obviously no simple matter. This is because, much as is the case with scientific theories, a metaphysical theory may do better than a rival on one vector but do worse on other vectors in such a way that determining which theory is, all things considered, the most plausible is a matter on which rational agents may justifiably disagree. For instance, though the Buddhists certainly offer a simpler metaphysical theory in that they posit far fewer kinds of entities than does Nyāya-Vaiśeṣika, Naiyāyikas object that Buddhist attempts to explain the unity of our mental lives in terms of a mere 'unity of system' fail to do justice to the phenomenology of our experience, particularly our pervasive sense of our *ownership* of our own mental states, both at a time and over time. (Buddhists, of course, do not need to deny the existence of such a felt sense of self, but they will insist that, ultimately, it is in fact an illusion that needs *explaining away*, rather than explaining.)

Be that as it may, a few words about the specific nature of Nyāya-Vaiśeṣika psycho-physical dualism are appropriate here. As we have seen, Nyāya-Vaiśeṣika conceives of the self as a permanent, immaterial substance that possesses perceptible qualia like cognition and desire. This view obviously has a certain resemblance to Cartesian mind–body dualism in Western philosophy – the theory that there is a sharp distinction between the mind and the body, with the body being one kind of substance and the mind quite another. There are, however, also important differences between Descartes' views and the views of Nyāya-Vaiśeṣika.

One respect in which Nyāya dualism is significantly distinct from Cartesian dualism is in holding that the immaterial self has location, though not extension. This apparently enables them to evade the familiar 'locus of interaction' problem that plagues Cartesian interactionism: exactly *where* can the immaterial and unextended Cartesian self causally interact with the material and extended body? However, if the immaterial-location claim is to be intelligible, Nyāya dualism surely also owes us a developed ontology of immaterial points that are distinct from material points, even though the spatial properties of the two kinds of points are indistinguishable.

Another difference from Cartesianism is that whereas Descartes held thinking to be the essence of the soul, Naiyāyikas hold thought to be an adventitious attribute of the self – as evidenced in dreamless sleep, where the self endures but is not characterized by any type of consciousness (a claim Descartes denied). Thus for Nyāya, while the self is an immaterial substance that may become conscious, it is not itself mental in nature. This is because the Nyāya-Vaiśeṣika metaphysical argument for the self we rehearsed earlier seems to conceive of the self quite minimally as being just that entity – a centre – which guarantees diachronic and synchronic identity. But this minimalist conception of the self was in turn a point of contention with other Hindu schools, who argued that it threatens to undermine the very desirability of *mokṣa*: thus the Advaitin jibe that liberation for Nyāya-Vaiśeṣika is to become like a stone, since it is to become a pure substance devoid of all qualities including consciousness and feeling. On this latter score, at least, the dualism of the Sāṃkhya-Yoga school is a little better off in that in their system sentience is conceived of as the very substance of the self and hence the liberated self cannot be insentient.

Sāṃkhya-Yoga dualism

Whereas Nyāya dualism is, notwithstanding its distinctness, strongly reminiscent of Cartesian dualism, Sāṃkhya-Yoga dualism is rather different from any Western dualism. Sāṃkhya-Yoga, the most ancient Indian philosophical school, is uncontroversially a kind of metaphysical dualism since it posits just two fundamental categories of reality: *puruṣa* (self, consciousness) and *prakṛti* (nature, matter). Suffering is caused by our confusion of *puruṣa* with *prakṛti* and emancipation follows from correct understanding of the real nature of *puruṣa* and its difference from *prakṛti*. In the Sāṃkhya texts – especially in Īśvarakṛṣṇa's *Sāṃkhyakārikā* (Larson 1979) – rational arguments are presented for some of the school's major theses. Thus the existence of *puruṣa* is argued for (*Kārikā* 18) on the grounds that consciousness exists and distinctions in the world are *for* this consciousness, which is itself apart from the world. Moreover there must be a plurality of *puruṣas* because otherwise whatever happens to one consciousness will happen at the same time to every consciousness, which is contrary to the perceived diversity of births, deaths and faculties (18).

Prakṛti, on the other hand, is a unitary material substance which evolves in the world we perceive through our senses. The proximity of *puruṣa* acts as a catalyst in releasing the causal transformation of primordial nature (*mūlaprakṛti*) into the whole of the perceptible world (20). The order in which *prakṛti* evolves is laid down in the following scheme. First, the pure contentless consciousness of the *puruṣa* becomes focused on the *prakṛti* and out of this delimitation evolves *mahat* or *buddhi* (intellect). The *buddhi* then evolves the ego consciousness (*ahaṃkāra*), which leads to the misidentification of the true self with the ego. From *ahaṃkāra* evolves the *manas* (mind); from *manas*, the five sensory organs and the five motor organs; then the five *tanmātrās* or subtle elements (sound, touch, form, taste and smell) and the five *bhūtas* or gross elements (ether, air, fire, water and earth). Sāṃkhya thus recognizes twenty-four principles (*tattvas*) in all, evolving out of *mūlaprakṛti* in this order. The twenty-fifth (and independent) *tattva* is *puruṣa*.

The school of Yoga (classically expounded in Patañjali's *Yogasūtra*) broadly accepts this Sāṃkhya ontology. Moreover, as well as being in fundamental agreement on most ontological matters, Sāṃkhya and Yoga also agree on the nature of the *summum bonum*. This is a radical isolation (*kaivalya*) of the true self from ordinary human experience. Liberation, the highest good, occurs when the *puruṣa* recognizes its real nature as absolutely distinct from *prakṛti*. In other words, transcendent value is associated with the realization of our essential nature as pure consciousnesses ontologically separate from our physical bodies.

It is important to note, however, that while Sāṃkhya-Yoga insists on a dualism of *puruṣa* and *prakṛti*, this is not a Western-style mind–body dualism. The active, personal self-consciousness in Sāṃkhya is associated with the material principles of *buddhi*, *ahaṃkāra* and *manas*, that is, the first evolutes of *prakṛti* (collectively termed the *antaḥkaraṇa*). This raises an interesting question: exactly where do Sāṃkhya-Yoga dualists stand on the mind–body problem?

Sāṃkhya-Yoga and the mind–body problem

To answer the question, 'Exactly where do Sāṃkhya-Yoga dualists stand on the mind-body problem?', we first need a characterization of the problem. There are various possibilities in the literature. A popular one is the *Mental States Characterization*. According to this view, the mind–body problem is posed by the following question: 'Are there mental states distinct from physical states?' At least three possible answers can be found defended in the modern Western philosophical literature. These are:

Dualism: There are mental states and they are not physical states.

Reductionism: There are mental states but they are physical states.

Eliminativism: There are no mental states, only physical states.

(The difference between reductionism and eliminativism is perhaps best captured in semantic terms. Reductionists do not object to continued talk of mental states, though they think all such states are reducible to physical states. Eliminativists instead hope to eliminate all talk of mental states and replace it with a suitably physicalist vocabulary.)

The mental states characterization, however, is not the only way the mind–body problem can be posed. A different way is the *Person Characterization*. According to this view, the mind–body problem is posed by the following question: 'Do persons have mental states distinct from physical states?' Again, at least three possible answers are defended in recent Western philosophy:

Dualism: Persons have mental states and these are not physical states.

Reductionism: Persons have mental states, but these are physical states.

Eliminativism: Persons do not have mental states, only physical states.

It is important to notice that the first two characterizations are not logically equivalent. One could consistently be a dualist or a reductionist on the mental states characterization without correspondingly being a dualist or a reductionist on the person characterization: for instance, all one (implausibly) needs to do is to affirm the existence of mental states but deny that persons have them. (Eliminativists on the mental states characterization, of course, are logically committed to being eliminativists on the person characterization: if there are no mental states, persons cannot have them.) As a matter of historical fact, of course, Western philosophers have naturally tended to align their positions so that they come out the same on both characterizations. But these historical correlations should not be allowed to blur the logical distinctness of the two characterizations, for this will become a matter of some significance when we look at Sāṃkhya-Yoga.

So where does Sāṃkhya-Yoga stand on the mind–body problem? The answer is that it depends on how we characterize the problem. Consider first the mental states characterization: 'Are there mental states distinct from physical states?' Sāṃkhya-Yoga clearly admits the existence of mental states, but the Sāṃkhya-Yoga answer to this question is further complicated by the fact that they are willing to admit both intentional mental states (*citta-vṛtti* or *antaḥkaraṇa-vṛtti*) that are object-directed and non-intentional mental states (*puruṣa* or 'pure consciousness') that are not object-directed. Given this admission of both intentional and non-intentional mental states, the original question about mental states needs to be disambiguated.

The Sāṃkhya-Yoga position on the existence of mental states, then, is that they affirm both of the following two theses:

(T_1) There are non-intentional mental states and they are not physical states.

(T_2) There are intentional mental states and they are physical states.

In other words, in terms of the mental states characterization of the mind–body problem Sāṃkhya-Yoga is *dualist* with respect to non-intentional mental states, but *reductionist* with respect to intentional mental states. (This is because pure consciousness states are states of the non-physical *puruṣa*, but intentional mental states are states of the most subtle evolutes of *prakṛti* and hence physical.)

When we pose the mind–body problem in terms of the person characterization, however, Sāṃkhya-Yoga comes out differently. Of course, it depends on what 'person' means here and, as eliminativists about persons like to remind us, the common-sense notion of a person is none too well defined. We can perhaps get some purchase on the notion, though, with the following strategy: I am a person and you are too, and so is anything that significantly resembles us. The theory of personhood is thus the explication of just what these significant resemblances are. In Indian thought the notion of a person is similarly vague, but one entirely natural, non-technical Sanskrit translation of 'person' is '*puruṣa*'. Sāṃkhya-Yoga begins from this ordinary sense of '*puruṣa*' and then offers a theory of what personhood consists in.

How, then, does Sāṃkhya-Yoga answer the question: 'Do persons have mental states distinct from physical states?' Once again, they insist on distinguishing two types of mental states and then they affirm the following two theses:

(T_3) Persons (*puruṣas*) have non-intentional mental states and these are not physical states.

(T_4) Persons (*puruṣas*) do not have intentional mental states and these are physical states.

In other words, in terms of the person characterization of the mind–body problem, Sāṃkhya-Yoga is *dualist* with respect to non-intentional mental states, but *eliminativist* with respect to intentional mental states.

Much of the interest in asking where Sāṃkhya-Yoga stands on the mind–body problem is because it seems difficult to fit it easily into the familiar Western categories (it is clearly dualist with respect to the *puruṣa–prakṛti* division, but this is not a Cartesian mind–body dualism; and so on). Our analysis clarifies precisely where Sāṃkhya-Yoga stands on the mind–body problem: in terms of the mental states characterization of the mind–body problem, Sāṃkhya-Yoga is dualist and reductionist; in terms of the person characterization of the mind–body problem, Sāṃkhya-Yoga is dualist and eliminativist. The possibility of being reductionist about the mind–body problem on one familiar characterization and eliminativist on another equally familiar characterization is not one that we find instanced in the history of Western philosophy. (Of course, part of the explanation for this is that we do not find that the notion of non-intentional pure consciousness states has enjoyed much general currency in Western philosophy.)

The Sāṃkhya-Yoga dualism, then, is perhaps less of a mind–body dualism than a consciousness–mind dualism. In Sāṃkhya-Yoga the representational mental states typically associated with the mind in Western philosophy are all states of the more refined evolutes of matter (*prakṛti*). Consciousness is instead essentially associated with the non-representational pure awareness of the *puruṣa*. The intentional mental states associated with the material *antaḥkaraṇa* are unconscious (*acetana*) and not to be confused with the pure consciousness of the *puruṣa* (*Sāṃkhyakārikā* 20).

Advaita Vedānta non-dualism

Common to both Nyāya-Vaiśeṣika and Sāṃkhya-Yoga is a belief that there are many selves. Common to both Sāṃkhya-Yoga and Advaita Vedānta (but not Nyāya-Vaiśeṣika) is a belief that the self is essentially pure consciousness. An obvious difficulty for the Sāṃkhya-Yoga doctrine of a plurality of immaterial pure consciousnesses is what could possibly distinguish one such consciousness from another. The Advaitin response is to accept the intelligibility of a pure, contentless consciousness, but to insist that there can be only *one* such conscious self. The crux of Advaita is the assertion of non-duality between this single Self (*ātman*) and the Absolute (*Brahman*). Advaita interprets the famous Upaniṣadic dictum '*tat tvam asi*' ('that art thou') to mean that *Brahman* and *ātman* are in reality one. The highest truth (*paramārtha*) is that there exists only one supreme contentless consciousness, although in terms of our ordinary (*vyāvahārika*) knowledge it is proper to talk of individual transmigrating selves (*jīvas*).

How do Advaitins argue for such an extremely radical metaphysics of the self? Over the long history of Advaita Vedānta a variety of strategies have been employed, but the original strategy of Śaṃkara, the effective founder of the school, was essentially apologetic: he argued (i) that Advaita gives us the best account of various scriptural passages, and (ii) that nothing in the theory is contradicted by our experience.

The first claim is necessary for Śaṃkara because he is an adherent of a school of Vedānta and all the schools of Vedānta claim to be based upon the Upaniṣads, notwithstanding their often very different interpretations of those texts. For Śaṃkara's view of the Self, two Upaniṣads are particularly important inspirations. One is the *Chāndogya Upaniṣad*, especially the sixth chapter of that text where the young Śvetaketu is instructed by his father as to the true nature of his deepest Self:

> That which is the finest essence – this whole world has that as its Self. That is reality. That is *ātman*. That art thou [*tat tvam asi*] Śvetaketu. (6.8.7)

Śaṃkara understands this famous 'great saying' (*mahāvākya*) as teaching an identity between *Brahman* and the individual self, ultimately denying any difference between the consciousness of the individual self and the consciousness that is *Brahman*. (Vedāntins of other schools often understand this passage as merely affirming some type of similarity, rather than identity, between *ātman* and *Brahman*.)

The other Upaniṣad particularly influential on Śaṃkara's view of the self is the *Māṇḍūkya Upaniṣad*, which outlines a four-level analysis of consciousness: waking consciousness, dream consciousness, deep sleep, and transcendental consciousness (*turīya*, 'the fourth'). The leading idea here seems to be that there is no discontinuity of consciousness, but just one consciousness (associated with *ātman*) that appears in different states. And in deep dreamless sleep we do have a glimpse of this pure consciousness without a content.

Once again, Vedāntins of other subschools dispute this reading of the text. The eleventh-century Viśiṣṭādvaitin philosopher Rāmānuja, for example, emphatically rejects the idea of a pure, contentless consciousness. Instead consciousness is irreducibly intentional: it is always *someone's* consciousness of *something*. Here he appeals to ordinary usage: '... as appears from ordinary judgments such as "I know the jar", "I understand this matter", "I am conscious of (the presence of) this piece of cloth"' (*Śrībhāṣya* 1.1). Moreover, Rāmānuja rejects the Advaitin analysis of the deep sleep state. Instead, when content is lost from consciousness, as when the individual passes from the waking or dreaming state into the state of deep dreamless sleep, what we say is not that he is now aware of contentless consciousness, but that he is *unconscious*. As evidence, Rāmānuja draws our attention to the way in which we express the state of deep dreamless sleep to ourselves and others. This is 'by the thought presenting itself to the person risen from sleep, "For so long a time I was not conscious of anything"' (*Śrībhāṣya* 1.1).

Whatever may be the most plausible exegesis of these Upaniṣadic texts, however, it is the second plank of Śaṃkara's original strategy that is of more directly philosophical interest: namely, his surprising insistence that nothing in the Advaitin theory of the self is contradicted by our experience. Replying to the obvious objection that we are not directly aware of the Self he describes, he invokes an anti-reflexivity principle accepted by most Indian philosophers (both Hindu and Buddhist): the self as *subject* cannot be a *object* for itself, much as a knife cannot cut itself. Thus it is only to be expected that I cannot directly apprehend myself in my discriminated awareness as being a subject, an *ātman*. Śaṃkara goes on to claim, though, that we nevertheless do have an immediate intuition of an 'I' that is prior to all particular contents of consciousness (this is the implication of his '*cogito*' argument cited earlier).

But what of the appearance in our experience of a multiplicity of individual selves? According to Advaita, such individual selves are unreal; or more precisely, the individual human person (the *jīva*) is a combination of reality and appearance. It is real insofar as *ātman* is its ground, but it is unreal insofar as it is identified as finite, conditioned and relative.

There still remains, of course, a cluster of problems about the nature of the *jīva* and its relation to *ātman/Brahman*. Two influential models were offered. The first is reflectionism (*pratibimbavāda*), whereby the *jīva* is said to reflect the *ātman*. It is thus (like a reflection in a mirror) not entirely distinct from the prototype, but neither is it to be identified with the prototype. The second is limitationism (*avacchedavāda*), whereby the *ātman* is said to be like space and individual *jīvas* like space in jars. When the jars are destroyed, the space which they enclosed remains part of space. Two important subschools of Advaita divide in particular upon which model to prefer: the Vivaraṇa school favours reflectionism and the Bhāmatī school favours limitationism. The discussion of the merits and demerits of each model is one of the major concerns of post-Śaṃkara Advaita.

Post-Śaṃkara debates on Self and selves

As far as these post-Śaṃkara Advaita philosophers are concerned, there are some very important issues at stake here. It is not enough just to find an analogy to indicate that there is no contradiction implied in holding that the one Self is somehow 'in' many individual *jīvas*. The relevant analogy has also to guarantee that liberation is feasible.

Now Śaṃkara is emphatic that only *ātman/Brahman* is real, that the appearance of multiple individual selves is a product of ignorance (*avidyā*), and that liberation involves realizing these truths. But ignorance has to be the ignorance *of* someone *about* something: it must have a conscious locus (*āśraya*) in which it exists and an object (*viṣaya*) which it conceals. So, in terms of the Advaitin metaphysics of the self, whose is the ignorance here? Presumably not *Brahman*'s, for surely *ātman/Brahman* is free of any ignorance. But presumably not the individual selves' (*jīva*) either, for they are a *product* of ignorance and cannot be the locus of what is logically and causally prior to them.

Faced with this dilemma, Advaitins of the Vivaraṇa school effectively accept the first horn and argue that *Brahman* is the locus of ignorance, while those of the Bhāmatī school effectively accept the second horn and argue that the *jīva* is the locus of ignorance. (Both schools, of course, have no difficulty in agreeing that *Brahman* is the *object* of ignorance.)

Consider first the Bhāmatī position, associated with the commentary of that name by Vācaspati Miśra (tenth century) on a portion of Śaṃkara's

Brahmasūtrabhāṣya (Sastri and Raja 1933). Vācaspati accepts that the individual selves are the locus of ignorance, since *Brahman* cannot be ignorant. He also insists that there are many such selves, for otherwise – contrary to both experience and testimony – the liberation of one would entail the liberation of all. Finally, there are many ignorances, a different one for each self. The Bhāmatī limitationism model is in turn supposed to explain how the many selves are related to the one Self: the *ātman* is said to be like space and individual *jīvas* like space in jars so that when the jars are destroyed, the space which they enclosed remains part of space. The limitations are only conceptual: the Self is essentially unlimited and real.

But what about the circularity objection to accepting the first horn of the dilemma above? The Bhāmatī reply is that the appearance of circularity is defused once we realize there are actually two distinct series here: (i) a series of successive individual lives of the same self as it reincarnates, and (ii) a series of ignorances. These two series are different in that my present ignorance causes my future birth, but my present birth is the product of my past ignorance in my past birth. Both series are, of course, beginningless and hence too is their interaction. Since there is no time when ignorance is and the self is not (or vice versa), all we have here is a virtuous infinite regress, not a vicious circle.

Whether the threat of circularity is thus averted so easily was a matter of controversy among other Advaitins. But putting that issue aside for a moment, it is obvious that the Bhāmatī position would be threatened if there were only *one* individual self. Although Vācaspati accepts that both experience and testimony make it reasonable to support the common-sense view that there are many selves, he does not go quite so far as to assert the *impossibility* of there being only a single self. That possibility was in fact an option explored by some Advaitins. Thus Sarvajñātman (tenth century) believed that a consistent Advaitin monism implies that ignorance must reside in *Brahman*, not the *jīva*; that there is only one ignorance; and there is only one individual self. So while it may seem that some are freed while others remain bound, this appearance is in fact nothing but the kind of confusion about the temporal order of events that we sometimes experience in dreams (*Saṃkṣepaśārīraka* II.129–31; Veezhinathan 1972).

An even more extreme example of this 'one self' trend is the case of Prakāśānanda (sixteenth century) and his version of metaphysical solipsism (*dṛṣṭisṛṣṭivāda*, the theory that perception is creation). According to his

Vedāntasiddhāntamuktāvalī (Venis 1898), there is only one real entity, *Brahman*, which we call the 'self' under the delusion of ignorance. Hence there is really only one liberation, that of the one self, and *jīvanmukti* or living liberation on the part of other selves is but a sham liberation.

Metaphysical solipsism, however, is very much a minority option within Advaita. Instead, Advaitins of the Vivaraṇa school, like Prakāśātman (thirteenth century), typically accept a plurality of *jīvas* while also holding that the individual self is nothing different from the Self (*ātman*). It is because of ignorance that we see our individual selves rather than their prototype, the Self. This is where the reflectionist model is invoked to explain how the *jīva* is said to reflect the *ātman*. It is (like a reflection in a mirror) not entirely distinct from the prototype, but neither is it to be identified with the prototype. Liberation is then identified with the realization that the individual self is just a reflection (*pratibimba*) of the one Self, rather than with a sudden transcendence of ordinary consciousness. Hence it makes sense too to suppose that other selves continue to exist after one becomes liberated.

The Vivaraṇa's reflection analogy here is, of course, self-admittedly imperfect in that the image in a mirror is insentient and hence cannot (like the self) think of itself as different from its prototype (the Self), nor discover that it is identical. But ultimately Advaitins of either subschool are willing to concede that analogies are inevitably limited and in the end are only of instrumental value insofar as they are conducive to the realization of the identity of the self with the Self.

The Bhāmatī and Vivaraṇa subschools do not, however, exhaust the variety of views in post-Śaṃkara Advaita. Another trend takes its inspiration from the work of Sureśvara (ninth century), a direct disciple of Śaṃkara, and pushes even further the instrumentalist themes implicit in Bhāmatī and Vivaraṇa. Thus at the beginning of Book 3 of his *Naiṣkarmayasiddhi*, Sureśvara addresses the issue of whether ignorance resides in *Brahman* or the selves and concludes that 'it is the Self alone which is both the locus (*āśraya*) of and the object (*viṣaya*) concealed by ignorance'. This might seem to align him with the Vivaraṇa position and hence open him to the Bhāmatī objections that he is thereby unfortunately committed (i) to *Brahman* being ignorant and hence having to be freed, and (ii) to everyone being freed at the same time as *Brahman* is.

Sureśvara, however, has little patience with such dialectical moves. First, his own position is that, strictly speaking, *Brahman* is not a kind of thing that can or cannot be a locus (*pace* both Bhāmatī and Vivaraṇa). Second, since ignorance is not a thing at all, the dispute between Bhāmatī and Vivaraṇa about how many primal ignorances there are is a meaningless fuss about a question that does not even arise.

Consider here Sureśvara's brisk response to an objector trying to press the question of whether it is *Brahman* or the *jīva* that is liberated:

> *Objection*: Is the teaching for the highest Self or for the lower self? *Answer*: What are you driving at? *Objection*: If the teaching is for the highest Self, then because it is already liberated anyway without the teaching, the teaching is useless. But if the teaching is for the lower self, then, the lower self being irrevocably transmigrant by nature, the teaching has no chance to succeed. So both views are faulty. *Answer*:... The statement of the Veda [about the higher and lower self in their nondiscriminated condition] becomes intelligible if it be assumed that it is made in accordance with the standpoint of one not discriminating (the ego, the Self and the reflection of consciousness). The teaching of 'that art thou', however, has to be directed to one who through lack of deep discrimination has made only superficial intellectual discrimination between Self and not-Self. The holy texts are meaningful to those who know the difference between the Self and the not-Self. When the difference between the Self and the not-Self is not known, pronouncing the holy text is about as useful as singing songs before an assembly of the deaf. (*Naiṣkarmyasiddhi* 4.19–21; Alston 1971)

The central lesson here is that while Advaitins of both the Bhāmatī and Vivaraṇa subschools identify enlightenment with the realization of the identity of self and Self, Sureśvara identifies it with the absolute disappearance of even the appearance of not-Self: 'And between the world (as false superimposition) and the rock-firm Self there is no connection except ignorance, and wherever (in the Veda) a positive identity or connection is affirmed between the two, that is to be interpreted as forming part of an injunction to perform symbolic meditation' (*Naiṣkarmyasiddhi* 3, comm.). Predictably, the implication for later Advaita of this way of thinking is to significantly limit the scope of philosophical reasoning. Metaphysical theorizing about the self comes to be thought of as being of only very limited, instrumental use. Instead – particularly in the cases of the late Advaitin dialecticians Śrīharṣa (twelfth century) and Citsukha (thirteenth century) – the appropriate role of philosophical reasoning is taken to be largely negative; critically reducing to incoherence the metaphysical pretensions of non-Advaitin opponents in order to clear the ground for the reality of non-distinctness to be discovered in meditation.

Buddhist 'no-self' theory

In contrast to the Hindu views of the self that we have been discussing so far, the Indian Buddhist tradition is traditionally associated with the doctrine of 'no-self' (*anātman*). But what is the nature of the self that Indian Buddhists take themselves to be denying? If we are asking about the views of Gautama Buddha as reported in the early Pali texts, then the answer seems to be that the Buddha denied the existence of anything like the Upaniṣadic Self. More specifically, the Buddha denied that there is any element that is part of a person, such that (1) it is permanent, (2) the person has control over that element, and (3) it does not lead to suffering (*duḥkha*) – all three features being characteristic, of course, of the Upaniṣadic *ātman*.

Instead the Buddha offers an analysis of the person as a bundle of five types of psycho-physical states. These are the five aggregates (*skandhas*): material form, feelings, perceptions, intentions/volitions, and consciousness. And none of these five aggregates can plausibly be a candidate for the role of the *ātman* since none of them is permanent, obeys the person of whom they are the aggregates, and is free from suffering.

The Buddha described impermanence, suffering and no-self as being the three marks of conditioned things, but he was not interested in elaborate abstract philosophizing about them. Hence fuller articulation of the metaphysics of the Buddhist no-self doctrine in India is to be found in the work of later Buddhist philosophers. As we saw earlier, in the Indian Abhidharma traditions impermanence is understood to imply momentariness and no-self to imply the decomposition of all partite entities into impartite *dharmas*. Thus the person is ultimately nothing more than a bundle of momentary *dharmas* and so not a candidate for being a universal Self in the Upaniṣadic sense, nor even an individual self in the manner of Nyāya-Vaiśeṣika or Sāmkhya-Yoga.

Right at the beginning of the ninth chapter of the *Abhidharmakośa*, Vasubandhu insists on the crucial soteriological importance of this *anātman* doctrine:

> [There is] no liberation to be found outside of this [teaching of the Buddha]... Owing to preoccupation with false views of the self... [our

> opponents] have not determined that the conceptual construction 'self' refers to the bundle-continuum alone... They imagine that the self is a discrete substance. Moreover the negative afflictions are born from grasping-as-self. (Kapstein 2001: 350)

Vasubandhu then goes on to present the main reasons for believing the *anātman* doctrine to be true: 'Because there is neither acquaintance with nor inference to [the posited self]'. Vasubandhu's reasoning here is that there are, according to Buddhist epistemologists, only two valid sources of knowledge (*pramāṇa*): perception and inference. Clearly, we do not perceive the self since everything we perceive is impermanent, uncontrollable and prone to suffering – features incompatible with the Hindu conception of a self. Nor is there any reasonable inference to the existence of the self, since the diachronic and synchronic unity of our experiences is more economically explicable as a unity of system, rather than a unity of centre.

The *ātmavādin* philosophers responded to both of Vasubandhu's claims. First, they invoke their anti-reflexivity principle: the self as *subject* cannot be an *object* for itself, any more than a knife can cut itself. Thus it is only to be expected that I cannot directly apprehend myself in my discriminated awareness as being a subject, an *ātman*. In other words, non-apprehension of the self does not establish its non-existence, but only that it is not a sensory object.

Secondly, they deny that there is no good inferential argument for the existence of the self. Instead they claim that a variety of phenomena – including memory, rebirth, and reference to apparently persisting subjects – are better explained in terms of the existence of enduring substantial selves than in terms of successive bundles of causally connected aggregates or *dharmas*. Vasubandhu squarely faces up to this latter challenge and tries to show that in fact the Buddhist no-self theory is both more economical ontologically and at least as explanatorily adequate as its rivals. Hence it is more reasonable to believe there is no self than to believe that there is.

Consider, for instance, the phenomenon of first-person memory, which both Naiyāyikas and Advaitins argue is incompatible with the Buddhist no-self theory. Vātsyāyana offers a brisk statement of the Nyāya version of the objection in these words:

> It is a commonplace [when speaking of] of a single being that memory is of what of he himself has perceived, not of what another has perceived.

> Similarly, it is a commonplace [when speaking of] of diverse beings, that what one has perceived is not remembered by another. Neither of these two [commonplaces] can be established by the non-self advocate. Therefore it is proven: The self is. (*Nyāyabhāṣya* 1.1.10; Kapstein 2001: 379)

Śaṃkara's statement of the Advaitin version of the argument is somewhat fuller:

> The philosopher who maintains that all things are momentary only would have to extend that doctrine to the perceiving person . . . also; that is, however, not possible, on account of the remembrance which is consequent on the original perception. That remembrance can take place only if it belongs to the same person who previously made the perception; for we observe that what one man has experienced is not remembered by another man. How, indeed, could there arise the conscious state expressed in the sentences, 'I saw that thing, and now I see this thing,' if the seeing person were not in both cases the same? That the consciousness of recognition takes place only in the case of the observing and remembering subject being one, is a matter known to every one; for if there were, in the two cases, different subjects, the state of consciousness arising in the mind of the remembering person would be, 'I remember; another person made the observation.' But no such state of consciousness does arise. (*Brahmasūtrabhāṣya* II.2.25)

Both versions of the objection, however, seem to share a common leading idea: namely, that when I now remember eating my breakfast yesterday morning I do more than just remember that breakfast was eaten that morning – I also remember 'from the inside' *my* eating it. In other words, I remember that I am the *very same person* who ate that breakfast. (My memories of you eating your breakfast, in contrast, are not memories 'from the inside' in this fashion.) So veridical first-person memories of this sort imply the existence of an enduring self, which is the subject of the memory.

Vasubandhu rejects such an account of memory as being possible only if there is a continuously existing substance that both had the experience and is now remembering it. Instead he analyzes a person as being a series of causally related momentary person-stages, with memory the result of a chain of momentary impressions (*vāsanās*) occurring in a series of person-stages. The original experience of a person-stage at one time gives rise to a memory experience for a person-stage at a later time, where the later person-stage is causally related to the earlier person-stage in the right sort of way. Those parts of the causal series that cause the memory get treated as the subject of experience, but there is no ultimately real thing that has experiences and later remembers them. It is only the *dharmas* in the causal series that are ultimately real.

Vasubandhu says analogous things too in response to another of his critics' objections: namely, the objection that the no-self theory cannot adequately account for the nature of karma and rebirth. Both Vasubandhu and his opponents accept that rebirth occurs and that it is supposed to be governed by karmic causal laws such that people get what they deserve. But his opponents ask how can rebirth occur if it is not one and the same being who dies and is reborn? And how can karma operate justly if it is not one and the same being who both performs the action and reaps the punishment or reward? Surely, they say, only the presence of a continuously existing self can guarantee that the being in question is indeed the very same being.

Vasubandhu rejects these claims of his opponents. For him a person is just a collection of momentary *dharmas* and a reborn person is linked to the being that died by a causal process. The reborn person is not strictly identical with the dead person, but because there is the right sort of causal dependence, neither is he or she completely different in the way you and I are different persons. Instead, the reborn one is, as the canonical Buddhist formula in the *Milindapañha* (II.2.1) puts it, 'neither the same nor another' (*na ca so na ca añño*). Similarly, in matters of karma all that is required for just punishment or reward is that my karmic heir be linked to me by the right sort of causal dependence, not that he or she be strictly identical with me.

That Buddhist no-self theory can really vindicate the doctrines of karma and rebirth in this way was disputed not only (predictably enough) by the Hindu *ātmavādins*, but also by a school of Buddhists known as the Pudgalavādins – indeed, much of the ninth chapter of Vasubandhu's *Abhidharmakośa* is devoted to an attack on the Pudgalavāda doctrine. Very few of the texts of the Pudgalavāda school survive and hence most of our knowledge of their views comes from the (quite possibly biased) texts of their Buddhist opponents. According to Vasubandhu, however, the Pudgalavādins affirmed the existence of a *pudgala* (person) who is neither a primary existent (a *dravya*) nor a secondary existent (a *prajñapti*). This *pudgala* is in turn supposed to be neither the same nor different from the aggregates. It is the subject of experiences, the agent of wholesome or unwholesome acts, that which undergoes karmic consequences, and that which is reborn.

Vasubandhu is predictably unimpressed by this doctrine and presents the Pudgalavādins with a dilemma: either the *pudgala* is reducible to the *dharmas* that make up the aggregates, or it has a separate reality. On the first alternative, the Pudgalavādin position collapses into the usual Buddhist no-self doctrine; on the second alternative, the *pudgala* is just another name for the Hindu *ātman* rejected by all Buddhists.

Whether or not this is a fair summary of their situation, it is significant that the Pudgalavādins seem to have been at least partially motivated by a sense of dissatisfaction with the way that standard Buddhist no-self theory deals with the doctrines of karma and rebirth. Apparently underpinning their dissatisfaction here is a widely held assumption about the appropriate normative implications of an adequate theory of the self – an assumption common to all the Indian philosophers (both Hindu and Buddhist) whose views on the self we have been discussing so far in this chapter. As we shall see, however, it is not an assumption that was unchallenged by *all* Indian philosophers.

The normative implications of theories of the self

In Western philosophy it has typically been assumed that an adequate metaphysics of the self should not only account for our diachronic and synchronic identity but also capture the link between identity and what have been called 'the four features': survival, moral responsibility, self-interested concern, and compensation (Schechtman 1996: 2). Indeed this is true of both *reductionist* and *non-reductionist* theories of the self in Western philosophy: that is, both theories that hold our identity just consists in the holding of certain facts that can be described without making reference to our identity, and theories that deny this (Parfit 1984). Thus, on the one hand, non-reductionism assumes that our normative practices are in need of a 'deep' metaphysical justification and posits 'superlative selves' to do the job. Indeed many have held that without such superlative selves we cannnot ground the four features properly in our identity. Reductionism, on the other hand, denies the existence of such superlative selves, but nevertheless instead tries to ground the four features in other metaphysical facts. In other words, both non-reductionism and reductionism share a common assumption:

> *The Grounding Assumption*: The justification of our normative practices with respect to the four features requires that they be grounded in facts about our identity, or in those facts to which identity is reducible.

How does all this relate to Indian thinking about the philosophy of the self? Firstly, the Western debate about reductionist and non-reductionist theories of our identity parallels in many respects the debate in classical Indian philosophy between those (the *ātmavādins*) who explain diachronic identity by reference to an enduring substantial self and those (the *anātmavādins*) who deny the existence of such a self, taking instead a mode-oriented view of reality. The orthodox Hindu philosophers take the former view: although they disagree on the nature and number of such selves, they are all non-reductionists of some sort. (This includes the Advaitins, who are certainly non-reductionists about the Self, even if – as we saw – the precise ontological status of the empirical self is a matter of intramural controversy for them.) In contrast, most Indian Buddhist philosophers (including the Theravādins, the Vaibhāṣikas, the Sautrāntikas, the Yogācārins and the Svātantrika-Mādhyamikas) take the latter view and hence are plausibly classifiable as reductionists about our identity.

These Buddhist philosophers also would have agreed that reductionism has normative significance. It is a familiar claim of the Buddhist tradition that the correct understanding of the self is necessary for liberation from suffering; it is also a claim made by Hindu non-reductionists. The normative importance of a correct analysis of our identity, particularly with respect to the four features, is thus common ground between the Indian reductionists and non-reductionists. But the form of the Grounding Assumption they share is a little different from the one shared by Western reductionist and non-reductionists. Both parties to the Indian dispute about our identity share the assumption that our identity needs to be explained in terms of metaphysical simples that have an essential ontological independence, or what Mādhyamika Buddhists call 'inherent existence' (*svabhāva*). Call this

> *The Indian Grounding Assumption*: The justification of our normative practices with respect to the four features requires that they be grounded in inherently existent facts about our identity, or in those inherently existent facts to which our identity can be reduced.

It is obvious enough that the Hindu non-reductionists' espousal of the *ātman* theory commits them to such essential haecceities, but it may be less obvious that the Buddhist reductionists are also so committed. However, the Theravādins, the Vaibhāṣikas, the Sautrāntikas and the Yogācārins are all committed to the view that facts about persons can be reduced to facts about the causal continuum, which is in turn made up of phenomena that exist independently with essential natures of their own. True, the Svātantrika-Mādhyamikas at least deny that ultimately the constituents of the continuum exist independently, but they still assert that these constituents possess conventional inherent existence: that is, they possess natures of their own in virtue of appearing to the consciousnesses in dependence upon which they exist.

Minimalism and Madhyamaka

A crucial Buddhist exception to this general Indian consensus are the Prāsaṅgika-Mādhyamikas: as Mādhyamikas, they deny the inherent existence of phenomena at the ultimate level; as Prāsaṅgikas, they also deny the inherent existence of the phenomena at even the conventional level. In other words, they deny the Indian Grounding Assumption common to both Buddhist reductionists and Hindu non-reductionists. In doing so the Prāsaṅgikas take themselves to be faithful to the original teachings of Nāgārjuna, the founder of Madhyamaka.

In chapter 18 of his *Mūlamadhyamakārikā* (Siderits and Katsura 2013), Nāgārjuna denies both that the self is the same as the psycho-physical constituents to which the Buddhist reductionists try to reduce it, and that it is other than those constituents in the way that the Hindu non-reductionists claim. He does not mean by this that we do not exist, but that we do not exist inherently in any way. In the *Vigrahavyāvartanī* (Bhattacharya 1978), Nāgārjuna rejects the opponent's demand that the doctrine of emptiness (i.e., the doctrine that everything is empty of inherent existence) be grounded in the foundationalist framework of Indian *pramāṇa* theory. Trying to meet such a demand, Nāgārjuna argues, will lead either to a justificatory infinite regress, or to the incoherent notion of an inherently existent ground for our epistemic practices. In the *Ratnavālī*, Nāgārjuna warns: 'Beyond good and evil, profound and liberating, this [doctrine of emptiness] has not been tasted by those who fear what is entirely groundless' (1.79; Huntington and Wangchen 1989: 26).

The great Prāsaṅgika Candrakīrti (seventh century) takes up some of these themes in chapter 6 of his *Madhyamakāvatāra*. His analysis of persons there utilizes an elaborate sevenfold negation of the self. According to this analysis, the self is: (1) not essentially other than the aggregates; nor (2) identical with them; nor (3) does it inherently possess them; nor (4) is it inherently dependent upon them; nor (5) is it the basis upon which they inherently depend; nor (6) is it the mere collection of them; nor (7) is it their shape. Candrakīrti says this is analogous to the case of a cart, in that a similar sevenfold analysis of the relation of a cart to its parts is possible (6.120–64). The implication in both cases is the same: the identities of the self and the cart are mere verbal conventions, 'dependent designations' (*prajñaptir-upādāya*); both they and their parts are conventionally existent, but empty of inherent existence. Moreover, in order to pre-empt further reification, Candrakīrti states explicitly that emptiness is itself empty (6.185–6). In other words, emptiness is not different from conventional reality, but just the fact that conventional reality is conventional.

According to Candrakīrti, then, we cannot ground our ascriptions of identity in inherently existent facts about our identity, or in those inherently existent facts to which our identity can supposedly be reduced. However, he also makes it clear that we can still preserve our ordinary conventional beliefs about what we are, provided that they are understood as merely conventions:

> Things such as jugs, cloth, tents, armies, forests, rosaries, trees, houses, trolleys and guest-houses should be understood to exist in the way they are commonly spoken of by people because the Buddha did not argue with the world over these matters. Furthermore, by applying the analysis of the cart to part-possessors and their parts, quality-possessors and their qualities, people with attachment and their desires, bases of characteristics and their characteristics and fuel and the fire it burns, one finds that they do not exist in any of the seven ways. But as long as they are not subjected to such analysis, they do exist in another way: namely, in terms of their being well known to the world. (*Madhyamakāvatāra* 6.166–7; Rabten 1983)

Living in terms of this insight requires wisdom (*prajñā*). According to the Buddhist tradition, such wisdom is a matter of both intellectual understanding and action. The enlightened *bodhisattva*, then, is characterized by both intellectual discernment (knowledge-that) and a non-inferential actualization of what has been discerned (knowledge-how).

These Prāsaṇgika themes are much closer to what is known in Western philosophy as *minimalism*, than they are to reductionism. According to minimalism (Johnston 1992, 1997), metaphysical pictures of the justificatory undergirdings of our practices do not represent the real conditions of justification of those practices. Any metaphysical view that we may have of persons is not indispensable to the practice of making judgments about our identity and organizing our practical concerns around these judgments. *Pace* both reductionists and non-reductionists, then, the presence or absence of 'deep facts' about personal identity is largely irrelevant to justifying our ordinary normative practices because these are not founded on a metaphysics of persons, but on our circumstances and needs.

Minimalism implies that the normative significance of the division between reductionism and non-reductionism has been exaggerated. On the one hand, non-reductionism assumes that our normative practices are in need of a 'deep' metaphysical justification and posits 'superlative selves' to do the job. Reductionism, on the other hand, denies the existence of such superlative selves. However, reductionism instead tries to ground the four features in other metaphysical facts. According to minimalism, both make much the same mistake: both appeal to a metaphysics which is just window-dressing so far as the real justification of our normative practices is concerned. In other words, both non-reductionism and reductionism share a common assumption (the Grounding Assumption) whereas minimalism rejects the Grounding Assumption.

Minimalism, then, is a deflationary account of the normative significance of ontological reductionism. Indeed the Prāsaṇgika Madhyamaka position on our identity is arguably a Buddhist analogue of the Western minimalist position on personal identity. Both believe that any metaphysical view that we may have of persons is not indispensable to the practice of making judgments about personal identity and organizing our practical concerns around these judgments. Both believe that the presence or absence of 'deep facts' about our identity is largely irrelevant to justifying our ordinary normative practices because these are not founded on a metaphysics of persons, but on our circumstances and needs. Both are, in this sense, deflationary about the normative pretensions of metaphysical reductionism and non-reductionism. Both acknowledge, however, that this does not mean that the philosophy of personal identity must leave everything as it is. Our everyday practices are open to criticism and revision, even if neither they nor their alternatives are groundable in the inherent existence of things in themselves.

Hence although reductionism is analogous to certain Buddhist views about 'no-self', this was not the only influential Buddhist view about our identity present in India: the Prāsaṅgika-Mādhyamikas held a view more closely comparable to minimalism. As such, they rejected both Buddhist reductionism and Hindu non-reductionism in order to tread a middle way between these opposed extremes.

Subjects and agents

Why did only the Prāsaṇgika Mādhyamikas effectively advocate minimalism in India and reject the Indian Grounding Assumption about our identity common to both Buddhist reductionists and Hindu non-reductionists? Here is a conjecture.

It is obvious enough that we can think about ourselves in two rather different ways: as *subjects* or as *agents*. According to the former conception, we are the detached subjects of our experiences, transcending those experiences and their contents. According to the latter conception, we are doers, psychophysical beings both in the world and of it.

The intuitive distinction between these two viewpoints was not unknown in ancient India. Thus the Hindu philosophers recognize a tension between what they call the *pravṛtti* and *nivṛtti* traditions. The *pravṛtti* tradition is the activist strand of Hindu thought, exemplified in the Vedic ritualistic tradition; the *nivṛtti* tradition is the quietism exemplified in the later Upaniṣadic renunciant tradition. It is also true that the Hindu philosophers acknowledge that the human person is characterized by both agency (*kartṛtva*) and enjoyment (*bhoktṛtva*). However, although both the activist and quietist strands are present in Hindu thought, in general it is the quietist tradition that is valorized by the *darśana* tradition of speculative philosophy. The self (*ātman*) is most typically conceived of by the Hindu philosophers as a pure subject, detached from the objects of its consciousness, enduring and changeless amidst the flux of our mental states. (Curiously enough, this is broadly true even of Mīmāṃsā, the philosophical school most concerned with ritual action. To be sure, Mīmāṃsā vehemently insists that the eternal self is an agent as well as an enjoyer, and even that knowing is an action. However, Mīmāṃsā also claims that the self is in no way essentially related to the world, a fact about it that is supposed to be realized in liberation.)

The picture of the self as witness subject, rather than doer, thus dominates Hindu philosophy and liberation is typically identified with the realization of the self's true nature as pure subject. Correspondingly, it is reasonable to infer that the Hindu non-reductionists would not be sympathetic to any suggestion that the demands of practical reason should place constraints upon the metaphysics of persons.

At first sight the case of the Buddhist reductionists looks rather different to that of the Hindu non-reductionists. After all, the Buddhists deny that there is an enduring *ātman*, reducing the self instead to the psycho-physical states and the causal relations between them. But, in an important sense, the same valorization of the person as subject, rather than agent, persists in early Buddhism. This is particularly evident in the emphasis on Buddhist meditators' detachment from their own mental and physical states. Of course, there is a well-known tension within the early Buddhist tradition between two types of meditation: one involving the cultivation of tranquillity (*samatha-bhāvanā*), the other involving the cultivation of insight (*vipassanā-bhāvanā*). The former emphasises the pursuit of liberation through enstatic techniques designed to destroy the passions by withdrawal from all contact with the external world; the latter emphasises the pursuit of liberation through analytic techniques designed to remove ignorance by the cognition of the way things really are. The enstatic techniques clearly reinforce the view of the person as subject, rather than agent. But so too does the analytic stress on cognition, with its attendant picture of the meditator as a knower detached from the objects of knowledge.

Perhaps this convergence between the Hindu non-reductionists and the Buddhist reductionists on the matter of the person as primarily subject is to be explained by the common historical origins of both traditions. Following Dumont 1980, it is sometimes suggested that the dominance within philosophical Hinduism of the quietist strand over the earlier activist strand is to be explained as a response to the challenge to Brahmanical authority represented by the rival renunciant tradition, especially Buddhism. But if that is right, then it should be unsurprising that we find within early Buddhism what is, in one sense, a not too dissimilar picture of the person than that of the Hindu quietists.

Of course, there is indeed a crucial metaphysical difference between Hindu non-reductionism and Buddhist reductionism about the nature of personal identity: this is the subject of the fiercely contested debate about *ātmavāda* and *anātmavāda* that the texts of both parties make so much of. However, what this debate obscures is a shared quietistic assumption that the person is properly to be seen as detached from his or her experiences, a witness rather than a doer. This assumption is arguably, in its own way, as embedded in early Buddhist meditation theory as in Hindu quietism. It is because of this deeper shared assumption about the nature of persons that the Indian Grounding Assumption is unquestioned by both Hindu non-reductionists and Buddhist reductionists: both parties to the Indian reductionism–non-reductionism debate assume that a person is most properly conceived of as a subject, rather than an agent. Hence they assume too that 'the four features', which are associated with personal agency and which need to be linked to our identity, are in reality derivative features. Although the Hindu non-reductionists and the Buddhist reductionists disagree strongly about precisely which facts about persons ground the four features, they nevertheless agree that the agent-centred features of persons must be grounded in the more fundamental subject-centred features of persons. Moreover, whatever facts about our identity serve to ground the four features must, on pain of a regress, be self-grounding (i.e., inherently existent).

Why do the Prāsaṅgika-Mādhyamikas dissent from this common assumption? Probably because Prāsaṅgika-Madhyamaka is so closely associated with the systematization of Mahāyāna Buddhism and its attendant religious ideal of the *bodhisattva*, a being tirelessly active in the compassionate service of suffering sentient beings. Candrakīrti's *Madhyamakāvatāra*, for instance, explicitly integrates Madhyamaka philosophy into the Mahāyāna spiritual path. Similarly, the major work of Śāntideva (eighth century) – that other great Prāsaṅgika – is the *Bodhicaryāvatāra*, a statement of the *bodhisattva*'s path to enlightenment which includes a chapter expounding a Prāsaṅgika-Mādhyamika understanding of the emptiness of all phenomena, including the self. In other words, Prāsaṅgika-Madhyamaka combines a Mahāyānist commitment to the kind of activism associated with the *bodhisattva* with a philosophical commitment to the absence of inherent existence. The two commitments fuse to create a system which acknowledges the primacy of practice (even *prajñā* involves knowledge-how), without feeling any need to seek to ground our practices in anything metaphysically 'deeper' than those practices themselves.

Prāsaṅgika-Madhyamaka, then, is much more a Buddhist minimalism than a Buddhist reductionism (or non-reductionism). In this way Prāsaṅgika invites us to tread a middle path with respect to the issue of personal identity: a path between the extremes of both reductionism and non-reductionism, dwelling in emptiness and fearless of groundlessness.

Conclusion

A path, of course, must lead somewhere, but there need not be somewhere that all paths lead to. For most Indian philosophers a proper path should ultimately lead to the state of liberation (*mokṣa*). Nevertheless there was still a very significant diversity of Indian views about the precise nature of that ultimate goal and its relation to other fundamental features of reality. Our final chapter will address some of those issues.

Suggestions for further reading

For an engaging overview of classical Indian debates about the self, see Ganeri 2007. A good extended study on Nyāya-Vaiśeṣika dualism is Chakrabarti 1999; see also Chakrabarti 1982. On Sāṃkhya dualism, see Larson 1979 and, Larson and Bhattacharya 1987. On Advaita non-dualism, see Deutsch 1969, Deutsch and van Buitenen 1971 and Potter 1981, 2006. On Buddhist views, see Kapstein 2001, Siderits 2007, Duerlinger 2003 and Collins 1982. Two very stimulating books that engage with Sanskrit texts on the self in philosophically creative ways are Siderits 2003 and Ganeri 2012. Useful collections of essays on this topic include Siderits, Thompson and Zahavi 2010 and Kuznetsova, Ganeri and Ram-Prasad 2012.

7 Ultimates

Introduction

Contrary to much popular Western belief, classical Indian philosophy was not indistinguishable from Indian religion – as even a cursory glance at the earlier chapters of this book will demonstrate. But religious concerns did motivate the work of many Indian philosophers (as they did too the work of many of the great Western philosophers), and there surely is something that can be described as 'Indian philosophy of religion', that is, 'philosophy of Indian religions' (Matilal 1982, Perrett 1989, 2001 (vol. IV)). However, important differences between the major Indian religions (Hinduism, Buddhism, Jainism) mean that the shape of Indian philosophy of religion is often significantly different from that of Western philosophy of religion.

One fundamental difference is that theism is not central to all the Indian religions in the way that it is to the major Western religions. While there certainly were classical Indian philosophers who were staunch monotheists (e.g., the Viśiṣṭādvaitins, the Dvaitins, the Śaiva Siddhāntins), overall this was not the dominant trend. In the first place, Buddhism and Jainism are both non-theistic religions. Then, within Hinduism, orthodoxy is determined by an acknowledgement of the authority of the Vedas, not a belief in God. Hence among the orthodox Hindu schools, Sāṃkhya and Mīmāṃsā are both atheistic, Advaita Vedānta is ultimately non-theistic, and Yoga and Nyāya-Vaiśeṣika are minimally theistic in the sense that they allow only significantly attenuated powers to God. Two implications of this for Indian philosophy of religion are evident. First, Indian philosophy of religion is much less centred on philosophical theology than is Western philosophy of religion. Second, even when the Indians engage in philosophical theology, it often has a rather different flavour (see Pereira 1976, Clooney 1993, 1996).

Consider, for instance, Indian discussions of the problem of evil (Herman 1976, Matilal 1982). The theistic problem of evil is how to reconcile the existence of evil with the existence of an omnipotent and benevolent God. Jaina and Buddhist atheists appealed to the existence of evil as an atheological argument, but Indian theists responded by limiting God's powers, holding that even God is constrained by individuals' karma. Nor did they accept that the existence of evil in the world showed that the world is not God's creation. The world is God's *līlā* or divine play, a creation with no purpose, and hence something for which God bears no moral responsibility.

On the other hand, Indian theists were not always persuaded of the soundness of the natural theologians' arguments for the existence of God. The philosophical theologian Rāmānuja, for example, criticized teleological arguments for God's existence, basing his belief in God instead on the authority of scripture. Part of his motivation was to retain a proper creaturely dependence: salvation should rest solely with God, and not with human reasoning. Nyāya-Vaiśeṣika, however, has a long tradition of natural theology, including elaborate causal and cosmological arguments for the existence of God. But the God (*Īśvara*) of the Naiyāyikas has distinctly attenuated powers: he does not, for instance, create the world *ex nihilo*, though he is the author of the Vedas. Yoga has an even thinner conception of God: *Īśvara* is nothing but a self (*puruṣa*) that has never been confused with nature (*prakṛti*), and his only role is as a meditative focus for the *yogin*.

Other Hindu philosophers effectively manage without God altogether. Classical Sāṃkhya is atheistic, and Mīmāṃsā even more aggressively so. The Advaitin monists hold that *Brahman* is ultimately non-personal, while the Kāśmīrī Śaivite monists identify the God Śiva with our true self (*ātman*), thus dissolving the usual theistic gap between God and his creation.

Ultimate concern and maximal greatness

Earlier we asserted that there surely is something that can be described as 'Indian philosophy of religion', that is, 'philosophy of Indian religions'. But what is meant here by the term 'religion'? This is a difficult and highly contested question. The twentieth-century Christian theologian Paul Tillich offered the following as his 'definition' of religion:

> Religion is the state of being grasped by an ultimate concern, a concern which qualifies all other concerns as preliminary and which itself contains the

> answer to the question of the meaning of our life. Therefore this concern is unconditionally serious and shows a willingness to sacrifice any finite concern which is in conflict with it. The predominant religious name for the content of such a concern is God – a god or gods. In nontheistic religions divine qualities are ascribed to a sacred object or an all-pervading power or a highest principle such as the Brahma or the One. (Tillich 1963: 4)

As a Socratic definition that specifies necessary and sufficient conditions for being a religion, this likely falls short. However, according to the Indian theory of definition (developed most fully by Nyāya), a satisfactory definition (*lakṣaṇa*) does not need to capture the essence of the object to be defined (Matilal 1985). Instead, it only needs to characterize what is being defined by picking out a unique mark of that object. Indeed, Nyāya even allows for the possibility of parallel defining properties of the same set of objects. In terms of this Indian sense of a definition, then, Tillich's definition of religion may be more suggestive than it might at first appear.

There is, however, a crucial ambiguity in Tillich's phrase 'ultimate concern': it might refer to an *attitude* of concern, or to the (real or imagined) *object* of that attitude. Tillich himself came to adopt both these possible meanings by identifying the attitude of ultimate concern with the object of ultimate concern, but even then this suggestion can still be developed in different directions. Thus we might emphasize the *attitude* and define the object as whatever it is that one is ultimately concerned about; or we might emphasize the *object* and its deservingness of the attitude. The latter approach typically invokes the conviction that a worthy object of our ultimate concern needs to possess *maximal greatness*. But when it comes to specifying precisely which properties confer maximal greatness there are – in both India and the West – various competing views. For example, in Christianity we have the tradition of 'perfect being theology' (Morris 1987), wherein God is claimed to be *omniperfect* (i.e., omnipotent, omniscient and omnibenevolent). In the Indian tradition, however, we have a variety of differing conceptions of a maximally great being. Among the most important of these proposed objects of ultimate concern are *Īśvara*, *Brahman*, Buddha and *Jina* (or *Tīrthaṅkara*). The first two are associated with Hinduism, the third and fourth with Buddhism and Jainism respectively. In what follows we shall consider what the Indian philosophers said about the nature of each of these four ultimates.

Īśvara and Yoga

The Sanskrit term *Īśvara* can be rendered as 'Lord' (from the verbal root *īś* = 'to rule'), but it is also often translated as 'God'. However, as already mentioned, *Īśvara* in both Yoga and Nyāya-Vaiśeṣika is a being with distinctly attenuated powers when compared with the usual Western conceptions of God.

Consider first the nature and role of *Īśvara* in classical Yoga. The *Yogasūtra* of Patañjali (third century) broadly accepts the Sāṃkhya dualist metaphysics of *puruṣa* and *prakṛti*. The two principal differences between the systems of Sāṃkhya and Yoga are usually said to be (i) that Yoga puts the emphasis on practical meditational techniques whereas Sāṃkhya stresses intellectual discrimination, and (ii) that Yoga is theistic while Sāṃkhya is atheistic. But what does 'theism' mean in this context?

The *Yogasūtra* (Feuerstein 1989) makes the following claims about the nature of *Īśvara*:

> The Lord [*Īśvara*] is a special self [*puruṣa*] untouched by defilement [*kleśa*], the results of karma and the store of mental deposits. In him the seed of omniscience is unsurpassed. He was also the teacher of the former ones because of his non-boundedness by time. His symbol is the *praṇava* [the syllable *oṃ*]. The recitation of that produces an understanding of its meaning. Then comes the attainment of inward-mindedness [*pratyak-cetanā*] and also the removal of the obstacles. (I.24–9)

This suggests that *Īśvara* possesses various great-making properties (including omniscience and being unlimited by time) and that a meditative focus on him can eliminate obstacles to a *yogin*'s progress towards enlightenment. *Īśvara* is not, however, creator of the world (cosmogenesis flows from the primordial *prakṛti* of the shared Sāṃkhya-Yoga ontology); nor is he claimed to be omnipotent or omnibenevolent, though he can and does assist *yogins* who take him as the object of their concentration. Nor, as a permanently unembodied, detached *puruṣa*, can *Īśvara* be a personal God in any meaningful sense.

In the *Yogabhāṣya* the later commentator Vyāsa (eighth century) elaborates two interesting arguments for some claims that are simply asserted about *Īśvara* in *Yogasūtra* I.24–5. The first of these arguments – which has been seen by some as reminiscent of Anselm's famous ontological argument for the existence of God as *that-than-which-nothing-greater-can-be-conceived* – is for the thesis that *Īśvara*'s existence is implied by his pre-eminence (*āiśvarya*):

> Now this his pre-eminence . . . is altogether without any equal to it or excelling it. For, to begin with, it cannot be excelled by any other pre-eminence, because whatever might [seem] to excel it would itself prove to be that very [pre-eminence we are in quest of]. Therefore that is the *Īśvara* wherein we reach this uttermost limit of pre-eminence. Nor again is there any pre-eminence equal to his. [Why not?] Because when one thing is simultaneously desired by two equals . . . if the one wins his way, the other fails in his wish and so becomes inferior. And two equals cannot obtain the same thing simultaneously, since that would be a contradiction of terms. Therefore . . . in whomsoever there is a pre-eminence that is neither equalled nor excelled, he is the *Īśvara*, and he is, as we have maintained, a special kind of self. (*Yogabhāṣya* I.24; Woods 1927: 50)

The most perfect being, then, is *Īśvara*, and he is unique.

The second argument is for the claim that *Īśvara* is omniscient:

> He, verily, in whom this germ as it increases progressively reaches its utmost excellence is the omniscient. It is possible for the germ of the omniscient to reach this [uttermost] limit, for it admits of degrees of excellence, as in the case of any ascending scale. He in whom the limit of thinking is reached is the omniscient and he is a special kind of self. (*Yogabhāṣya* I.25; Woods 1927: 50)

Grades of knowledge, in other words, supposedly imply an upper limit (omniscience) and this upper limit belongs to a perfect self, who (as the previous argument has shown) is *Īśvara*.

It is clear enough that Vyāsa has added here some extra great-making properties to Patañjali's original list. Now *Īśvara* is not only omniscient and unlimited by time, but also unique and unequalled in power (though not, strictly speaking, thereby *omnipotent*). In addition, Vyāsa explains *Īśvara*'s willingness to assist *yogins* thus: '[To him] the gratification of living beings is a sufficient motive. He may be conceived as resolving, "By instruction in knowledge and right-living . . . I will lift up human beings, who are whirled into the vortex of existence"' (*Yogabhāṣya* I.25; Woods 1927: 56). While this description sits uncomfortably with Patañjali's description of *Īśvara* as a detached *puruṣa*, and hence a seer rather than a doer, it presumably points towards Vyāsa's own sense of the importance of benevolence (albeit not, strictly speaking, *omnibenevolence*) as a great-making property.

Notwithstanding these two metaphysical arguments for the existence of *Īśvara*, it is clear that Vyāsa ultimately views the scope of rational theology as quite limited. Firstly, the proof of *Īśvara*'s pre-eminence is in the end said by Vyāsa (I.24) to be the scriptures, which are in turn authoritative in virtue of being present in *Īśvara*'s perfect *sattva* – an apparent circularity! Secondly, the degrees of knowledge argument for *Īśvara*'s omniscience is admitted to be powerless by itself to prove that it is *Īśvara*, rather than some other being, that is the perfectly omniscient one (I.25). Again, an appeal to scripture is needed for that task.

The manner in which Vyāsa raises the issue of how to justify the claim of *Īśvara*'s greatness is revealing here: '"That universally admitted eternal superiority (*utkarṣa*) of the *Īśvara* which results from his assuming a *sattva* of perfect (*prakṛṣṭa*) quality – has it any proof [to authorize it], or is it without proof?" [The reply is, His] sacred-books are its proof' (*Yogabhāṣya* I.24; Woods 1927: 50). Obviously, Vyāsa is well aware that there are those – including the Buddhists and the Jainas – who do not believe in *Īśvara*. But they are not part of his intended audience and he is unconcerned with any attempt to present a rigorous theistic proof that will convince them. Instead, his arguments are an elucidation of what he already believes. Once again, there is an Anselmian resonance here, for Anselm's motto was 'Faith seeking understanding' ('*fides quaerens intellectum*') and he too utterly rejected the assumption that his proper intellectual task was to replace a testimony-based belief in God with an inferentially based belief in God. Vyāsa's arguments about *Īśvara* are not really intended to convince Buddhist and Jaina unbelievers, but instead are intended for the edification of those (like Vyāsa himself) who already believe in God and the authority of the scriptures.

Īśvara in Nyāya-Vaiśeṣika

Nyāya-Vaiśeṣika, in contrast, has far greater confidence in the scope of natural theology, and a less attenuated conception of God. Consider first the nature of God. The *Īśvara* of the Naiyāyikas has far more great-making properties than the *Īśvara* of Yoga, being not only omniscient and the benevolent author of the Vedas, but responsible too for the operations of karmic justice. Another of his roles is to be the fixer of the linguistic conventions that connect words and their meanings. *Īśvara* is also said to be the creator of the world in the sense that he is the agent responsible for setting the world in motion at the beginning of each repeated cosmic cycle of creation and dissolution by bringing about the first combinations of atoms. He is not the creator, however, of many of the world's basic constituents – including atoms, ether, space, time, universals and individual selves – and hence, although very powerful, he is not omnipotent. Finally, and perhaps most surprisingly, he is not a liberated self because he has karma (albeit all of the meritorious kind) and desires (necessary for agency, according to Nyāya) – all properties incompatible with the Nyāya description of the liberated state.

Some have felt that Nyāya-Vaiśeṣika theism is an artificial graft on to the originally atheistic system of Vaiśeṣika atomism, and that *Īśvara* is blatantly a 'God of the gaps' invoked to fill explanatory holes in that largely naturalistic metaphysics of atomism. Historically, however, the developed Nyāya position has consistently been that the existence of *Īśvara* is accessible to inference from the physical world, and showing this has been a concern over the centuries of most of the major Naiyāyika philosophers – including Uddyotakara, Jayanta, Vācaspati Miśra, Udayana and Gaṅgeśa. Hence although Nyāya happily admits testimony as a *pramāṇa*, it is inference (*anumāna*) that is taken to be the principal *pramāṇa* for establishing the existence of God. The *locus classicus* here is the *Nyāyakusumāñjali* of Udayana (eleventh century), who both explicitly asserts this commitment to rational theology and gestures towards the form of the inference to be developed as follows:

> The existence of a creator of the universe is established by inference (*anumāna*): the universe, whose status as having a maker is disputed, does have a maker, since it is a product. (Dravid 1996: 380)

In the *Nyāyakusumāñjali*, Udayana draws freely on the work of his Naiyāyika predecessors to develop an elaborate set of theistic proofs of the existence of God. These are arranged in two groups of nine proofs each. The first series of proofs seeks to establish *Īśvara* as the creator, sustainer and destroyer of the universe, the instructor of living beings and the author of the Vedas; the second series of proofs seeks to establish *Īśvara* as the author of the Vedas. The most central proof of all as far as the Nyāya tradition itself is concerned is a 'cosmoteleological' argument that combines into one argument elements of both the cosmological and the teleological arguments for God's existence. It can be presented as a formal five-part 'inference for others' of the form we encountered in Chapter 3 above:

(1) Hypothesis: earth and the like have an intelligent maker as an instrumental cause.

(2) Ground or reason: because they are effects.

(3) Corroboration: whatever is an effect has an intelligent maker as an instrumental cause, like a pot (which has an intelligent maker as an instrumental cause), and unlike an atom (which is not an effect).

(4) Application: earth and the like, since they are effects, have an intelligent maker as an instrumental cause (i.e., they fall under the general rule of pervasion in (3)).

(5) Conclusion: therefore earth and the like have an intelligent maker as an instrumental cause.

Alternatively, the argument can be presented less formally as a three-membered syllogism:

(1) Hypothesis: earth and the like have an intelligent maker as an instrumental cause.

(2) Ground or reason: because they are effects.

(3) Examples: (a) like a pot (b) unlike an atom.

Either way, and as in any Indian formal inference, the structure of this argument requires specifying (i) the *pakṣa* or subject of the inference (here *earth and the like*), (ii) the *sādhya* or property that qualifies the *pakṣa* (here *having an intelligent maker as an instrumental cause*), and (iii) the *hetu* or property that is related in an appropriate way to the *sādhya* (here *being an effect*). Each of these three elements of the argument occasioned protracted debate over many centuries by Naiyāyikas and their opponents (especially the Buddhists).

The subject of the inference here is said to be the world; or more precisely (and as Udayana's use of 'earth and the like' (*kṣityādi*) reminds us), all those things in the world that are produced. For Nyāya, the universe is beginningless since nothing comes out of nothing, and so *Īśvara* does not create the world *ex nihilo*. Instead things like the atoms of the four elements (including earth) are eternal. But the many things compounded out of the eternal atoms, and so on, do come into existence and their coming into existence is then supposed to require the postulation of a maker (*kartā*), an agent whose intentional activity can adequately explain the purported effects in question. Vācaspati Miśra (tenth century) suggests that we can group together (i) things that are known to be made by conscious makers (pots, palaces and the like) and (ii) things where there is doubt as to whether they are made by conscious makers (trees, mountains and the like) in order to contrast them with (iii) things eternal and uncreated (atoms, selves and the like). Then the former (combined) group of composite things can be counted as the subject of the inference.

The *sādhya* or property to be inferred here is *having an intelligent maker as an instrumental cause*. This is taken to imply that the maker must have direct knowledge of the material causes of the product, a requirement that (in the case of many composite things in the world) is beyond the powers of a merely human agent.

The *hetu* or reason here is *being an effect*. But, of course, the Naiyāyika has to be very careful to interpret the reason so as not to beg the question: for example, interpreting *being an effect* as *being an effect of conscious volition* is clearly going to be unacceptable to an atheist, who will cite trees, mountains and the like as counterexamples. This is where Vācaspati's proposal mentioned earlier is relevant, for it amounts to counting all such apparent counterexamples as included in the set of things taken to be the inferential subject. Then the atheist cannot assume – without begging the question – that what is included within the subject of the inference is not qualified by the property to be inferred. After all, a good inference (*anumāna*) is supposed to make us come to know something about an inferential subject that we did not know previously. Hence we cannot just assume we know, prior to the inference, whether the inferential subject is or is not qualified by the property to be inferred.

One objection to this Nyāya cosmotheological argument is that it cannot establish a conclusion as strong as it purports to: at best, it can only establish the existence of one or more sentient agent, not the existence of a single *Īśvara*. Udayana concedes this point, but thinks that a supplementary argument can be made for the claim that a single *Īśvara* is the best candidate for the role of the intelligent maker. After all, this is the simplest hypothesis and the principle of 'lightness' tells us we should assume only as much about a posited cause as is necessary to account for the effect in question. Moreover, not just any maker or intelligent being could be the cause of the universe: such a being would have to be eternal and omniscient in order to do the job.

Three critics of Nyāya natural theology

Indian critics of natural theology (like their Western counterparts) were variously motivated. Some (like the Buddhists, the Jainas and the Mīmāṃsakas) were atheists and viewed their critiques of Nyāya natural theology as atheological arguments designed to show the unwarrantedness of belief in God; others (like the Viśiṣṭādvaitin theologian Rāmānuja) were theists who opposed Nyāya natural theology in the cause of revealed theology.

It is the later Buddhist logicians who challenge most directly the logical technicalities of the developed Nyāya inference to God. For example, Ratnakīrti (eleventh century), addressing the Nyāya theistic inference in his *Īśvarasādhanadūṣaṇa* (Patil 2009), asserts that there are clear counterexamples to the purported pervasion of the reason (*being an effect*) by the property to be inferred (*having an intelligent maker*). For instance, *growing grass* is an effect, but does not have an intelligent maker. We saw earlier how Nyāya responds to such a purported counterexample by including it within the inferential subject. But Ratnakīrti rejects such a move, dismissing it as the 'Naiyāyikas' trick' (*vidamabana*).

The central issue at stake here has to do with whether there is significant doubt about whether grass does not have an intelligent maker. Ratnakīrti argues that *growing grass* cannot legitimately be part of the inferential subject if there is no such doubt. More technically, the 'Naiyāyikas' trick' is to establish pervasion on the basis of one property (*having been observed to have an intelligent maker*) and extend it on the basis of another (*being an effect-in-general*).

> So, in this way, even though things such as pots, cloth, and mountains belong to the same class on the basis of properties such as 'being an effect' or 'being a thing', it is after recognizing a secondary distinction between the classes 'pot', 'cloth', and 'mountains' that pervasion-grasping perception functions for an ordinary person. (*Īśvarasādhanadūṣaṇa* 52–3; Patil 2009: 156–7)

Ratnakīrti goes on to offer an example to illustrate his case:

> A person who is gifted in common sense and free from the influence of philosophy determines that things that belong to the class of temples are made by a person. He then enters a forest from the city. Upon seeing a temple, he has the awareness of its having been made, but does not have this awareness upon seeing a mountain – even though he saw neither of these things being made. Now in virtue of being effects, both belong to a single

> class. But he is not able to establish either the absence or presence of the property 'an awareness of having been made' without first relying on a secondary distinction in the class, defined by 'being a mountain' and 'being a temple'. (*Īśvarasādhanadūṣaṇa* 53; Patil 2009: 159–60)

Ratnakīrti concludes, then, that there is no significant doubt about whether growing grass does not have an intelligent maker, at least a maker of the sort familiar to us through the likes of examples such as a pot and a potter.

The Mīmāṃsaka philosopher Kumārila Bhaṭṭa (seventh century) was not concerned to address the logical intricacies of the Nyāya cosmoteleological inference in the very detailed way that Ratnakīrti does. However, in his *Ślokavārttika* Kumārila does offer a battery of objections to the Nyāya arguments for the existence of a creator God, including two interesting claims about some difficulties with the set of great-making properties Nyāya attributes to *Īśvara*.

The first claim is that creation is not possible without a desire to create, but such a desire implies an imperfection in the alleged creator.

> If the activity of the Creator were due to a desire for mere amusement [*līlā*], then that would go against his ever-contentedness. And (instead of affording any amusement), the great amount of work (required for creation) would be a source of infinite trouble to him. And his desire to destroy the world (at *pralaya*) too would be hardly explicable. (*Ślokavārttika* 16.56–7; Jha 1983: 357)

More generally, a desire requires the presence in the desirer of a felt lack, and hence too a lack of perfect contentedness in the desirer.

Kumārila's second claim is that the doctrine of karma surely renders God irrelevant:

> If creation were dependent on God's wish, it would be useless to assume the (agency of) actions (*dharma* and *adharma*)... If by 'control' it is meant only the fact of some intelligent agency being the cause of creation, – then... all creation could be accomplished by the actions [karma] of all living beings. (16.72, 75; Jha 1983: 360–1)

On the other hand, if God were to ignore karma to rule, then he would be unjust.

We have already noted that the *Īśvara* of the Naiyāyikas, though supposedly a creator of many excellences, nonetheless possesses a more attentuated set of great-making properties than the omnigod of Western perfect being theology. So why should Nyāya not just reply by conceding that *Īśvara* is not omnipotent or omnibenevolent or free from karma? Because what Kumārila effectively seems to be arguing here is that these very restrictions render *Īśvara* unworthy of being an appropriate object of ultimate concern. For Mīmāṃsā, in contrast, the supreme value in life is not God or some such being, but an impersonal unconditional imperative prescribed by the Vedas to attain heaven through sacrificial acts.

The Mīmāṃsā position – an ultra-orthodox Hindu philosophical school of scriptural exegetes committed to deconstructing theistic arguments in order to shore up the independent authority of the Vedas – is certainly curious. Part of the impetus for this Mīmāṃsā project is the influence of the very differently motivated atheistic arguments of the Buddhists. While the Buddhists rejected both the existence of God and the authority of the Vedas, the Mīmāṃsakas laboured to show that the latter issue was logically independent of the former.

This is why Kumārila is so critical of the Nyāya claim that *Īśvara* is the omniscient author of the Vedas (*Ślokavārttika* 2.117–51; Jha 1983: 38–43). For if we allow that *Īśvara* might be omniscient, then so too might Buddha or Mahāvīra (just as their Buddhist or Jaina followers claim). But then the authority of the Vedas is jeopardized, for the claim of their authorship by an allegedly omniscient being would not distinguish them from the Buddhist and Jaina scriptures. Instead, according to Mīmāṃsā, the Vedas are authorless (*apauruṣeya*) and their authority derives from precisely this property, for if they did have an author they would be fallible (as are other authored texts of our acquaintance). Since they do not have an author, however, they must be infallible because their falsity could have no possible cause (the possibility of falsity always depending on some person or other).

Mīmāṃsā concedes that there is no positive proof of the validity of the Vedas, for this would require the assumption of something prior or external to the eternal revelation. This is epistemically unproblematic for them, however, since they hold a negative theory of confirmation according to which no theory can ever be positively proved true. Non-falsification is the criterion of truth and every statement is assumed true unless contradicted by another statement. (This is the theory of the self-validity of knowledge known as *svataḥprāmāṇyavāda* that we encountered in Chapter 2 above.)

All this rests heavily on the intelligibility of the notion of an authorless revelation and the plausibility of the involved theory of language Mīmāṃsā offers in support of the idea. Moreover, even on the conjectural view of enquiry *svataḥprāmāṇyavāda* favours, Vedic texts seem to be contradicted by other (heterodox) texts. For the Mīmāṃsā, however, this latter point is not seen as a problem since both Jainism and Buddhism hold that their scriptures are the products of (highly developed) authors. Hence, on Mīmāṃsā principles, they are fallible in a way that the authorless Veda cannot be.

It is interesting to note that the atheistic Buddhists and Jainas take a view of their scriptures that is similar to the theistic Nyāya account and opposed to the atheistic Mīmāṃsā view of revelation. Thus for Jainism the scriptures are the products of the totally omniscient *tīrthaṅkaras* and their omniscience guarantees the reliability of the scriptures in much the same way as God's omniscience guarantees the reliability of the Vedas for the Nyāya theists. This is one motive for the Jaina attribution of the total omniscience usually reserved for divine beings to the human *arhats* and *tīrthaṅkaras*. Similarly, Buddhism attributes the reliability of its scriptures to the reliability of their origin: the Buddha himself.

As a Vedāntin, Rāmānuja (eleventh century) broadly accepts the Mīmāṃsā view that the scriptures are authorless (though for him they do have personal promulgators). Rāmānuja is also a theist who accepts the existence of a personal *Brahman*. He refuses, however, to allow that either perception or inference is able to give us knowledge of *Brahman*, for only scripture can do that. Accordingly, he rejects the Nyāya cosmoteleological argument for the existence of God.

Rāmānuja's critique of the Nyāya argument (*Śrībhāṣya* I.1.3; Thibaut 1971: 161–74) is arguably focused rather more on its teleological dimension than on its cosmological dimension. He makes a number of telling points, including the following. First, we cannot justifiably infer that the world has a creator on the grounds that it has parts (like a pot which has a potter as its instrumental cause), for we have actually no idea how or why the parts of nature were formed. Anyway, there would be no reason to suppose that only one designer was involved. Moreover, the only designers we have direct experience of have physical bodies, which God presumably does not. Finally, the more like us God is supposed to be, the less appropriate it is to worship him: a being worthy of worship would transcend the ordinary world.

Rāmānuja himself has, of course, no doubt that there exists a personal God – *Brahman* the supreme person – whom he describes as:

> That highest Person who is the ruler of all; whose nature is antagonistic to all evil; whose purposes come true; who possesses infinite auspicious qualities, such as knowledge, blessedness, and so on; who is omniscient, omnipotent, supremely merciful; from whom the creation, subsistence, and reabsorption of this world proceed he is Brahman: such is the meaning of the Sūtra. (*Śrībhāṣya* I.1.2; Thibaut 1971: 156)

Rāmānuja's point is instead that scripture is our only source of knowledge of such a being.

Specifically addressing the case of inference (*anumāna*), Rāmānuja succinctly summarizes why it fails to be a source of knowledge of the supreme being:

> [I]nference either of the kind which proceeds on the observation of special cases or of the kind which rests on generalizations [is not a source of knowledge of *Brahman*]... Not inference of the former kind, because such inference is not known to relate to anything lying beyond the reach of the senses. Nor inference of the latter kind, because we do not observe any characteristic feature that is invariably accompanied by the presence of a supreme Self capable of being conscious of, and constructing, the universe of things. (*Śrībhāṣya* I.1.3; Thibaut 1971: 162)

Brahman and the varieties of Vedānta

Rāmānuja is a Vedāntin and hence, like other Vedāntins, his object of ultimate concern is the maximally great *Brahman*. As we saw, Rāmānuja conceives of *Brahman* as the supreme person, that is, as a personal God. But there are several different varieties of Vedānta, and *Brahman* is conceived of somewhat differently in each of them.

The term *Vedānta* means 'the end of the Vedas' and refers to all those Hindu philosophical traditions concerned with the interpretation and systematization of three authoritative texts (the *prasthānas*): the Upaniṣads, the *Brahmasūtra* and the *Bhagavadgītā*. Each of the three most important schools of Vedānta – Advaita, Viśiṣṭādvaita and Dvaita – is associated with an *ācārya*, a foundational preceptor who composed commentaries on all three *prasthānas*, setting out a distinctive systematic interpretation of the texts. For Advaita, that person is Śaṃkara (eighth century), for Viśiṣṭādvaita it is Rāmānuja (eleventh century), and for Dvaita it is Madhva (thirteenth century).

All schools of Vedānta are committed to the pursuit of knowledge of *Brahman*, thus the opening verses of the *Brahmasūtra* read: 'Now then the desire to know *Brahman*, that from which occurs the origin, maintenance and dissolution of all that there is' (I.1.1–2). *Brahman* is the supreme principle in Upaniṣadic thought (sometimes conceived of as personal, sometimes as impersonal). It is the power implicit in the Vedic sacrificial ritual and, by extension, the sacred power sustaining the cosmos. For Vedāntins, knowledge of *Brahman* is alone the source of liberation, and hence *Brahman* is both the goal of existence and the means by which to attain it.

Vedāntins also agree that selfhood is the primary model for understanding the being of *Brahman* and that there is an analogical relationship between the finite self (*jīva*) and the supreme Self (*ātman*). But on the question of the precise relation of the Self to *Brahman*, the principal schools disagree significantly and in ways that their names suggest. Thus Advaita ('non-dualism') holds that the Self and *Brahman* are identical; Dvaita ('dualism') holds that they are non-identical, though similar; and Viśiṣṭādvaita ('qualified non-dualism') holds that the Self is a part of *Brahman*, and hence non-identical with it. These three subschools of Vedānta disagree too on *Brahman*'s relation to the world. Finally, a major divergence within Vedānta is between those who take a monistic position (like Advaita) and those who take a theistic position (like Viśiṣṭādvaita and Dvaita).

Śaṃkara on *Brahman*

The best-known subschool of Vedānta is surely Advaita Vedānta. Advaita has a long history and many distinguished advocates, who do not always agree with each other on everything. For convenience here, then, we shall focus just on the thought of the great Advaitin *ācārya* Śaṃkara.

Towards the beginning of his commentary on the *Brahmasūtra*, Śaṃkara offers a characterization of Vedāntic enquiry into the maximally great *Brahman* that would be unexceptionable to all Vedāntins:

> Knowledge thus constitutes the means by which the complete understanding of Brahman is desired to be obtained, [this being] the highest end of man . . . Brahman, which is all-knowing and endowed with all powers, whose essential nature is eternal purity, intelligence, and freedom, exists. For if we consider the derivation of the word 'Brahman' from the root *bṛh*, 'to be great', we immediately understand that eternal purity, and so on, belong to Brahman. (*Brahmasūtrabhāṣya* I.1.1; Thibaut 1971: 13–14)

After this point, however, there is a crucial divergence within Vedānta between those who think of such perfection as essentially personal and those that think it impersonal. The Advaitin view is that *Brahman* is ultimately impersonal, but the textual sources to which all Vedāntins are committed speak at times of a personal supreme being. Thus room has to be found too for a personal *Brahman*. The Advaitin solution is to introduce a distinction between a *Brahman* with qualities (*saguṇa Brahman*) and a *Brahman* without qualities (*nirguṇa Brahman*). Whereas *nirguṇa Brahman* is the transcendent ultimate being of which nothing positive can be affirmed, *saguṇa Brahman* is that transcendent being as conceived by us from our limited human perspective. Ultimately there is only the one unqualifiable *Brahman*, but a personal *Brahman* is required to account for the relative reality of created existence and the devotional experience. For Śaṃkara, however, talk of a *Brahman* with qualities is just a provisional concession, for such a qualified being must necessarily be inferior by virtue of lacking the transcendent nature that provides ultimate liberation.

What reason do we have to believe in such a maximally great transcendent being? For Śaṃkara, one very important reason is, of course, that such a belief supposedly makes the best exegetical sense of the scriptures Vedāntins consider authoritative – a claim strongly disputed by other Vedāntins. Another significant reason is the belief's potential cosmological fruitfulness for the explanation of the origination, subsistence and dissolution of the universe. This is so notwithstanding that there is something of a tension between Śaṃkara's claims that the lower *Brahman* – God (*īśvara*) – is both the efficient and material cause of the world, and that God is conditioned by ignorance.

A third reason is the way in which the belief supposedly accords with our experience of selfhood in order to provide a model for understanding the being of *Brahman* as that pure consciousness on which we superimpose the contents we take ourselves to be experiencing in our interactions with the world: 'Moreover the existence of Brahman is known on the ground of its being the Self of every one... And this Self (of whose existence all are conscious) is Brahman' (*Brahmasūtrabhāṣya* I.1.1; Thibaut 1971: 14). According to Advaita, *ātman* is identical to *Brahman* and hence is pure consciousness just as *Brahman* is. Thus Śaṃkara claims that one cannot coherently assert 'I do not exist' and then goes on to identify this 'I' with pure consciousness. In his *Upadeśasāhasrī* (Śaṃkara's major non-commentarial work), this is nicely brought out in the dialogue between the teacher and the pupil when the pupil argues that pure consciousness must be an accidental property of the self since it is not known in deep sleep. The teacher replies that it is impossible to deny that the self is pure consciousness. The pupil's supposed objection involves a contradiction:

> Although you are [in truth] seeing, you say, 'I do not see'. This is contradictory... You are seeing in the state of deep sleep; for you deny only the seen object, not the seeing. I said your seeing is Pure Consciousness. Thus as [it] does not depart [from you] [its] transcendental changelessness and eternity are established solely by itself without depending upon any means of knowledge. (II.93; Mayeda 1992: 243)

Finally, a central point clearly at issue in all Vedāntin debates about the description of *Brahman* is how to provide for an object of ultimate concern plausibly worthy of that role, that is, a being that is maximally great. Once again, the disagreement here is about what it really means to be a maximally great being.

Rāmānuja on *Brahman*

Viśiṣṭādvaita is a theistic subschool of Vedānta that is committed to a rather different conception of *Brahman* than Advaita's. It too has a long history and a variety of distinguished adherents, but for convenience here we shall once again focus just on the thought of the subschool's great *ācārya*: in this case, Rāmānuja.

For Rāmānuja a proper understanding of *Brahman*'s supremacy is not to be found by emphasizing the impersonal nature of a transcendent *Brahman* without qualities. Instead Rāmānuja chooses to emphasize the distinctively personal attributes of *Brahman*, seeking thereby to reflect both the supremacy and accessibility of the divine nature. (For Rāmānuja, this personal God is identified with Viṣṇu-Nārāyaṇa.) The system of Viśiṣṭādvaita thus attempts a synthesis of personal theism with the absolutist philosophy of *Brahman*. (Since the three foundational texts of Vedānta include passages that favour both impersonal and personal understandings of *Brahman*, the exegetical situation is a relatively open one.)

Rāmānuja accepts the standard Vedāntin claim that *Brahman* is that from which everything emanates, that by which everything is sustained, and that into which everything returns. But if the Vedāntic promise of liberation involves an individual 'attaining *Brahman*', then *Brahman* must also have an immanental dimension wherein the individual shares some qualities in common with *Brahman*.

Advaita, of course, holds that there is but one entity – *Brahman* – devoid of all difference (*bheda*) and change. This is supposed to be the meaning of the Upaniṣadic 'great saying' '*tat tvam asi*' ('That art thou'): the essential Self (*ātman*) is numerically identical with *Brahman*. Rāmānuja rejects this Advaitin interpretation of '*tat tvam asi*' as a misreading of the syntax of the Sanskrit text, which involves 'co-ordinate predication' (*sāmānādhikaraṇya*).

Co-ordinate predication as a *syntactic* notion was originally defined by the Indian Grammarians: 'The experts on such matters define it thus: "The signification of an identical entity by several terms which are applied to that entity on different grounds is co-ordinate predication"' (*Vedārthasaṃgraha* 24; Raghavachar 1978: 24). According to Rāmānuja, this syntactic feature also has an important *ontological* implication: terms referring to the qualities of a substance also refer to the substance the qualities qualify. Co-ordinate predication, then, expresses the fact of one thing being characterized by two attributes: it implies differentiation both between individual objects and within the individual object. In other words, the attributes should be distinct from each and also different from the substance, though inseparable from it.

This semantic theory is then used by Rāmānuja to interpret those scriptural passages like '*tat tvam asi*' that Advaita takes to support monism. Since those passages certainly employ co-ordinate predication *grammatically*, they must also thereby be committed to the supposed *ontological* implications of this grammatical feature. This means that in the expression '*tat tvam asi*', '*tat*' refers to *Brahman* through certain qualities (*being cause of the universe*, for instance) that are possessed by *Brahman*, but which are different from the *Brahman* who possesses them. And '*tvam*' refers to *Brahman* through other qualities (*having an individual self as part of his body*, for instance) also possessed by *Brahman*, but which are different from the *Brahman* who possesses them. So, *pace* Advaita, both '*tat*' and '*tvam*' actually denote *Brahman* (through its qualities), and those qualities are both distinct from each other and also different – though inseparable from – from the *Brahman* that possesses those qualities.

The notion of inseparability (*apṛthak-siddhi*) plays a crucial role in the alternative model Rāmānuja provides of the relation of *Brahman* to the world and to the individual self. Inseparability implies that two entities are asymmetrically related in such a way that one is dependent on the other and cannot exist without the other also existing. Moreover, neither can the dependent entity be known without the other also being known. For Rāmānuja, substance and attribute are so related; so too are the body and the individual self.

Even more importantly, however, the relation of *Brahman* to the world and the individual self is of this type too: the physical world and the individual self are the body of which *Brahman* is the controlling self. For a devout theist like Rāmānuja, this has the theologically welcome consequence that God is as intimately related to us as we are to our own bodies. To say, then, that the world (or an individual) is *Brahman*'s body is to say that it is both non-different from and yet not identical with *Brahman*, on whom it is dependent.

Clearly, to make sense of this we have to understand the special sense Rāmānuja attaches to the term 'body' (*śarīra*): 'Any substance which a sentient soul is capable of completely controlling and supporting for its own purposes, and which stands to the soul in an entirely subordinate relation, is the body of that soul' (*Śrībhāṣya* II.1.9; Thibaut 1971: 424). The general relationship between a self (*ātman*) and its body – and hence between God and the world – is then spelled out by Rāmānuja in the following terms:

> This is the fundamental relationship between the Supreme and the universe of individual selves and physical entities. It is the relationship of soul and body, the inseparable relationship of the supporter and the supported, that of the controller and the controlled, and that of the principal entity and the subsidiary entity. That which takes possession of another entity entirely as the latter's support, controller and principal, is called the soul of that latter entity. That which, in its entirety, depends upon, is controlled by and subserves another and is therefore its inseparable mode, is called the body of the latter. Such is the relation between the individual self and its body. Such

> being the relationship, the supreme Self, having all as its body, is denoted by all terms. (*Vedārthasaṃgraha* 95; Raghavachar 1978: 76)

This model is supposed to guarantee that *Brahman* is both transcendent and immanent, a maximally great being worthy of being the object of ultimate concern. It is also explicitly intended to synthesize three competing strands of thought present in the scriptures that all Vedāntins hold to be authoritative: (1) that *Brahman* is 'one without a second' and to be identified with the individual self and the physical world; (2) that *Brahman* is to be distinguished from the individual self and the world; and (3) that *Brahman* is one, but its unity is such as to include variety ('identity-in-difference' or *bhedābheda*). Śaṃkara, of course, valorizes strand (1); Madhva (as we shall shortly see) valorizes strand (2); Bhartṛprapañca (sixth century) and Bhāskara (ninth century) valorize strand (3). Rāmānuja's 'qualified non-dualism' is explicitly supposed to harmonize all three strands:

> It may be asked, 'What is your final position? Do you uphold unity or plurality or both unity and plurality? Which of these three forms the substance of the Vedānta on your interpretation?' We reply that we uphold all the three as they are all affirmed in the Veda. We uphold unity because Brahman alone exists, with all other entities as its modes. We uphold both unity and plurality, as the one Brahman itself, has all the spiritual and physical substances as its modes and thus exists qualified by a plurality. We uphold plurality as the three categories, sentient selves and non-sentient existents and the supreme Lord, are mutually distinct in their substantive nature and attributes and there is no mutual transposition of their characteristics. (*Vedārthasaṃgraha* 117; Raghavachar 1978: 90)

Madhva on *Brahman*

The subschool of Dvaita Vedānta is less well known than either Advaita or Viśiṣṭādvaita. Dvaita Vedānta's great *ācārya* is Madhva and, like Rāmānuja, Madhva too takes *Brahman* to be a personal God (identified with Viṣṇu-Nārāyaṇa). Metaphysically, Dvaita is a realist form of pluralism. Theologically, it is a form of monotheism.

Dvaita ('dualism') is sharply and polemically opposed to Advaita ('non-dualism') and its monistic metaphysics. Instead, Madhva affirms what he calls the 'fivefold difference' (*pañcabheda*), differences that cannot be overcome even in liberation:

> The universe consists of five differences. They are the difference between God and the individual self, that between God and insentient matter, that among individual selves, that between insentient matter and individual self and that among the material entities themselves. This is real and unoriginated. If it were originated, it would perish. But it does not perish. Nor is it a fabrication of illusion. If it were so, it would have disappeared. But it does not disappear. Therefore, the view that there is no duality is the view of the ignorant. The view of the enlightened is that this world is comprehended and protected by Viṣṇu. Therefore it is proclaimed to be real. (*Viṣṇutattvavinirṇaya* 340; Raghavachar 1959)

Madhva has an interesting epistemological argument for the existence of these five differences: namely, that the very structure of knowledge reveals differences in reality. Firstly, a knowledge episode always involves both a knower and an object of knowledge different from the subject who knows. In other words, the nature of knowledge implies differences in reality. Secondly, these differences cannot be coherently denied by appeal to the supposed unreliability of our recognized means of knowledge (*pramāṇa*). The whole point of a *pramāṇa* is that it is a means of comprehending the objects of knowledge just as they are (*yadārtha*) and so it is self-defeating to deny the validity per se of a recognized *pramāṇa*. But everybody accepts that perception and inference are *pramāṇas*, and both tell us that the world is a world of differences.

As a Vedāntin, of course, Madhva accepts that scriptural testimony is also a valid *pramāṇa*. But although only scripture can give us knowledge of *Brahman*, our access to this scriptural knowledge is always mediated through our perceptions of the sacred words and our ability to draw inferences from those words. Thus scriptural testimony cannot overturn the deliverances of perception and inference without undermining itself, since the latter two *pramāṇas* are involved in all our knowledge of scripture:

> Further, if difference is established by perception and inference, scripture asserting non-difference must be construed as false just on the ground of its contradiction to what is established by these other means of knowledge . . . Even if a scripture is stronger than the other means of

> knowledge like perception, it cannot have validity if it conflicts with the *pramāṇa* on which it depends and on whose foundation it is itself built up. (*Viṣṇutattvavinirṇaya* 65–8)

Unsurprisingly, then, Madhva rejects too the Advaitin reading of Upaniṣadic texts like '*tat tvam asi*' as asserting the identity of Self and *Brahman*. Instead he ingeniously proposes that the *Chandogya Upaniṣad*'s statement '*sa atmātat tvam asi*' should not be read as '*sa atmaa-tat tvam asi*' ('It is the Self; thou are that'), but – by carrying over the '*a*' from the preceding word – as '*sa atma atat tvam asi*' or 'It is the Self; thou are *not* that'. (Sanskrit texts written in the traditional *devanāgari* script do not clearly mark all word divisions and when two vowels make a juncture in a sentence they often coalesce into a single lengthened vowel, so either reading would be transcribed in the same way in *devanāgari*.)

Although Madhva affirms the 'five differences', not all of these differences are equally fundamental. Madhva's ontology is built on a more crucial dualism: 'There are two distinct orders of reality – the independent [*svatantra*] and the dependent [*paratantra*]' (*Tattvaviveka* 1; Sharma 1997: 31). Independent reality consists of *Brahman* alone, whereas dependent reality consists of the individual selves (*jīvas*) and insentient matter (*jada*). Since dependent reality would not exist apart from *Brahman*'s will, this very dependence creates a fundamental distinction between *Brahman* and all else.

Like Rāmānuja, Madhva insists that *Brahman*'s transcendence is to be expressed in terms of his splendid personal qualities. Moreover, acknowledgement of this personal *Brahman*'s maximal greatness (especially his lordship over all) is necessary for liberation:

> He who knows Viṣṇu as full of excellences, gets rid of *saṃsāra* and becomes a enjoyer of painless bliss for all eternity. He rejoices in proximity to Viṣṇu. Viṣṇu is the support for the liberated selves. He surpasses them and he is their Lord. All of them are under his control. He is always the supreme ruler. (*Viṣṇutattvavinirṇaya* 461)

Such supreme perfections, however, are beyond the attainment of dependent selves. It is only God (Nārāyaṇa) who is all-surpassingly perfect in this way:

> All the Vedas aim at revealing Nārāyaṇa who is all-surpassing, free from all evil, abounding in all excellences and different from all else by reason of his uniqueness . . . [He] is above [other deities] because he is infinite in all his

> glorious attributes like independence, power, knowledge and bliss. They are all under his control . . . Thus, it is established that Nārāyaṇa is free from every imperfection and that he is perfect and abounds in infinite excellences. (*Viṣṇutattvavinirṇaya* 437–64)

Particularly important here is God's unique independence (*svatantra*), the attribute that distinguishes him ontologically from all other existents (all of which are dependent on him). This perfect independence is a fundamental part of his maximal greatness and its presence implies many of his other attributes – including his omniscience, sovereignty, divine grace, immutability and freedom from karma.

We saw earlier that Rāmānuja too emphasized the presence of an asymmetrical dependence relation between God and the individual selves and the material world such that they are dependent on God and cannot exist without God also existing. For Madhva, however, Rāmānuja's own account of the nature of that dependence relation effectively fails to do justice to the idea of God as a maximally great being worthy of ultimate concern. This is because when Rāmānuja says that the world (or an individual) is *Brahman*'s body, he is also saying that the world is both non-different from and yet not identical with *Brahman*, on whom it is dependent. As far as Madhva is concerned, this kind of qualified non-dualism compromises God's supremacy and undermines his unique devotional status.

Madhva's emphasis on God's total independence, however, has its own costs. In order to guarantee the individual selves' complete creaturely dependence upon God, Madhva argues that their liberation is determined by God. Knowledge, action and devotion are all powerless to bring about liberation without the grace of God. Moreover, selves are further classified according to their unique inherent characteristics and to their devotional capacity. Some selves are predestined for eternal punishment in hell, others for eternal transmigration, yet others for various grades of liberation. Madhva thus embraces both a theory of differentiated liberation and a doctrine of predestination.

Perhaps this move preserves our absolute dependence upon God. It may even be that by thus excluding any sense that liberation is automatic, some aspirants will be encouraged to undertake spiritual practice. However, in the absence of knowledge as to one's fitness for liberation, it seems that such predestinarianism is just as likely to discourage a rational agent from undertaking the rigorous path to liberation altogether. Why incur the costs of liberation-oriented practice unless there is good reason to suppose you are not already among the damned?

Jina

Īśvara and *Brahman*, the candidates that we have considered so far for being maximally great beings worthy of ultimate concern, are clearly not human beings. In contrast, the next two such candidates we shall consider – *Jina* and Buddha – are supposed to be human beings, albeit very highly developed ones.

The ideal of Jainism is to achieve liberation (*mokṣa*) by becoming an enlightened being. Jainas call such a being a *Jina* ('conqueror') or a *Tīrthaṅkara* ('ford-builder'), with these names indicating that the enlightened being has conquered all attachments and built a ford across the river of *saṃsāra*. A *Jina*, then, is one who, having following a path of ascetic purification over many lives, is now free of all karma and all attachments that defile the soul, and hence will no longer be reborn. In the meantime such a highly developed human being now possesses various important great-making properties, including omniscience.

We have already seen how various Hindu theists claimed omniscience (*sarvajñatva*) to be a great-making property of divine beings like *Īśvara* or *Brahman*. Such theists, of course, also deny omniscience to anyone but a deity. The non-theistic traditions of Buddhism and Jainism, however, claim for their great human teachers Gautama Buddha and Mahāvīra the status of omniscient beings. Moreover, Buddha and Mahāvīra are human beings who *attained* omniscience, unlike the eternally omniscient deities. In the case of Buddhism, however, the kind of omniscience involved was often thought to be not entirely unrestricted. Jainism, on the other hand, is both atheistic and committed to affirming that the *Jinas* are unrestrictedly omniscient.

The usual Jaina terms for omniscience are *kevalajñāna* ('knowledge isolated from karmic interference') or *anantajñāna* ('infinite knowledge'). The favoured illustrative image is of a mirror in which each one of the innumerable existents, in all its qualities and modes, is simultaneously reflected. Moreover, when each of the veiling obstructions of karma has been removed, the self directly and effortlessly perceives all the past, present and future knowables reflected in itself. In this sense, the omniscient being is one who has complete *self*-knowledge.

It is obvious that this account of the nature of the omniscience of a perfected human being depends heavily on a particular (and controversial) metaphysics of the self. But the Jaina philosopher Samantabhadra (sixth century) also offers an epistemological argument for the existence of an omniscient being: 'The objects that are minute, concealed or distant must be amenable to somebody's perception, because they are amenable to inferential knowledge, just like fire etc. It is this argument that establishes the existence of an omniscient personage' (*Āptamīmāṃsā* 5; Shah 1999: 4). Clearly, Samantabhadra's statement of his syllogism is highly compressed, but what he seems to be arguing here is that when we can infer the existence of fire on the mountain from our perception of smoke on that mountain, it is also the case that someone on the mountain can directly perceive the fire. Thus, in general, when we can infer the existence of any object we cannot directly perceive, that object can be perceived by somebody. For Samantabhadra, it is also the case that everything in the universe can be an object of inference: in other words, there are no unknowables, though there are things that are not directly perceived by all. Hence there must be somebody who perceives every object.

Unfortunately, the argument so construed would fail to establish that there is somebody (i.e., *some single person*) who perceives every object: at best, it would only establish that every object is perceived by *somebody or other*, without it needing to be the same person for each object. Nor could the argument establish that only the *Jina* (and not *Īśvara* or the Buddha) is omniscient.

Samantabhadra's next verse, however, does at least try to address this latter gap:

> And such an omniscient personage are you alone whose utterance is neither in conflict with logic nor in conflict with scripture. As for the proof of such an absence of conflict, it is the circumstance that what you seek to establish is never contradicted by what is known to be the case. (*Āptamīmāṃsā* 6; Shah 1999: 5)

But now an apparent vicious circle threatens: only a *Jina* is omniscient because only a *Jina*'s utterances do not contradict logic or (Jaina) scripture – scripture the authority of which is supposed to be guaranteed by the fact that it has an omniscient author, a *Jina*!

Be that as it may, Jaina philosophers after Samantabhadra continue to affirm the existence of the omniscient person, though increasingly they follow the lead of Hemacandra (eleventh century) and – particularly when arguing against the Mīmāṃsakas – concentrate on the more modest strategy of trying to establish that at least we have no valid means of knowledge that demonstrates the *non-existence* of an omniscient being.

Many Indian philosophers (including Kumārila the Mīmāṃsaka and the Buddhists Dharmakīrti and Śāntarakṣita) have offered trenchant criticisms of the Jaina account of total omniscience. But over the centuries, and notwithstanding the uniqueness of the idea in India, the Jainas have remained firmly committed to this doctrine of a (highly developed) human being who is unrestrictedly omniscient. Why so? Various possible answers might be suggested, all of them compossible.

Firstly, part of the appeal of the idea of an omniscient *Jina* historically was to guarantee the authority of the Jaina scriptures. Both Buddhism and Jainism were renunciant movements opposed to the orthodox Hindu insistence that only the Vedic scriptures were authoritative. Hindu orthodoxy split into two major camps about what made the Vedas unique: Mīmāṃsā held that they were unauthored and hence infallible, Nyāya held that they were authored by an omniscient and benevolent God and hence infallible. Either way, humans were unable to know right and wrong unaided by Vedic guidance. Both Buddhism and Jainism rejected this and appealed to the guidance of their own scriptures, authored by their human teachers. But ordinary human teachers are fallible, so both Buddhism and Jainism insist that the human authors of their own scriptures are omniscient beings. The Jainas then seek to justify the superiority of their own scriptures in terms of the unrestricted omniscience of the *Jina* in contrast to the restricted omniscience of the Buddha.

Secondly, it has been suggested (Fujinaga 2006) that a different Jaina motive for affirming the existence of an omniscient being might be to do with its potential usefulness in dealing with a certain predestinarian difficulty in Jainism, a difficulty analogous in many respects to that mentioned earlier as confronting Madhva's Dvaita Vedānta. Jainas hold both that it is a necessary condition of liberation that the soul possesses the capability to become free (*bhavyatva*), and that not all souls possess this quality. Those who do not are called *abhavya* and will never attain salvation. No ordinary person, however, can know through perception or inference whether someone will be liberated in the future. Thus it seems irrational for any ordinary person to choose to incur the considerable costs of embarking upon the rigorous Jaina path of purification. The way out here, of course, is to invoke the Jaina omniscient, who knows everything and can tell us about our prospects for future liberation.

Finally, it seems that the Jainas intuitively take omniscience to be a great-making property that a maximally great object of ultimate concern like the *Jina* should possess: after all, at the very least a perfect being surely needs to be *epistemically perfect*, and to possess only restricted omniscience is to be less than epistemically perfect. So whereas others have often portrayed Jaina claims about the omniscience of the *Jina* as outrageously extravagant, Jainas have consistently regarded the uniqueness of these claims as evidence for the superiority of their path.

Buddha

The Indian Buddhist tradition represents Gautama Buddha as being a human being who attained perfect enlightenment, earning the honorific 'Buddha' ('awakened one'). But what properties must an individual possess in order to be a Buddha? The answer to that question presumably gives us a list of those great-making properties that Buddhists think a maximally great being must possess (see Griffiths 1987, 1994).

The early Pali texts frequently offer a set of nine exalted epithets used of Gautama Buddha. He is (1) worthy, (2) fully and completely awakened, (3) accomplished in knowledge and virtue, (4) well gone, (5) knower of worlds, (6) unsurpassed guide for those who need restraint, (7) teacher of gods and men, (8) awakened one, and (9) lord. The later Theravādin tradition then glosses and elaborates on this ninefold list of superlatives in a way that seeks to provide a list of the Buddha's attributes as a perfect being. Over time, this kind of thinking develops into a more systematic Buddhist attempt to delineate systematically those attributes something must have to be a maximally great being.

The most elaborate Indian effort in this direction – by now no longer working with the original ninefold list of the Pali Nikāyas – is to be found in the Yogācāra tradition's doctrinal digests. There the central great-making properties attributed to Buddha are (1) purity, (2) omnipresence, (3) universal awareness, (4) inseparability from everything that exists, and (5) absence of volition or effort.

It is immediately noticeable how much this Yogācāra list tends to downplay individuality, agency, temporality and volition as great-making properties. In contrast, Western theists listing the great-making properties of an all-perfect God have tended to nominate attributes like conscious agency, benevolence, omniscience, omnipotence, and being a creator. To be sure, there are some similarities between the two lists, but there are also striking disagreements: particularly, with respect to the status of agency and personality as great-making properties. These divergences are related to certain fundamental differences in beliefs about the nature of the world. For instance, the Buddhist metaphysics of 'no-self' treats ordinary instances of what we call 'agency' as just the occurrence of impersonal events, rather than a property of ontologically independent persons, and so there is not the Western tendency to think of agency as a great-making property.

One apparent commonality between the two lists, however, is omniscience: both Buddha and God are all-knowing. The Sanskrit term often used for this property is *sarvajñatva* (*sarva*, 'all', plus *jñatva*, 'knowing') and it is cognate with the Latinate *omniscience*. But even this may be a bit deceptive, since the Yogācārins hold that a Buddha's knowledge of all things is through direct awareness free from conceptual construction (*vikalpa*).

Putting that aside for the moment, however, it is important to note that the early Buddhist scriptures attach more significance to the knowledge of *dharma* than to the knowledge of all. So when the Buddha is described as *sarvajña*, this is understood primarily in the sense of 'knower of the *dharma*', that is, knower of the noble truths that lead to liberation. It is this restricted conception of omniscience that the Jainas contrast with their own conception of an unrestrictedly omniscient being.

Reluctant to have the Buddha seem less great than Mahāvīra but unable to accept the Jaina metaphysics of the self, the Theravādins begin to restrict the scope of the Buddha's omniscience differently from the early Pali scriptures. They define the omniscience of the Buddha as an ability to know *all* objects, but only one object at a time. Thus when in the *Milindapañha* the king Milinda asks if the Buddha was omniscient, the Venerable Nāgasena replies: 'Yes, O king, he was. But the insight of knowledge was not always and continually (consciously) present with him. The omniscience of the Blessed One was dependent on reflection. But if he did reflect he knew whatever he wanted to know' (IV.1.19; Rhys Davids 1890: II, 154). Later Theravādins, however, seem to find his position more than a little artificial. Thus the commentator Dhammapāla (sixth century) is happy to insist: '[The] Buddha, whether he wishes to know the objects all together, or separately, all at once or one by one, knows them all as he wishes. Therefore he is called *sammā-sambuddha* [a perfectly enlightened one]' (Jaini 1974: 85). Obviously, Dhammapāla here takes unrestricted omniscience to be a great-making property that a Buddha should possess. But just how he is to square his bold claims about it with apparently incompatible passages from the scriptures is unresolved.

The writings of the Mahāyāna Buddhist philosophers present a reconsideration of the problem. While they felt the need to take account of the Mīmāṃsā attack on the idea of a totally omniscient being, their metaphysics was not realist in the manner of the Theravādins. Accordingly, they were unimpressed by a purported ability to know 'the all'. Instead there is a return to the earlier position of the Pali scriptures: the Buddha's omniscience is once again restricted in scope to what is necessary for salvation. Thus the demand that an authoritative teacher must be unrestrictedly omniscient is disparagingly rejected in Dharmakīrti's *Pramāṇavārttika* (seventh century):

> People, afraid of being deceived by false teachers in the matter of directing the ignorant, seek out a man with knowledge, for the sake of realizing his teaching. What is the use of his wide knowledge pertaining to the number of insects in the whole world? Rather, enquire into his knowledge of that which is to be practised by us. For us, the most desired authority is not the one who knows everything [indiscriminately]; rather, we would have a Teacher who knows the Truth which leads to prosperity in this world, as well as to insight into things to be forsaken and things to be cultivated. Whether he sees far or whether he sees not, let him see the desired Truth. If one becomes an authority merely because of seeing far and wide, let us worship these vultures who can do it better. (II.32–5; Jaini 1974: 86–7)

Total omniscience, then, is not a great-making property that a maximally great being like the Buddha needs to possess. Restricted omniscience with respect to all matters relevant to the nature of salvation and the means of attaining it, however, is a great-making property that a maximally great Buddha does need to possess.

Śāntarakṣita, writing a century or so later, expresses a similar view in his huge polemical compendium the *Tattvasaṃgraha*:

> If the attempt were made to prove that one has the knowledge of the details of all individuals and components of the whole world, – it would be as futile

> as the investigation of the crow's teeth... By proving the existence of the person knowing only *dharma* and *adharma*, whom the Buddha postulates, – one secures the reliability and acceptability of the scripture composed by him; and by denying the said person, one secures the unreliability and rejectability of the said scripture. Thus when people [e.g., the Jainas] proceed to prove the existence of the person knowing all the little details of the entire world, they put themselves to the unnecessary trouble of writing treatises on the subject and carrying on discussions on the same. (*Tattvasaṃgraha* 3138–41; Jha 1986: 1397–8)

Śāntarakṣita, however, does not actually deny that total omniscience is possible. Moreover, he tries to show that the Mīmāṃsaka arguments against this possibility are inconclusive. But he does insist that a totally omniscient being is not required to guarantee the trustworthiness of scripture. And by implication, he also agrees with Dharmakīrti that unrestricted omniscience is not a great-making property that a maximally great being like the Buddha is required to possess.

But if the authority of the Buddhist scriptures derives from the (restricted) omniscience of the Buddha, then how can we know this? After all, both the Jainas and some Hindus also claim omniscience for the authors of their quite divergent scriptures. Śāntarakṣita's answer is that the individual teachings of the Buddha must be established one by one as compatible with empirical and rational investigation and the whole system must be shown to be internally consistent. This is the burden of the huge bulk of argumentation presented in the *Tattvsaṃgraha*.

Satisfied with the results of his investigation, Śāntarakṣita concludes that the (restricted) omniscience of the Buddha is the basis for the reliability of the scriptures. However, he also concludes that *our* knowledge of the truth of the doctrines expressed in the scriptures is based upon independent logical and empirical investigation. Omniscience, then, while it may be possible, is not of much significance to us in deciding which scriptural doctrines we ought to believe (though it may be of religious significance in helping to preserve the ideal of the perfect Buddha as an object of ultimate concern).

Conclusion

This concludes our survey of some prominent problems and arguments in Indian philosophy of religion, particularly those centred around competing

Indian conceptions of ultimate concern and maximal goodness. Once again, we have seen at least a little of the considerable philosophical rigour and ingenuity that the Indian authors brought to these issues - much the same kind of rigour and ingenuity that they brought to bear on all of the many philosophical issues they addressed.

With the conclusion of this final chapter we also have come to the end of our general introduction to Indian philosophy. The reader who has attentively read this book all the way through will likely now have a rather different picture of Indian philosophy than they started out with. And a reader who wishes to pursue the subject further should hopefully now be in possession of a chart with which to begin to navigate for themselves the broad and deep ocean of Indian philosophy: *śubhayātrā*!

Suggestions for further reading

On ultimate concern, maximal greatness and alternative concepts of God, see further Wainwright 2013. For more on the role of *Īśvara* in Yoga, see Larson and Bhattacharya 2008 and Phillips 2009. On the Nyāya arguments for the existence of *Īśvara*, see Bhattacharyya 1961, Chemparathy 1972, Vattanky 1984, Chakrabarti 1989 and Dasti 2011. On Buddhist atheism, see Hayes 1988b, Jackson 1986 and Patil 2009; on Mīmāṃsā atheism, see Bilimoria 1990. For Hindu views about revelation (with special reference to Advaita), see Murty 1974. A good comparative review of the rival views of Śaṃkara, Rāmānuja and Madhva on *Brahman* is Lott 1980. On Śaṃkara, see further Potter 1981 and Alston 2004. On Rāmānuja, see further Carman 1972, Lipner 1986 and Yamunacharya 1988. On Madhva, see further Sharma 1997, 1986, 1981 and Sarma 2003. For more on the nature of the *Jina* and the Jaina path of purification, see Jaini 1998 and Dundas 2002; on the Jaina view of omniscience, see Jaini 1974, Singh 1974 and Fujinaga 2006. On the Buddha as a maximally great being, see Griffiths 1989, 1994. For the Buddhist epistemologists' views about reason and scripture, see Hayes 1983. On the omniscience of the Buddha, see further Jaini 1974 and McClintock 2010.

Glossary

For much more complete glossary of Sanskrit philosophical terms, see Grimes 1996.

abādhitatva	unfalsifiedness
abhāva	absence
Abhidharma	Buddhist analytic metaphysics of momentary *dharmas*
Ābhidharmika	a specialist in Abhidharma
Advaita	non-dualism; a school of Vedānta
Advaitin	an adherent of Advaita
ahiṃsā	non-injury
ākāṅksā	mutual expectancy
anātman	'no-self'; the Buddhist denial of a permanent and substantial self
anavasthā	infinite regress
anekantavāda	Jaina nonabsolutism
antaḥkaraṇa	inner sense
anumāna	inference
anupalabdhi	presumption
anvitābhidhāna	related designation theory
apoha	exclusion
āpta	an expert whose testimony is reliable
artha	wealth; meaning; aim, goal
arthakriyā	successful action; causal efficacy
arthāpatti	presumption
asatkāryavāda	the non-identity theory of causation which denies the pre-existence of the effect
āsatti	contiguity

āstika	orthodox, i.e., one who accepts the authority of the Vedas
ātman	self
avacchedavāda	limitationism
avidyā	ignorance
Bhāmatī	a subschool of Advaita
Bhāṭṭa	an adherent of the Bhāṭṭa subschool of Mīmaṃsā
bhedābheda	identity-in-difference
bodhisattva	Mahāyāna Buddhist ethical ideal of a being aspiring to enlightenment for the sake of all sentient beings
Brahman	the Absolute
Buddha	an enlightened being in Buddhism
caitanya	consciousness
catuṣkoṭi	the Buddhist tetralemma
cetanā	volition, intention
darśana	philosophical school
dharma	morality; duty; (in Buddhism) a momentary simple
dravya	substance
dravyasat	primary existent
duḥkha	suffering
Dvaita	dualism; a school of Vedānta
guṇa	quality
hetu	reason; that other property which is related in an appropriate way to the *sādhya* of an inference
hetvābhāṣa	fallacy
Īśvara	God
Jaina	an adherent of Jainism
jāti	class; universal
Jina	'spiritual victor', an enlightened being in Jainism
jīva	individual self
jīvanmukti	living liberation
jñāna	cognition
kāma	pleasure
kāraṇa	cause
karma	action; accumulation of past actions

khyātivāda	theory of perceptual error
lakṣaṇa	secondary meaning; definition
līlā	play
Madhyamaka	'the middle'; alongside Yogācāra, one of the two principal Mahāyāna Buddhist schools
Mādhyamika	an adherent of Madhyamaka
Mahāyāna	'great vehicle'; a broad school of Buddhism
Mīmaṃsā	orthodox school of Vedic exegetes
Mīmaṃsaka	an adherent of Mīmaṃsā
mithyā	false
mokṣa	liberation
mukti	liberation
nāstika	heterodox, i.e., one who denies the authority of the Vedas
Naiyāyika	an adherent of the Nyāya school
nirguṇa	without qualities
nirvāṇa	liberation in Buddhism
nirvikalpaka	indeterminate; non-conceptual
niṣkāma karma	desireless action
nivṛtti	quietism
Nyāya	the orthodox school of logic
padārtha	category
pakṣa	the subject of an inference; minor term
paramārthasat	ultimately real
parataḥprakāśa	other-illumination
parathaḥprāmāṇyavāda	extrinsic truth apprehension theory
paryudāsa-pratiṣedha	implicative negation
phala	fruit; result
Prabhākāra	an adherent of the Prabhākāra subschool of Mīmāṃsā
prajñaptisat	secondary or 'conventional' existent
prakṛti	nature, matter (in Sāṃkhya philosophy)
pramā	a knowledge episode
pramāṇa	means of knowledge
pramāṇavāda	epistemology
prāmāṇya	truth
prameya	object of knowledge

prasajya-pratiṣedha	non-implicative negation
prasaṅga	*reductio ad absurdum*
Prāsaṅgika Madhyamaka	a subschool of Madhyamaka Buddhism (associated with the philosophers Candrakīrti and Śāntideva)
pratibimbavāda	reflectionism
pratijñā	thesis; hypothesis
pratītyasamutapāda	the Buddhist doctrine of causality
pratyakṣa	perception
pravṛtti	activism
pudgala	person
puruṣa	self (in Sāṃkhya-Yoga)
puruṣārtha	the ends of human life
śabda	word; testimony
śābdabodha	linguistic understanding
sādhya	the property that qualifies the subject of an inference; major term
saguṇa	with qualities
sallekhanā	ritual death by fasting in Jainism
sāmānādhikaraṇya	co-ordinate predication
sāmānya	a universal
samavāya	inherence
Sāṃkhya	orthodox dualist philosophical school
saṃsāra	the cycle of birth and death
saṃśāya	doubt
saṃvṛtisat	conventionally real
sapakṣa	the positive example in an inference
saptabhaṅgi	sevenfold predication in Jainism
sarvajñatva	omniscience
Sarvāstivāda	a Buddhist Abhidharma school (also known as Vaibhāṣika)
sat	being, reality
satkāryavāda	the identity theory of causation, which affirms the pre-existence of the effect
Sautrāntika	Buddhist school that denied the authority of the Sarvāstivādin Abhidharma
savikalpaka	determinate; conceptual

sphota	the linguistic sign as meaning-bearer, that from which the meaning 'bursts forth'
śubhayātrā	*bon voyage*
śūnyatā	emptiness
svabhāva	inherent existence
svadharma	own-duty
svaprakāśa	self-illumination
svataḥprāmaṇyavāda	intrinsic truth apprehension theory
syādvāda	Jaina theory of conditional assertion
'*tat tvam asi*'	'that art thou' (one of the Upaniṣadic 'great sayings')
tātparya	intention
trairūpya	triple condition
upādhi	an inferential undercutting condition
upamāna	analogy
Vaiśeṣika	orthodox school of atomism
varṇāsrama-dharma	the Hindu social system of caste and stage-of-life duties
Vedānta	orthodox Hindu philosophical schools (including Advaita, Viśiṣtādvaita and Dvaita) founded on the teachings of the Upaniṣads
vikalpa	conceptual construction
vipakṣa	negative example in an inference
Viśiṣṭādvaita	qualified non-dualism; a school of Vedānta
Vivaraṇa	a subschool of Advaita
vivartavāda	the appearance theory of causation
vyāpti	pervasion; the invariable concomitance that grounds inference
vyāvahārika	the relative or conventional viewpoint
yoga	ascetic practice
Yoga	an orthodox school of Hindu philosophy
Yogācāra	Buddhist idealism; alongside Madhyamaka, one of the two principal Mahāyāna Buddhist schools
yogyatā	semantical appropriateness

Bibliography

Alston, A. J. (1971). trans. *The Realization of the Absolute: The 'Naiṣkarmya Siddhi' of Śrī Sureśvara*. 2nd edn. London: Shanti Sadan.

(2004). ed. and trans. *A Śaṅkara Source Book*. 2nd edn. 5 vols. London: Shanti Sadan.

Arnold, Dan (2005). *Buddhists, Brahmin, and Belief: Epistemology in South Asian Philosophy of Religion*. New York: Columbia University Press.

Basham, A. L. (1971). *The Wonder that was India*. 3rd edn. London: Fontana.

Bhaduri, Sadananda (1975). *Studies in Nyāya-Vaiśeṣika Metaphysics*. 2nd edn. Poona: Bhandarkar Oriental Research Institute.

Bhartiya, M. C. (1973). *Causation in Indian Philosophy*. Ghaziabad: Vimal Prakashan.

Bhatt, Govardhan P. (1989). *The Basic Ways of Knowing*. 2nd rev. edn. Delhi: Motilal Banarsidass.

Bhattacharya, Gopinath (1989). trans. *Tarkasaṁgraha-Dīpikā on Tarkasaṁgraha by Annaṁbhaṭṭa*. 2nd rev. edn. Calcutta: Progressive Publishers.

Bhattacharya, Kamaleswar (1978). *The Dialectical Method of Nāgārjuna (Vigrahavyāvartanī)*. 4th edn. Delhi: Motilal Banarsidass.

Bhattacharya, Ramkrishna (2002). 'Cārvāka Fragments: A New Collection'. *Journal of Indian Philosophy* 30: 597–640.

(2010). 'What the Cārvākas Originally Meant: More on the Commentators on the Cārvākasūtra'. *Journal of Indian Philosophy* 38: 529–42.

Bhattacharyya, Gopikamohan (1961). *Studies in Nyāya-Vaiśeṣika Theism*. Calcutta: Sanskrit College.

Bhattacharyya, Janaki Vallabha (1978). trans. *Jayanta Bhaṭṭa's Nyāya-Mañjarī*. Delhi: Motilal Banarsidass.

Bhattacharyya, Sibajiban (1990). 'Some Features of the Technical Language of Navya-Nyāya'. *Philosophy East and West* 40: 129–49. (Reprinted in Perrett 2001, vol. II.)

Bhusan, Nalini and Jay L. Garfield (2011). eds. *Indian Philosophy in English: From Renaissance to Independence*. Oxford University Press.

Bilimoria, Puruṣottama (1990). 'Hindu Doubts About God: Towards a Mīmāṃsā Deconstruction'. *International Philosophical Quarterly* 30: 481–99. (Reprinted in Perrett 2001, vol. IV.)

Broad, C. D. (1927). *The Mind and its Place in Nature*. London: Routledge.

Brown, D. Mackenzie (1953). *The White Umbrella: Indian Political Thought from Manu to Gandhi*. Berkeley: University of California Press.

Carman, John B. (1972). *The Theology of Rāmānuja*. New Haven, CT: Yale University Press.

Chakrabarti, Arindam (1982). 'The Nyāya Proofs for the Existence of the Soul'. *Journal of Indian Philosophy* 10: 211–38.

(1989). 'From the Fabric to the Weaver?' In Roy W. Perrett (ed.), *Indian Philosophy of Religion*. Dordrecht: Kluwer.

(1997a). *Denying Existence*. Dordrecht: Kluwer.

(1997b). 'Rationality in Indian Philosophy'. In Eliot Deutsch and Ron Bontekoe (eds.), *A Companion to World Philosophies*. Oxford: Blackwell.

Chakrabarti, Kisor Kumar (1975). 'The Nyāya-Vaiśeṣika Theory of Universals'. *Journal of Indian Philosophy* 3: 363–82. (Reprinted in Perrett 2001, vol. III.)

(1977). *The Logic of Gotama*. Honolulu: University of Hawai'i Press.

(1999). *Classical Indian Philosophy of Mind: The Nyāya Dualist Tradition*. Albany: State University of New York Press.

(2010). *Classical Indian Philosophy of Induction: The Nyāya Viewpoint*. Lanham, MD: Rowman & Littlefield.

Chari, V. K. (1990). *Sanskrit Criticism*. Honolulu: University of Hawai'i Press.

Chatterjee, Satischandra (1950). *The Nyāya Theory of Knowledge*. 2nd edn. Calcutta University Press.

Chattopadhyaya, Debiprasad and Mrinalkanti Gangopadhyaya (1967). trans. *Nyāya Philosophy*. Calcutta: Indian Studies Past and Present.

(1994). eds. *Cārvāka/Lokāyata*. New Delhi: Indian Council of Philosophical Research.

Chemparathy, George (1972). *An Indian Rational Theology*. Vienna: De Nobili Research Library.

Clooney, Francis X. (1993). *Theology after Vedānta: An Experiment in Comparative Theology*. Albany: State University of New York Press.

(1996). *Seeing Through Texts: Doing Theology Among the Śrīvaiṣṇavas of South India*. Albany: State University of New York Press.

Collins, Steven (1982). *Selfless Persons: Imagery and Thought in Theravādin Buddhism*. Cambridge University Press.

Conze, Edmund (1951). *Buddhism: Its Essence and Development*. New York: Harper.

Coulson, Michael (1976). *Sanskrit: An Introduction to the Classical Language*. London: Hodder & Stoughton.

Coward, Harold G. and K. Kunjunni Raja (1990). eds. *The Philosophy of the Grammarians*. Delhi: Motilal Banarsidass.

Crawford, S. Cromwell (1982). *The Evolution of Hindu Ethical Ideals*. 2nd rev. edn. Honolulu: University of Hawai'i Press.

Das, Gurcharan (2009). *The Difficulty of Being Good: On the Subtle Art of Dharma*. Oxford University Press.

Dasgupta, Surendranath (1922–55). *A History of Indian Philosophy*. 5 vols. Cambridge University Press.

Dasti, Matthew R. (2011). 'Indian Rational Theology: Proof, Justification, and Epistemic Liberality in Nyāya's Argument for God'. *Asian Philosophy* 21: 1–21.

Datta, D. M. (1960). *The Six Ways of Knowing*. 2nd rev. edn. Calcutta University Press.

Davis, Donald R. (2010). *The Spirit of Hindu Law*. Cambridge University Press.

De Bary, W. T. (1958). ed. *Sources of Indian Tradition*. New York: Columbia University Press.

Deutsch, Eliot (1969). *Advaita Vedānta: A Philosophical Reconstruction*. Honolulu: East-West Center Press.

Deutsch, Eliot and J. A. B. van Buitenen (1971). eds. *A Source Book of Advaita Vedānta*. Honolulu: University of Hawai'i Press.

Doniger, Wendy and Brian K. Smith (1991). trans. *The Laws of Manu*. Harmondsworth: Penguin.

Dravid, N. S. (1995). trans. *Ātmatattvaviveka of Udayanācārya*. Shimla: Indian Institute of Advanced Study.

(1996). trans. *Nyāyakusumāñjali of Udayanācārya*. New Delhi: Indian Council of Philosophical Research.

Dravid, Raja Ram (1972). *The Problem of Universals in Indian Philosophy*. Delhi: Motilal Banarsidass.

Dreyfus, Georges B. J. (1997). *Recognizing Reality: Dharmakīrti's Philosophy and its Tibetan Interpretations*. Albany: State University of New York Press.

Duerlinger, James (2003). *Indian Buddhist Theories of Persons: Vasubandhu's 'Refutation of the Theory of a Self'*. London: RoutledgeCurzon.

Dummett, Michael (1981). *Frege: Philosophy of Language*. 2nd edn. London: Duckworth.

Dumont, Louis (1980). *Homo Hierarchicus*. rev. edn. University of Chicago Press.

Dundas, Paul (2002). *The Jains*. 2nd edn. London: Routledge.

Dunne, John D. (2004). *Foundations of Dharmakīrti's Philosophy*. Boston, MA: Wisdom Publications.

Edelglass, William and Jay L. Garfield (2009). eds. *Buddhist Philosophy: Essential Readings*. Oxford University Press.

Edgerton, Franklin (1965). *The Beginnings of Indian Philosophy*. Cambridge, MA: Harvard University Press.

Feuerstein, Georg (1989). trans. *The Yoga-Sūtra of Patañjali: A New Translation and Commentary*. Rochester, VT: Inner Traditions International.

Fort, Andrew O. and Patricia Y. Mumme (1996). eds. *Living Liberation in Hindu Thought*. Albany: State University of New York Press.

Framarin, Christopher G. (2009). *Desire and Motivation in Indian Philosophy*. London: Routledge.

Franco, Eli (1994). *Perception, Knowledge and Disbelief: A Study of Jayarāśi's Scepticism*. 2nd edn. Delhi: Motilal Banarsidass.

(2013). ed. *Periodization and History of Indian Philosophy*. Vienna: De Nobili Research Library.

(forthcoming). 'Jayarāśi and the Skeptical Tradition'. In Matthew T. Kapstein (ed.), *The Columbia Guide to Classical Indian Philosophy*. New York: Columbia University Press.

Frauwallner, Erich (2007). *The Philosophy of Buddhism*. Delhi: Motilal Banarsidass.

Frege, Gottlob (1960). *Translations from the Philosophical Writings of Gottlob Frege*. 2nd edn. Oxford: Blackwell.

Fujinaga, Sin (2006). 'Why Must There be an Omniscient in Jainism?' In Peter Flügel (ed.), *Studies in Jaina Philosophy and Culture*. London: Routledge.

Ganeri, Jonardon (1999). *Semantic Powers: Meaning and Means of Knowing in Classical Indian Philosophy*. Oxford University Press.

(2001a). ed. *Indian Logic: A Reader*. London: Curzon.

(2001b). *Philosophy in Classical India: The Proper Work of Reason*. London: Routledge.

(2002). 'Jaina Logic and the Philosophical Basis of Pluralism'. *History and Philosophy of Logic* 23: 267–81.

(2004). 'Indian Logic'. In Dov M. Gabbay and John Woods (eds.), *Handbook of the History of Logic, Volume* 1. Amsterdam: Elsevier.

(2006). *Artha: Meaning*. Oxford University Press.

(2007). *The Concealed Art of the Soul*. Oxford University Press.

(2011). *The Lost Age of Reason: Philosophy in Early Modern India 1450–1700*. Oxford University Press.

(2012). *The Self*. Oxford University Press.

Gangopadhyaya, Mrinalkanti (1971). trans. *Vinītadeva's Nyāyabindu-ṭīkā*. Calcutta: Indian Studies Past and Present.

Garfield, Jay L. (1995). trans. *The Fundamental Wisdom of the Middle Way*. Oxford University Press.

(2002). *Empty Words*. Oxford University Press.

Gerow, Edwin (1997). 'Indian Aesthetics: A Philosophical Survey'. In Eliot Deutsch and Ron Bontekoe (eds.), *A Companion to World Philosophies*. Oxford: Blackwell.

Gillon, Brendan S. (1991). 'Dharmakīrti and the Problem of Induction'. In Ernst Steinkellner (ed.), *Studies in the Buddhist Epistemological Tradition*. Vienna: Verlagder Österreichischen Akademie der Wissenschaften.

Goldman, Robert P. and Sally J. Sutherland (1987). *Devavāṇīpraveśikā: An Introduction to the Sanskrit Language*. 2nd edn. Berkeley: Center for South and Southeast Asia Studies, University of California.

Goodman, Charles (2009). *Consequences of Compassion: An Interpretation and Defense of Buddhist Ethics*. Oxford University Press.

Granoff, P. E. (1978). *Philosophy and Argument in Late Vedānta: Śrī Harṣa's Khaṇḍanakhaṇḍakhādya*. Dordrecht: D. Reidel.

Griffiths, Paul J. (1989). 'Buddha and God: A Contrastive Study in Ideas about Maximal Greatness'. *Journal of Religion* 69: 502–29. (Reprinted in Perrett 2001, vol. IV.)

(1994). *On Being Buddha: The Classical Doctrine of Buddhahood*. Albany: State University of New York Press.

Grimes, John (1996). *A Concise Dictionary of Indian Philosophy*. rev. edn. Albany: State University of New York Press.

Gupta, Bina (1991). *Perceiving in Advaita Vedānta: Epistemological Analysis and Interpretation*. Lewisburg, PN: Bucknell University Press.

Halbfass, Wilhelm (1988). *India and Europe: An Essay in Understanding*. Albany: State University of New York Press.

(1992). *On Being and What There Is: Classical Vaiśeṣika and the History of Indian Ontology*. Albany: State University of New York Press.

Hamblin, C. L. (1970). *Fallacies*. London: Methuen.

Harvey, Peter (2000). *An Introduction to Buddhist Ethics: Foundations, Values and Issues*. Cambridge University Press.

Hattori, Masaaki (1997). 'The Buddhist Theory Concerning the Truth and Falsity of Cognition'. In J. N. Mohanty and Purushottama Bilimoria (eds.), *Relativism, Suffering and Beyond: Essays in Memory of Bimal K. Matilal*. Oxford University Press.

Hayes, Richard P. (1983). 'The Question of Doctrinalism in the Buddhist Epistemologists'. *Journal of the American Academy of Religion* 52: 645–70. (Reprinted in Perrett 2001, vol. IV.)

(1988a). *Dignāga on the Interpretation of Signs*. Dordrecht: D. Reidel.

(1988b). 'Principled Atheism in the Buddhist Scholastic Tradition'. *Journal of Indian Philosophy* 16: 5–28. (Reprinted in Perrett 2001, vol. IV.)

(1994). 'Nāgārjuna's Appeal'. *Journal of Indian Philosophy* 22: 299–378.

Hayes, Richard P. and Brendan S. Gillon (1991). 'Introduction to Dharmakīrti's Theory of Inference as Presented in Pramāṇavārttika Svopajñavṛtti 1–10'. *Journal of Indian Philosophy* 19: 1–73.

Herman, Arthur L. (1976). *The Problem of Evil and Indian Thought*. Delhi: Motilal Banarsidass.

Hiriyanna, M. (1932). *Outlines of Indian Philosophy*. London: George Allen & Unwin.

(1975). *Indian Conception of Values*. Mysore: Kavyalaya Publishers.

Horner, I. B. (1938). trans. *The Book of the Discipline (Vinayapiṭaka)*, vol. i. London: Pali Text Society.

Houben, Jan E. M. (1997). 'The Sanskrit Tradition'. In Wout van Bekkum et al. (eds.), *The Emergence of Semantics in Four Linguistic Traditions*. Amsterdam: John Benjamins.

Huntington, C. W., Jr and Geshé Namgyal Wangchen (1989). *The Emptiness of Emptiness*. Honolulu: University of Hawai'i Press.

Ingalls, Daniel H. H. (1951). *Materials for the Study of Navya-Nyāya Logic*. Cambridge, MA: Harvard University Press.

Jackson, Roger (1986). 'Dharmakīrti's Refutation of Theism'. *Philosophy East and West* 36: 315–48.

Jacobi, Hermann (1884). trans. *Jaina Sūtras*, part I. Oxford University Press.

Jagadānanda, Swāmi (1941). trans. *Upadeśa Sāhasrī of Śrī Śaṅkarācārya*. Mylapore: Sri Ramakrishna Math.

Jaini, Padmanabh S. (1973). 'Śramaṇas: Their Conflict with Brāhmaṇical Society'. In Joseph W. Elder (ed.), *Chapters in Indian Civilization*. Madison: Department of Indian Studies, University of Wisconsin.

(1974). 'On the Sarvajñatva (Omniscience) of Mahāvīra and the Buddha'. In L. Cousins (ed.), *Buddhist Studies in Honour of I. B. Horner*. Dordrecht: D. Reidel.

(1998). *The Jaina Path of Purification*. Delhi: Motilal Banarsidass.

James, William (1950). *The Principles of Psychology*. New York: Dover.

Jha, Ganganatha (1942). trans. *The Chāndogyopanishad: A Treatise on Vedānta Philosophy Translated into English with the Commentary of Śankara*. Poona: Oriental Book Agency.

(1964). *Pūrva-Mīmāṁsā in its Sources*. 2nd edn. Varanasi: Banaras Hindu University.

(1983). trans. *Ślokavārttika*, 2nd edn. Delhi: Sri Satguru Publications.

(1986). trans. *The Khaṇḍanakhaṇḍakhādya of Shri Harṣa*. 2nd edn. Delhi: Sri Satguru Publications.

(1986). trans. *The Tattvasaṅgraha of Śāntarakṣita with the Commentary of Kamalaśīla*. Delhi: Motilal Banarsidass.

Jing Haifeng (2006). 'From "Philosophy" to "Chinese Philosophy": Preliminary Thoughts in a Postcolonial Linguistic Context'. *Contemporary Chinese Thought* 37: 60–72.

Johnston, Mark (1992). 'Reasons and Reductionism'. *Philosophical Review* 101: 589–618.

(1997). 'Human Concerns Without Superlative Selves'. In Jonathan Dancy (ed.), *Reading Parfit*. Oxford: Blackwell.

Kagan, Shelly (1998). *Normative Ethics*. Boulder, CO: Westview Press.

Kangle, R. P. (1960–5). *The Kauṭilīya Arthaśāstra*. Bombay: University of Bombay.

Kapstein, Matthew T. (2001). *Reason's Traces: Identity and Interpretation in Indian and Tibetan Buddhist Thought*. Boston, MA: Wisdom Publications.

Katsura, Shōryū (1984). 'Dharmakīrti's Theory of Truth'. *Journal of Indian Philosophy* 12: 215–35. (Reprinted in Perrett 2001, vol. I.)

Keown, Damien (2001). *The Nature of Buddhist Ethics*. New York: Palgrave Macmillan.

(2005). *Buddhist Ethics: A Very Short Introduction*. Oxford University Press.

Koller, John M. and Patricia Koller (1991). eds. *A Sourcebook in Asian Philosophy*. New York: Prentice-Hall.

Kripke, Saul (1982). *Wittgenstein on Rules and Private Language*. Cambridge, MA: Harvard University Press.

Kuznetsova, Irina, Jonardon Ganeri and Chakravarthi Ram-Prasad (2012). eds. *Hindu and Buddhist Ideas in Dialogue: Self and No-Self*. Farnham: Ashgate.

Larson, Gerald J. (1979). *Classical Sāṃkhya*. 2nd rev. edn. Delhi: Motilal Banarsidass.

Larson, Gerald J. and Ram Shankar Bhattacharya (1987). eds. *Sāṃkhya: A Dualist Tradition in Indian Philosophy*. Delhi: Motilal Banarsidass.

(2008). eds. *Yoga: India's Philosophy of Meditation*. Delhi: Motilal Banarsidass.

Lewis, David (1969). *Conventions: A Philosophical Study*. Cambridge, MA: Harvard University Press.

Lindtner, Christian (1981). 'Buddhapālita on Emptiness'. *Indo-Iranian Journal* 23: 187–217.

Lingat, Robert (1973). *The Classical Law of India*. Berkeley: University of California Press.

Lipner, Julius J. (1986). *The Face of Truth: A Study of Meaning and Metaphysics in the Vedāntic Theology of Rāmānuja*. Albany: State University of New York Press.

Lott, Eric J. (1980). *Vedāntic Approaches to God*. London: Macmillan.

Mādhavānanda, Swāmī (1977). trans. *Bhāṣa-Pariccheda with Siddhānta-Muktāvalī by Viśvanātha Nyāya-Pañcānana*. 3rd edn. Calcutta: Advaita Ashrama.

(1988). trans. *The Bṛhadāraṇyaka Upaniṣad: With the Commentary of Śaṅkarācārya*. 7th edn. Delhi: Advaita Ashrama.

(2000). trans. *Vedānta-Paribhāṣa of Dharmarāja Ādhvarīndra*. 4th edn. Kolkata: Advaita Ashrama, 2000.

Madhusūdana Sarasvatī (1937). *Advaitasiddhi of Madhusūdanasarasvatī*, ed. M. M. Anant Kṛiṣṇa Sāstrī. 2nd edn. rev. Bombay: Nirnaya-sagar Press.

Maitra, Sushil Kumar (1956). *The Ethics of the Hindus*. 2nd edn. Calcutta University Press.

Matilal, Bimal Krishna (1968). *The Navya-Nyāya Docrine of Negation*. Cambridge, MA: Harvard University Press.

(1981). *The Central Philosophy of Jainism (Anekānta-Vāda)*. Ahmedabad: Lalbhai Dalpatbhai Institute of Indology.

(1982). *Logical and Ethical Issues of Religious Belief*. Calcutta University Press.

(1985). *Logic, Language and Reality*. Delhi: Motilal Banarsidass.

(1986). *Perception: An Essay on Classical Indian Theories of Knowledge*. Oxford: Clarendon Press.

(1989). ed. *Moral Dilemmas in the Mahābhārata*. Delhi: Motilal Banarsidass.

(1990). *The Word and the World: India's Contribution to the Study of Language*. Oxford University Press.

(1998). *The Character of Logic in India*. Albany: State University of New York Press.

(2002a). *The Collected Essays of Bimal Krishna Matilal: Ethics and Epics*, ed. Jonardon Ganeri. Oxford University Press.

(2002b). *The Collected Essays of Bimal Krishna Matilal: Mind, Language and World*, ed. Jonardon Ganeri. Oxford University Press.

Matilal, Bimal Krishna and Arindam Chakrabarti (1994). eds. *Knowing from Words*. Dordrecht: Kluwer.

Matilal, Bimal Krishna and Robert D. Evans (1986). eds. *Buddhist Logic and Epsitemology*. Dordrecht: Kluwer.

Matilal, Bimal Krishna and P. K. Sen (1988). 'The Context Principle and Some Indian Controversies over Meaning'. *Mind* 97: 73–97. (Reprinted in Perrett 2001, vol. II.)

Mayeda, Sengaku (1992). trans. and ed. *A Thousand Teachings: The Upadeśasāhasrī of Śaṅkara*. Albany: State University of New York Press.

McClintock, Sara L. (2010). *Omniscience and the Rhetoric of Reason*. Boston, MA: Wisdom Publishing.

McDermott, A. C. Senape (1969). *An Eleventh-Century Buddhist Logic of 'Exists'*. Dordrecht: D. Reidel.

Mills, Ethan (2015). 'Jayarāśi's Delightful Destruction of Epistemology'. *Philosophy East and West* 65: 498–541.

Mohanty, J. N. (1989). *Gaṅgeśa's Theory of Truth*. 2nd rev. edn. Delhi: Motilal Banarsidass.

(1992). *Reason and Tradition in Indian Thought*. Oxford: Clarendon Press.

(1993). *Essays on Indian Philosophy*. Oxford University Press.

(2000). *Classical Indian Philosophy*. Lanham: Rowman & Littlefield.

Mookerjee, Satkari (1995). *The Jaina Philosophy of Non-Absolutism*. Delhi: Motilal Banarsidass.

Morris, Thomas V. (1987). 'Perfect Being Theology'. *Nous* 21: 19–30.

Murty, K. Satchidananda (1974). *Revelation and Reason in Advaita Vedānta.* Delhi: Motilal Banarsidass.

Nikhilananda, Swami (2006). trans. *The Vedānta-sāra of Sadānanda.* Kolkata: Advaita Ashrama.

Oetke, Claus (1996). 'Ancient Indian Logic as a Theory of Non-Monotonic Reasoning'. *Journal of Indian Philosophy* 24: 447–539.

Olivelle, Patrick (2005). ed. and trans. *Manu's Code of Law: A Critical Edition and Translation of the Mānava-Dharmaśāstra.* Oxford University Press.

Parfit, Derek (1984). *Reasons and Persons.* Oxford University Press.

Patil, Parimal (2009). *Against a Hindu God: Buddhist Philosophy of Religion in India.* New York: Columbia University Press.

Pereira, José (1976). ed. *Hindu Theology: A Reader.* Garden City, NY: Image Books.

Perrett, Roy W. (1989). ed. *Indian Philosophy of Religion.* Dordrecht: Kluwer.

(1998). *Hindu Ethics: A Philosophical Study.* Honolulu: University of Hawai'i Press.

(2001). ed. *Indian Philosophy: A Collection of Readings.* 5 vols. New York: Garland.

Phillips, Stephen H. (1995). *Classical Indian Metaphysics.* Chicago, IL: Open Court.

(2009). *Yoga, Karma, and Rebirth: A Brief History and Philosophy.* New York: Columbia University Press.

(2012). *Epistemology in Classical India: The Knowledge Sources of the Nyāya School.* London: Routledge.

Phillips, Stephen H. and N. S. Ramanuja Tatacharya (2002). *Gaṅgeśa on the Upādhi, The 'Inferential Undercutting Condition'.* New Delhi: Indian Council of Philosophical Research.

(2004). *Epistemology of Perception: Gaṅgeśa's Tattvacintāmaṇi, Jewel of Reflection on the Truth (About Epistemology): The Perception Chapter (Pratyakṣa-khanda).* New York: American Institute of Buddhist Studies.

Pillai, K. Raghavan (1971). trans. *Vākyapadīya. Critical Text of Cantos I and II,* with English translation, summary of ideas, and notes. Delhi: Motilal Banarsidass.

Potter, Karl H. (1963). *Presuppositions of India's Philosophies.* Englewood Cliffs, NJ: Prentice-Hall.

(1977). ed. *Indian Metaphysics and Epistemology: The Tradition of Nyāya-Vaiśeṣika up to Gaṅgeśa.* Princeton University Press.

(1981). ed. *Advaita Vedānta up to Śaṃkara and his Pupils.* Delhi: Motilal Banarsidass.

(2006). ed. *Advaita Vedānta from 800 to 1200.* Delhi: Motilal Banarsidass.

Potter, Karl H. and Sibajiban Bhattacharyya (1992). eds. *Indian Philosophical Analysis: Nyāya-Vaiśeṣika from Gaṅgeśa to Raghunātha Śiromaṇi.* Princeton University Press.

Priest, Graham (2008). 'Jaina Logic: A Contemporary Perspective'. *History and Philosophy of Logic* 29: 263–78.

(2010). 'The Logic of the Catuṣkoṭi'. *Comparative Philosophy* 1: 24–54.

Pruden, Leo M. (1991). trans. *Abhidharmakośabhāṣyam by Louis de La Vallée Poussin*. Berkeley, CA: Asian Humanities Press.

Quine, W. V. O. (1960). *Word and Object*. Cambridge, MA: MIT Press.

Rabten, Geshé (1983). *Echoes of Voidness*, trans. and ed. Stephen Batchelor. Boston, MA: Wisdom Publishing.

Radhakrishnan, Sarvepalli and Charles A. Moore (1957). eds. *A Source Book in Indian Philosophy*. Princeton University Press.

Raghavachar, S. S. (1959). trans. *Śrīmad-Viṣṇu-Tattva-Vinirṇaya of Śrī Madhvācārya*. 3rd edn. Mangalore: Sri Ramakrishna Asrama.

(1978). trans. *Vedārtha-Saṅgraha of Śrī Rāmānujācārya*. Mysore: Sri Ramakrishna Asrama.

Raghuramaraju, A. (2006). *Debates in Indian Philosophy: Classical, Colonial, and Contemporary*. Oxford University Press.

(2013). *Philosophy and India: Ancestors, Outsiders and Predecessors*. Oxford University Press.

Raja, C. Kunhan and S. S. Suryanarayana Sastri (1933). eds. and trans. *Mānameyodaya: An Elementary Treatise on the Mīmāṁsa by Nārāyaṇa*. Madras: Adyar Library and Research Centre.

Raja, K. Kunjunni (1969). *Indian Theories of Meaning*. 2nd. edn. Madras: Adyar Library and Research Centre.

Ram-Prasad, Chakravarthi (2001). *Knowledge and Liberation in Classical Indian Thought*. Basingstoke: Palgrave Macmillan.

Ramsey, Frank Plumpton (1931). *The Foundations of Mathematics and Other Logical Essays*. London: Kegan Paul.

Rangarajan, L. N. (1987). ed. and trans. *Kautilya: The Arthashastra*. Harmondsworth: Penguin.

Rao, Srinavasa (1998). *Perceptual Error: The Indian Theories*. Honolulu: University of Hawai'i Press.

Rhys Davids, T. W. (1969). trans. *The Questions of King Milinda*. Delhi: Motilal Banarsidass.

Robinson, Richard H. (1972). 'Did Nāgārjuna Really Refute All Philosophical Views?' *Philosophy East and West* 22: 325–31.

(1973). 'Classical Indian Philosophy'. In Joseph W. Elder (ed.), *Chapters in Indian Civilization*. Madison: Department of Indian Studies, University of Wisconsin.

Ruegg, David Seyfort (1977). 'The Uses of the Four Positions of the Catuṣkoṭi and the Problem of the Description of Reality in Mahāyāna Buddhism'. *Journal of Indian Philosophy* 5: 1–71.

Said, Edward (1978). *Orientalism*. New York: Pantheon.

Samten, Geshe Ngawang and Jay L. Garfield (2006). trans. *Ocean of Reasoning: A Great Commentary on Nāgārjuna's Mūlamadhyamakakārikā*. Oxford University Press.

Sarma, Deepak (2003). *An Introduction to Madhva Vedānta*. Aldershot: Ashgate.

(2011). ed. *Classical Indian Philosophy: A Reader*. New York: Columbia University Press.

Sastri, S. S. Suryanarayana (1942). ed. and trans. *Vedāntaparibhāṣā by Dharmarāja Adhvarin*. Madras: Adyar Library and Research Centre.

Sastri, S. S. Suryanarayana and C. Kunhan Raja (1933). eds. and trans. *Bhāmatī of Vācaspati on Śaṃkara's Brahmasūtrabhāṣya (Catuhsūtri)*. Madras: Adyar Library and Research Centre.

Scharf, Peter M. (1996). *The Denotation of Generic Terms in Ancient Indian Philosophy: Grammar, Nyāya, and Mīmāṃsā*. Philadelphia, PN: American Philosophical Society.

Schechtman, Marya (1996). *The Constitution of Selves*. Ithaca, NY: Cornell University Press.

Sen, Amartya (1997). 'Indian Traditions and the Western Imagination'. *Daedulus* 129: 1–26.

Sen, Prabal K. and Amita Chatterjee (2011). 'Navya-Nyāya Logic'. *Journal of the Indian Council of Philosophical Research* 27: 77–99.

Shah, Nagin J. (1999). trans. *Samantabhadra's Āptamīmāṁsā – Critique of an Authority*. Ahmedabad: Sanskrit-Sanskriti Granthamālā.

Sharma, B. N. K. (1981). *A History of the Dvaita School of Vedānta and its Literature*. 2nd rev. edn. Delhi: Motilal Banarsidass.

(1986). *The Philosophy of Śrī Madhavācārya*. rev. edn. Delhi: Motilal Banarsidass.

(1997). *Madhva's Teachings in His Own Words*. 4th edn. Mumbai: Bharatiya Vidya Bhavan.

Shaw, J. L. (1978). 'Negation and the Buddhist Theory of Meaning'. *Journal of Indian Philosophy* 6: 59–77.

Siderits, Mark (1991). *Indian Philosophy of Language*. Dordrecht: Kluwer.

(2003). *Personal Identity and Buddhist Philosophy: Empty Persons*. Aldershot: Ashgate.

(2007). *Buddhism as Philosophy: An Introduction*. Aldershot: Ashgate.

Siderits, Mark and Shōryū Katsura (2013). trans. *Nāgārjuna's Middle Way: Mūlamadhyamakakārikā*. Boston, MA: Wisdom Publications.

Siderits, Mark, Evan Thompson and Dan Zahavi (2010). eds. *Self, No-Self? Perspectives from Analytical, Phenomenological, and Indian Traditions*. Oxford University Press.

Siderits, Mark, Tom Tillemans and Arindam Chakrabarti (2011). eds. *Apoha: Buddhist Nominalism and Human Cognition*. New York: Columbia University Press.

Singh, Ramjee (1974). *The Jaina Concept of Omniscience*. Ahmedabad: Lalbhai Dalpatbhai Institute of Indology.

Skyrms, Brian (1996). *Evolution of the Social Contract*. Cambridge University Press.

Smart, Ninian (1964). *Doctrine and Argument in Indian Philosophy*. London: George Allen & Unwin.

Solomon, Esther (1976). *Indian Dialectics*. Ahmedabad: Gujarat Vidya Saha.

Spellman, John W. (1964). *Political Theory of Ancient India*. Oxford University Press.

Staal, Frits (1969). 'Sanskrit Philosophy of Language'. In Thomas A. Sebeok (ed.), *Current Trends in Linguistics: Vol. 5, Linguistics in South Asia*. The Hague: Mouton. (Reprinted in Perrett 2001, vol. II.)

(1988). *Universals: Studies in Indian Logic and Linguistics*. University of Chicago Press.

Stcherbatsky, Th. (1962). *Buddhist Logic*. New York: Dover.

Stoltz, Jonathan (2007). 'Gettier and Factivity in Indo-Tibetan Epistemology'. *Philosophical Quarterly* 57: 394–415.

Sundaram, P. K. (1980). *Iṣṭa Siddhi of Vimuktātman*. Madras: Swadharma Swaarajya Sangha.

Taber, John A. (2004). 'Is Indian Logic Nonmonotonic?' *Philosophy East and West* 54: 143–70.

(2005). *A Hindu Critique of Buddhist Epistemology: Kumārila on Perception*. London: RoutledgeCurzon.

(2013). 'On Engaging Philosophically with Indian Philosophical Texts'. *Études Asiatiques* 67: 125–63.

(forthcoming). 'Mīmāṃsā and the Eternality of Language'. In Matthew T. Kapstein (ed.), *The Columbia Guide to Classical Indian Philosophy*. New York: Columbia University Press.

Tachikawa, Musashi (1981). *The Structure of the World in Udayana's Realism: A Study of the Lakṣaṇāvalī and the Kiraṇāvalī*. Dordrecht: Reidel.

Thibaut, George (1968). trans. *Vedānta Sūtras with the Commentary by Śaṅkarācārya*. Delhi: Motilal Banarsidass.

(1971). trans. *The Vedānta Sūtras with the Commentary by Rāmānuja*. Delhi: Motilal Banarsidass.

Thomas, F. W. (1968). trans. *The Flower-Spray of the Quodammodo Doctrine: Śrī Malliṣeṇasuri's Syād-Vāda-Mañjarī*. Delhi: Motilal Banarsidass.

Tillemans, Tom J. F. (1999). *Scripture, Logic, Language: Essays on Dharmakīrti and his Tibetan Successors*. Boston, MA: Wisdom Publications.

(2000). trans. *Dharmakīrti's Pramāṇavārttika: An Annotated Translation of the Fourth Chapter (Parārthānumāna)*. Vienna: Verlag der Österreichischen Akademie der Wissenschaften.

(2011). 'How to Talk About Ineffable Things: Dignāga and Dharmakīrti on Apoha'. In Siderits, Tillemans and Chakrabarti.

(forthcoming). *'How Do Mādhyamikas Think?' and Other Essays on the Buddhist Philosophy of the Middle*. Boston, MA: Wisdom Publications.

Tillich, Paul (1963). *Christianity and the Encounter of the World Religions*. New York: Columbia University Press.

Trivedi, Saam (2013). 'Evaluating Indian Aesthetics'. *ASA Newsletter* 33: 1–4.

Van Buitenen, J. A. B. (1973). 'Vedic and Upaniṣadic Bases of Indian Civilization'. In Joseph W. Elder (ed.), *Chapters in Indian Civilization*. Madison: Department of Indian Studies, University of Wisconsin.

(1981). trans. *The Bhagavadgītā in the Mahābhārata: Text and Translation*. University of Chicago Press.

Vattanky, John. (1984). *Gaṅgeśa's Philosophy of God*. Madras: Adyar Library and Research Centre.

Veezhinathan, N. (1972). ed. and trans. *Saṁkṣepaśārīraka of Sarvajñātman*. University of Madras Publications.

Venis, Arthur (1898). trans. *The Vedānta Siddhāntamuktāvali of Prakāśānanda*. Benares: E. J. Lazurus.

Vidyabhusana, Satis Chandra (1978). *A History of Indian Logic*. Delhi: Motilal Banarsidass.

Wainwright, William (2013). 'Concepts of God'. In *The Stanford Encyclopedia of Philosophy*, ed. Edward N. Zalta. http://plato.stanford.edu

Wallace, Vesna A. and B. Alan Wallace (1997). trans. *A Guide to the Bodhisattva Way of Life (Bodhicaryāvatāra) by Śāntideva*. Ithaca, NY: Snow Lion.

Westerhoff, Jan (2009). *Nāgārjuna's Madhyamaka: A Philosophical Introduction*. Oxford University Press.

(2010). trans. *The Dispeller of Disputes: Nāgārjuna's Vigrahavyāvartanī*. Oxford University Press.

Williams, Paul M. (1981). 'On the Abhidharma Ontology'. *Journal of Indian Philosophy* 9: 227–57.

(1998a). *Altruism and Reality: Studies in the Philosophy of the Bodhicaryāvatāra*. London: Curzon.

(1998b). 'Indian Philosophy'. In A. C. Grayling (ed.), *Philosophy 2: Further Through the Subject*. Oxford University Press.

Wittgenstein, Ludwig (1961). *Tractatus Logico-Philosophicus*. London: Routledge & Kegan Paul.

(1980). *Culture and Value*. Oxford: Basil Blackwell.

Woods, James Haughton (1927). trans. *The Yoga System of Patañjali*. 2nd edn. Cambridge, MA: Harvard University Press.

Yamunacharya, M. (1988). *Rāmānuja's Teachings in His Own Words*. 3rd edn. Bombay: Bharatiya Vidya Bhavan.

Yao, Zhihua (2009). 'Empty Subject Terms in Buddhist Logic: Dignāga and his Chinese Commentators'. *Journal of Indian Philosophy* 37: 383–98.

Index